W9-CLN-272

HIT THE GROUND RUNNING

Other Books by Gene Garofalo

Sales Manager's Desk Book

*Sales Professional's Survival Guide or Things Your Sales Manager Never Told You
(with Gary Drummond)*

Secrets of Competitive Bidding: Strategies for Finding and Winning Million Dollar Contracts

The Sales Managers' Training and Coaching Kit

HIT THE GROUND RUNNING

WINNING SECRETS FOR KEEPING YOUR CAREER ON TRACK AND MOVING FORWARD

GENE GAROFALO

PRENTICE HALL
Englewood Cliffs, New Jersey 07632

Prentice-Hall International (UK) Limited, *London*
Prentice-Hall of Australia Pty. Limited, *Sydney*
Prentice-Hall Canada, Inc., *Toronto*
Prentice-Hall Hispanoamericana, S.A., *Mexico*
Prentice-Hall of India Private Limited, *New Delhi*
Prentice-Hall of Japan, Inc., *Tokyo*
Simon & Schuster Asia Pte. Ltd., *Singapore*
Editora Prentice-Hall do Brasil, Ltda., *Rio de Janeiro*

©1993 *by*
PRENTICE-HALL, Inc.
Englewood Cliffs, NJ

All rights reserved. No part of this book may be
reproduced in any form or by any means, without
permission in writing from the publisher.

10 9 8 7 6 5 4 3 2 1

Library of Congress Cataloging-in-Publication Data

Garofalo, Gene.
    Hit the ground running : surviving and thriving in the downsized
corporation / by Gene Garofalo.
      p. cm.
    Includes index.
    ISBN 0-13-299553-0   ISBN 0-13-299538-7
    1. Executive ability.   2. Executives—United States—Dismissal of.
3. Corporate culture—United States. I. Title.
HD38.25.U6G37   1993   92-40001
658.4'09—dc20   CIP

ISBN 0-13-299553-0

ISBN 0-13-299538-7   PBK

PRENTICE HALL
Professional Publishing
Englewood Cliffs, NJ 07632

Simon & Schuster. A Paramount Communications Company

Printed in the United States of America

PREFACE

In the next decade the trip up the corporate ladder will be more difficult than ever. In many cases the ladder itself has actually disappeared. Management jobs in large companies are disappearing faster than the ozone layer. Most of these jobs are gone forever. Seventy-five percent of those laid off by a *Fortune* 500 organization will never again be employed by a big company.

When corporations began reducing staff levels they called the trend "downsizing." The spin doctors changed that unfortunate phrase to "rightsizing." Whatever it's called there's been a bloody night-of-the-long-knives in just about every major company in America.

What do these cutbacks mean for the ambitious managers who survived and still want to advance in their careers? What about the young people just getting into the work force? Their career paths will certainly be less predictable. The old nose-to-the-grindstone system of doing the job and waiting your turn won't work anymore. There's not enough time for that strategy because there are no more guarantees of lifetime employment in exchange for absolute loyalty. Companies won't make that trade anymore.

There will be less patience on the part of the "rightsized" corporation. They won't give the inexperienced time to grow into a job. Employees will be expected to pull their weight immediately. Nurturing talent, giving it time to flower, is already a dimly remembered luxury. The warning is clear: Contribute now or get out! No one gets in on a free pass.

Fortunately, periods of drastic change always bring unique opportunities along with the disruption. Those missing ladders make it possible to skip a few of the traditional way stations on the way up. Thinner ranks mean those with talent will be recognized sooner. Promotion doesn't always require putting in the proper amount of time. Advancement is based on contribution.

Hit the Ground Running is a reference work for today's reality. Our aim with this book is to guide managers to success in the fastest changing environment in business history. We focus on what the corporations of the Nineties will expect from their managers. More important, it details what mangers can expect from their employers.

There's a new relationship between corporate manager and employer. It's based on mutual need. When the relationship doesn't benefit both parties, either is free to sever it and look elsewhere. Today's equation is immediate performance in return for *almost* immediate reward.

The first thing managers must do to get noticed is to be good at their jobs. This requirement hasn't changed much since Adam hired on his sons to till the fields. *Hit the Ground Running* offers suggestions on how to perform tasks with efficiency and style. The book shows how every assignment, however insignificant, can be used as a building block for career advancement.

Being a corporate manager today requires mastering a bewildering array of skills. Managers must learn how to make decisions from imperfect information. They must learn the importance of setting priorities. They must learn how to cope with stress. They must learn how to motivate staff members grown cynical from a decade of leveraged buyouts and senior management's golden parachutes. They must learn to develop techniques for digging out and interpreting facts. They must learn how to master the thousand and one details associated with management responsibility. They must master all of these things, but they aren't given the luxury of time to learn them.

Hit the Ground Running is a source that provides this information and much more. The book is intended to be the manager's constant companion, a resource and guide that provides answers to the new situations that all business executives will face over the next ten years.

This is a nuts-and-bolts book offering practical solutions to the new dilemmas faced by managers working for the modern corporation. It's a shortcut for experience because the information on business operations, the suggestions for mastering managerial skills, the advice on career strategies, the simple explanations of the technical changes shaping business, and the hundreds of additional suggestions would take years to learn.

Hit the Ground Running will be useful for both the person who has just been given a managerial assignment and the senior-level executive who wonders how he or she will fit into the brave new corporate world.

HOW TO USE THIS BOOK

Every author would like his or her book to be read cover to cover. How else can the reader obtain the benefit of the incalculable wisdom they offer? Going through every page, however, is just not practical for readers of most business books, including this one. Advice to do so would be questionable from a writer who advocates getting the maximum use from available time.

Please treat *Hit the Ground Running* as a reference work similar to a dictionary or a thesaurus. It has been divided into sections on career development, acquiring and mastering managerial skills and the nuts and bolts of what every manager needs to know. Our suggestion is to go directly to the section of the book that is of immediate interest. The other sections are there, patiently waiting for the reader to discover them when the time is appropriate.

If the table of contents appears to be exhaustive it's because the chapters within the sections are divided into very short "essays" or topics with convenient headings. We want to make it easier for the reader to find a specific topic of interest.

One last suggestion from someone who values time: Use the rifle rather than the shotgun approach to get the most value from this book. Extract the information you want today, but keep the book in a handy place. There's additional material here that you'll want to access tomorrow.

CONTENTS

2

Learning How to Communicate: The Key to Success in Any Career 35

3

How to Get More Done in Less Time 61

SECTION TWO

ACQUIRING AND MASTERING MANAGERIAL SKILLS **79**

4

The Manager's Role in a Changing Work Place **81**

5 Dealing with the Nineties 99

6

How to Manage a Project 119

7

How to Manage Under Pressure 133

8 A Blueprint for the Woman Manager 145

9 How to Work and Thrive within Your Company's Structure 159

10 Life in the Boardroom 171

Section Three

THE NUTS AND BOLTS STUFF EVERY MANAGER NEEDS TO KNOW 181

11 The Stuff About Company Operations Every Manager Needs to Know 183

14 Predicting the Future 249

Index 271

WHAT IS A MANAGER ANYWAY?

What a Manager Manages

When beginning *Hit the Ground Running* the first question that had to be answered was *what exactly does a manager manage?* Ask it in any office and expect a variety of replies, some of them surprising. One thing is for sure: There's more to being a manager than issuing orders from behind a desk in the corner office. Anyone who doesn't understand management's primary function isn't likely to advance very far, no matter how capable he or she is.

The traditional answer, the one that will get you a passing grade in most business schools' exams, is that a manager manages resources. Like many definitions, this one raises another question: *What are resources?*

For a corporation, resources are usually defined in terms of the Big Three. They are:

1. *Assets in any of their varied forms.* (Assets can be in the shape of cash in the bank, property, inventory, a valuable patent or copyright, etc.)

2 *Time*. (The days, hours, and minutes are always the most difficult things to manage because, except for those on rocket ships traveling at the speed of light, time is not expandable. We run out of every day exactly at midnight.

3 *People*. (Simultaneously the most aggravating and gratifying factor in the managerial equation because it is the least predictable.)

Examine any corporate management responsibility and it can almost always be fitted into one of these three categories. In fact, every job in every company involves manipulation of at least one of these resources.

We're making the explanation now at the beginning of this book because it simplifies the success equation. To get noticed and respected as a manager become an expert at managing people, time, or assets. Skill in one of these areas is an inoculation against the worst recession. The manager who handles two of these categories well is soon selecting from the ala carte menu in the executive dining room. Those with an easy familiarity with all three are CEO material.

The first step in career advancement is for managers to analyze their jobs from the perspective of resource responsibility. Which vital resource has the company given over to the manager for care and nurturing? The answer to that question determines where ambitious managers devote their time and energies.

HOW TO SELF-MANAGE YOUR CAREER

❖ 1 ❖

HOW TO SET AND ACHIEVE CAREER GOALS

Setting Career Goals

Outside of a few hopeless romantics, who would ever board a plane without knowing its destination? The rest of us wouldn't dream of doing anything so foolish. Then why on earth would anyone hire on with a company without having some idea of a career destination with that company?

A career is a journey. It is one of life's more important trips. Return tickets are not issued. Before hopping on board that career ride with an employer, better decide on the final destination you hope to reach and the route that will give you the best chance of getting there.

How to Decide on a Career Destination

The next decade will bring a confusing choice of career opportunities. It will also bring more intense competition for each available position. With all these possible choices and with more bodies fighting for every slot, what's the best way to select a career goal? It's an important question because each time a choice is made future options are limited.

Some people have a firm idea of what they want to accomplish with their lives from age fifteen; others in their mid-forties still can't make up their minds. They wander from one job to another, vaguely dissatisfied with each, working for employers who are vaguely dissatisfied with them because they have no sense of commitment.

Simple advice for the undecided is, *when unsure about career goals, embrace your passion.* Do what excites you. What occupation do you think would be fun? exhilarating? challenging? What absorbs you? That's the career for you. Don't worry about the pay. Money follows conviction. By using passion as a career guide you ensure that you won't be fed up with your choice five or ten years from now.

Of course, we must all learn to operate within our limitations. Most of us aren't tall enough or can jump high enough to play in the NBA, but someone really dedicated to a career in sports could aim for a job in the administrative office of a team, even if the starting point is selling tickets. Can't even get a job moving tickets with a major-league sports franchise? Start in the minors. That's how most of the players made the big time.

When to Lay Career Plans

The best time to lay career plans is well before you join any organization. That's because, as any map maker or systems designer knows, destination determines route. If your goal is to become the treasurer or controller of a company, you're not likely to get to one of those jobs from a starting point of a territory salesperson.

The first step in career planning, beyond the school-days phase, is to research any company that is a potential employer. Conduct the same kind of background check on them that they do on you as a job candidate. No, be far more thorough. They can afford the luxury of a mistake far better than you can.

Here's the kind of information you want to find out about a company:

Fourteen Things to Find Out About a Prospective Employer

1. *How big is the company?* What is its annual sales? Are its sales growing or declining?

2. *Is it profitable?* What are the company's five-year profit trends?

3. *How many divisions does it have?*

4. *Is the division where you'll be working profitable?* What are the division's five-year profit trends?

5. *Would you be located at headquarters or at a distant branch?*

6. *What is the division's position in the company?* Is it the dominant factor? A cash cow? A drain on profits?

7. *What is the company's position in the industry?* Is it an industry leader? Second banana? An also-ran?

8. *What's the condition of the industry of which the company is a member?* Is it a growth industry? Is it ailing? Holding steady? Is it under attack from foreign competitors?

9. *Is the company and/or the division expanding or cutting back on the number of employees?*

10. *What's the typical career path for someone starting out in your position?* Where do the successes go?

11. *How long has the direct supervisor you would report to been in that position?* What are his or her expectations? Does that person have a job you covet?

12. *Is the available position one in which the results can be quantified?* (In other words, will it be easy to determine good or poor job performance without relying on the word of a supervisor?)

13. *Does the company have internal training programs for promising people?*

14. *Does the company have a "fast-track" program for qualified business school graduates?* (Look out for this one unless you're designated as a fast-tracker. They automatically absorb many of the available first-line promotions. There aren't many good jobs left over for others, regardless of merit. This is a great policy if you're in the program, but it's not so hot if you joined the company via another route.)

Note: The size of an organization used to be directly related to the degree of job security a loyal employee could expect. This is no longer true. The largest companies are perhaps the most ruthless in cutting back on staff.

The ideal employer in the next decade will be the small- or medium-size company in a dominant position in a growth industry.

If the prospective employer's stock is publicly traded, many of the preceding questions can be answered through Standard & Poor reports and other records. Additional answers can be obtained during the interview process. Competitive companies, industry journals, trade associations, friends working for the organization are other sources.

Why It's Important to Investigate a Prospective Employer

The reason these questions are important is because there are more opportunities for advancement in growing companies than there are in companies that are retrenching. Young, vibrant industries are also more exciting and stimulating. Working for a stagnant company or in a mature industry makes one defensive, in the position of holding the line against progress. Pay attention to all the signals during an interview. The person who tells you that opportunity *teems* over at his shop, but who has been in the same position for more than ten years is not to be believed.

Picking a Winning Situation

Going with a company currently on top isn't always the best move. For example, a company that already controls more than 80 percent of market share isn't likely to do much better. What can you possibly do to improve performance when they own the market now? Meanwhile, a company that has been unprofitable for a few years isn't necessarily a poor risk as an employer. You could be coming on board at a point when that company is about to turn around. Perhaps you'll even be credited for having a part in the turnaround. Being considered a hero never harmed any career.

Low expectation often offers more opportunity than high expectation. There's no place to go when you already occupy the mountain peak. That's why Alexander the Great wept when he learned there were no more nations left to conquer.

This is not a suggestion that opportunities with successful organizations be ignored, only the thought that each situation must be carefully evaluated. Companies in an expansion mode usually offer the fastest opportunities for career advancement. They're also more fun to work for.

How to Design a Career-Planning Chart

Perhaps we should have used a train instead of a plane in the analogy of a career as a journey. The reason a train may be more appropriate is that, except for the sons and daughters of company founders, there are no nonstop flights on career journeys. Each trip requires stops at way stations, small towns, and fueling depots. Frequently, the train gets side-tracked. Occasionally, it is derailed. That's why it's important to draw a map before starting off.

Career-Planning Chart

The career planning chart is a simple graph to prepare. On the illustrated sample ten years are listed in reverse order in the left margin. (Don't plan a career with a single employer more than ten years ahead. We'll explain why later.)

In the example on the following page, the ambitious little devil who drew this chart wants to go from a territory salesperson to vice-president of sales in ten years. A few judicious questions put to the employer should reveal the necessary route, meaning required job experience and performance level, to reach that destination. Across the top of the chart the planner has listed the job titles between him and his career goal. As each promotion is achieved, the planner draws a line to that point.

One glance at the chart reveals how much further the planner has to go to reach a career goal and how much time is left to get there. If the planner feels dead-ended in a position or sees that the road ahead is blocked, he may decide to seek that next step up through joining another company.

Ten Obstacles That Stand in the Way of Career Promotion, Including Three the Company Rarely Reveals

The road to true love is seldom smooth, and neither is the road to promotion. There are rock slides, the highway gets washed out, repairs block off most of the available lanes, traffic jams impede progress, and the road signs occasionally misdirect the traveler. Here are ten of the common obstacles to career advancement:

> **1.** *An immediate supervisor is a jerk who won't give proper credit for your accomplishments or takes credit for herself.* This is a

Career Planning Chart

Title	Sales Rep.	Branch Mgr.	District Mgr.	Regional Mgr.	National Sales Mgr.	V.P. Sales
10						
9						
8						
7						
6						
5						
4						
3						
2						
1						
Year						

tough obstacle, particularly in a large organization where the only time the senior brass learns what a prize they have in you is when they are reading your annual performance review. Complain too vigorously about the injustice and expect a poor review from the jerk supervisor. Keep quiet and your brilliant light can't be seen under that bushel.

The way out of this one is to somehow get on projects that bring you in direct contact with the senior brass. When you get the opportunity, turn on the incandescence so the brass can't help but see the glow!

2. *The company, or a supervisor has given you an impossible task.* A fact of corporate life is that most of us are judged on the performance against a goal and it doesn't matter much if that goal is unattainable. If the job isn't done, then the person responsible must be ineffectual. Any other conclusion would admit something might be wrong with the plan.

The escape from this dilemma is to analyze every assignment before beginning the work. If the goals are not reachable make objections early. Be prepared to make your points with powerful arguments. Present them in writing. A reputation for being "negative" is a career killer so always suggest viable alternatives. Make sure a copy of your recommendations gets into all the right hands.

3. *The company roster is filled with players just approaching middle age, all of them with more seniority and clout than you.* These people still have twenty years or so left in their careers. Unless the company is expanding rapidly, there may be no way up the ladder when the rungs above are teeming with capable people who have seniority, but who are still in mid-career.

Young managers facing this plight are like rookies brought up to a major-league team filled with all-stars. The only way to get playing time may be to get traded to another team. In other words, think about moving on.

4. *The company is going through hard times and is cutting back on staff.* Fewer jobs mean fewer promotion opportunities. Actually, this situation is not as grim as it first seems—providing you're one of the survivors.

Opportunity still exists during a period of cutbacks because the down-sizing company will inevitably eliminate too many key people. The tasks these people performed are there to be seized by someone who takes initiative. This initiative will get noticed.

5. *The company is a poor also-ran in a tough, competitive industry.* It cuts every corner that can be cut to stay afloat. Companies in this position seem always to be on the fringe of disaster. Morale is terrible.

The best tactic in this situation may be to acquire enough job experience to become valuable to another company within the same industry, then jump ship.

6. *The company is a family-owned business, and the family is doing its best to aid and abet the population explosion.* There is no remedy for this one, unless there's a "junior" after your name. If you're an ambitious outsider, get out.

7. *Your company has just been bought out by another, larger outfit.* Forget about promotions for a while. The dominant organization will provide all the management you'll ever want or need. The one thing you can absolutely positively count on is that the

management of the takeover company will lie to the employees of the acquired outfit. They don't want a wholesale bailout of personnel until they find out where all the bones are buried.

There are also a few obstacles to promotion that most companies never talk about, they're just facts of corporate life. They include:

8. *The company has a fast-track program designed to recruit the top graduates from major schools.* A certain number of choice managerial positions are reserved for the fast-trackers because of their academic credentials. Other managers within the company, regardless of their actual performance on the job, need not apply.

9. *The company division is considered a cash cow, meaning it produces a good profit right now, but is considered to have a limited future.* What do you do with a cash cow? Milk it, of course. The exciting things, the grandiose plans, the big promotions, are all happening in the other divisions. Your division is supposed to run lean and mean, scrap for every penny to finance the exciting vision of the future that's happening across the hall.

10. *The company is sprucing up the books because it's looking for a buyer.* This is similar to the cash-cow situation related to a division, but the problem is now companywide. The financial wizards take over completely. All operations are trimmed to make bottom-line profits appear better than they are. There are few promotions, few salary raises, never enough budget to get things done during such a period because senior management is concentrating all efforts on looking for a sucker who will be seduced by the cooked numbers.

The Action Ladder: Eight Steps Toward Reaching Your Career Goals. (They needn't be over the backs of your peers.)

The first step even before formally accepting a job with a company is to set definite career goals. What comes after that? The answer is simple. It is to develop a specific action plan to reach those goals. The following steps will enhance the possibility of promotion for any career:

1. *Analyze your job responsibility.* What is the company really looking for related to your performance? (Remember what a manager manages.) Concentrate on giving your employers what they want. Sounds simple, doesn't it?

2. *Analyze your direct supervisor's responsibility and long-term goals.* What will make your boss look good to his or her superiors? What will get him or her out of the department so you can take over the corner office? Assist your boss toward that next promotion because it helps your case.

3. *Develop a reputation for cooperation among your co-workers.* When conflicts arise be ready to compromise. Never turn down a request for help from one of your peers. Praise their efforts.

4. *Learn how to communicate clearly and concisely.* The ability to write simply and directly is a wonderful asset. Make your reports sparkle. Be honest and realistic when evaluating situations, but do so in an upbeat manner. When sounding a warning, be sure you're correct.

5. *Look for the assignment that will bring you to the attention of senior management.* Never pass up an opportunity to make a presentation before the brass. This is the time to put in extra effort. Be prepared to dazzle when making these presentations.

6. *Don't play it safe.* Take calculated risks that you feel will genuinely benefit the company. A mistake in judgment doesn't necessarily ruin a career. (It's a maxim at GE that every manager worth his or her salt has made at least a one-million-dollar mistake.)

7. *Learn what motivates the people who report to you.* It isn't always money. Learn how to praise achievement. Better yet, learn how to give full credit to staff members who have done something noteworthy. They'll work harder on your behalf knowing their efforts will be recognized.

8. *Learn how to cut your way through the company bureaucracy.* The best way to do this is by making friends and allies with your peers in other departments. The best way to make lasting friends is to help your peers get through the red tape in your own department. The biggest handicap you can give yourself when starting a position with a new company is to memorize the regulations. In other words, never sacrifice substance for form.

How to Analyze Your Job from a Cynic's Perspective: Ten Questions Only a Confirmed Cynic Would Ask

Cynicism is an attitude that sits more comfortably on a weathered brow. The young manager is better advised to demonstrate, and genuinely feel eagerness and enthusiasm. Ambitious managers determined to succeed should, however, put enthusiasm aside for a time while they examine their responsibilities and prospects from a cynic's perspective. Here are some of the questions they should ask themselves:

1. *What's the average time in this job before a manager gets promoted to another position?* The answer may be available from historical data, or can be obtained through observation.

2. *What action could be taken that would lessen the time frame?* What kind of performance would satisfy management that the current position holder, namely you, was ready to move up?

3. *What could go wrong?* Were you handed a hot potato when given your position? Is this department a Gulag, a frozen land where they send the political prisoners? Where are the disasters waiting to happen? How can they be prevented?

4. *Does your boss have a hidden agenda?* What is it? What's his reputation in the company? Is the boss on the way up? On the way down? Treading water until retirement? Is it a smart move to be closely associated with this person?

5. *Who are the influential people who would have a voice in the next step up the ladder?* Who in the company would make a good "rabbi" to help your career? What would make that person want to be your mentor?

6. *Who are the people who know what's going on at the top where the eagles soar?* How can you become part of this communication link?

7. *Which of your peers have job responsibilities that impact your performance?* Do they have the power to make you look good or bad? How can you get these people on your side?

8. *Who is your competition for the next step up the ladder?* What can you do to make yourself appear a better candidate for promotion without in any way trying to undercut them?

9. *What dead-end assignments should be avoided at all costs?*

10. *Who are the ambitious people on your staff who can help you with career goals in return for a boost up themselves?*

A Complete Job-Analysis Kit and Worksheet

A completion of the following worksheet will give any manager a feel for what needs to be done to win that next promotion. It also helps the manager analyze which personal alignments could enhance career potential.

Job Analysis Worksheet

List of primary job responsibilities _____

_____

_____

_____

_____

_____

Obstacles in the way of meeting responsibilities _____

_____

_____

_____

_____

_____

What direct supervisor wants in way of performance_____

_____

_____

_____

_____

_____

What can go wrong_____

_____

_____

_____

_____ *continued*

Important deadlines

When they occur   *What needs to be done*   *Obstacles for getting it done*

_____

_____

_____

_____

_____

_____

List of company departments whose cooperation is crucial

Department   *Department head*

_____

_____

_____

_____

_____

_____

List of possible assignments or committees that would bring me to the attention of senior management _____

_____

_____

_____

_____

_____

List of potential mentors

Name   *Possible motive for helping*

_____

_____

_____

_____

_____

_____

Possible promotions from current position
Title   Performance needed

_____

_____

_____

_____

_____

_____

Possible allies
Name   Department   Title

_____

_____

_____

_____

_____

Possible competitors for next promotion
Name   Title   Assets

_____

_____

_____

_____

_____

_____

The completion of this form gives the manager a synopsis of both the job performance and the political alliances that must be made to have a successful career. Note that in the list of possible competitors, only their assets are analyzed. An evaluation of a job competitor's weaknesses is not appropriate because of the temptation to bring this information to the attention of senior management.

How to Analyze the Company and Its Management

To the job applicant, companies may appear in a certain light, but they can be completely understood only once one is actually inside and working. The apparently efficient organization may be mismanaged, the apparently fiscal conservatives may be borrowing wildly to finance high-risk ventures. There is no way of managers knowing for sure what an organization is like until they become members of the team. That's why it's pointless to be envious of any peer's position. To quote the performer Little Richard, "The other guy's grass may look greener, but it's just as tough to cut."

The new executive intent on advancement should analyze the company and its management style. Knowing how a company operates can help that executive map the best route to career goals. Here are the critical things the new executive needs to know:

1. *Who calls the shots?* Departments seem to have equal authority, but in almost every company some "are more equal than others." In other words, one department will enjoy larger operating budgets, employ more personnel, and seem to have a bigger voice in the decisions that affect the direction of the company. The department head is usually a senior V.P. and is extremely influential. In many companies it's Sales or Marketing, others Finance; with some high-tech outfits, it's R & D; with a few retailers, Purchasing calls the tune. These influential departments are the ones to be in to get on the fast promotion track. If that's not possible, this department is the 900-pound gorilla to stay clear of.

2. *What's the average age of the senior management team?* Why is this important? The older they are, the more conservative they're likely to be. While caution is not a terrible thing, risk takers may not be welcome here. On the other hand, demonstrating prudent and thoughtful judgment may be rewarded.

3. *How bureaucratic is the company?* Does it take five signatures and six initials from department heads to get a dozen pencils from the supply room? Companies that haven't streamlined their operations and are still mired in bureaucracy will have difficult times in the Nineties because red tape slows things down. These bureaucratic dinosaurs may not be the best vehicle for the career-minded manager.

4. *Whom does your boss report to?* The second line of management, the boss's boss, is an important factor in any executive's career

success. The important question is, what does the boss's boss want? How can the new manager help him or her get it? Help if you can, but in a way that doesn't undermine a direct supervisor's authority.

5. *What's the mood inside the company?* The morale of personnel within a company can tell a new manager much about the organization. People aren't pessimistic inside a company that is achieving its goals and moving forward. There's a Gloomy Gus or two in every outfit, but if everyone appears cynical, showing up at work only for the paycheck, then coming on board may have been a mistake.

6. *How does management motivate?* Do they encourage their employees through praise, do they recognize achievement, do they reward accomplishment? Or do they threaten, try to intimidate, use the K.I.T.A. (Kick In The Arse) motivation technique? Are the goals that management sets realistic? Do people frequently leave the company because they "can't stand the pressure"? Is the standard managerial facial expression a big scowl?

The answer to these questions will help new managers understand the work places they've entered and what needs to be done to get ahead.

How to Find Out What's Going On in Other Divisions

Mid- and even senior-level executives working for smoothly operating, profitable divisions of large companies have often been shocked when the corporation suddenly announces a gigantic loss, a major cutback of personnel, a sale of assets, or even bankruptcy. The corporate version of fiscal peek-a-boo starts with a statement from the chief executive officer (drafted by the head of public relations) such as, "Hey, fellas, forget about the profit we projected up to ten minutes ago; we lost a ton of money last quarter."

The red ink waved before the employees like a red flag before a bull is an excuse for an austerity program with wage freezes, budget cuts, personnel reductions, and in many cases, a suspension of common decency.

The scenario has become so common that corporate managers must develop an intelligence system that will help them learn what's going on in other divisions throughout the company. If they're in trouble, you may be in trouble regardless of how well your own operation is functioning. It's not enough today to concentrate merely on what's happening in your own backyard. Events halfway across the country, even across the world, can have a dramatic impact on your career plans.

Information about potential problems isn't easy to come by because large losses seem consistently to surprise even the Wall Street analysts who follow the fortunes of major corporations.

Warning: What follows is heresy. Don't repeat in the presence of senior management: One reason problems take so long to surface is because of our inherent faith in the bonus system as a way to motivate managers. Managers rewarded for performance over a short period often find it to their financial advantage to temporarily sweep problems under the rug rather than solve them. When faced with losses, "creative bookkeeping" and just plain skullduggery often takes over. Obsolete inventory is carried at full value, expenses are underreported, problem loans are ignored, charge-backs are put off until the next quarter, poor credit risks are shipped large quantities of merchandise to make sales projections. According to the books, everything is peachy right up to the collapse.

How can a lower or mid-level manager learn what's really going on in another division of the corporation when it is to the advantage of the division brass to keep the true situation a secret? Look for these telltale signs of trouble:

1. *The division is in a problem industry such as real estate, or a supercompetitive industry such as computers or automobiles.* If the division head makes a statement to the effect that "the problems that affect our industry haven't touched us," don't believe the rascal.

2. *The division is late with its report to the corporation.* (Get friendly with someone in the corporate controller's or treasurer's office.) Maybe they're late because they're trying to make the numbers look better.

3. *The division's auditing firm is fired or resigns.* In this case the messenger has been killed or decided to flee before the bad news is delivered.

4. *The division's revenues have been growing at more than a 40 percent annual rate for the past few years and it is absorbing most of the corporation's investment capital.* Spectacular growth is almost impossible to sustain more than several years in a row without cutting corners. The corporation can't keep putting all their money into one division forever. Most division heads suffer from withdrawal symptoms if the financing that fueled their growth is cut back. The growth collapses, but the expenses go on.

5. *The division is contributing a higher share of profit than the industry average.* Maybe this phenomenon is caused by excellent management, but maybe the division head is taking inordinate risks or, worse, cooking the books.

6. *Rumors are flying everywhere that the division is in trouble.* Gossip is not reliable, but that's no reason not to check out the stories.

7. *Several senior-level executives leave the division for what appear to be petty reasons.* There are stories of squabbles in the executive suite. Adversity brings out latent hostility.

8. *The chief executive officer of the corporation spends an inordinate amount of time working with one division.*

9. *Senior-level executives in other divisions have derogatory things to say about the person heading up one division.* These are the jackals nipping at the heels of a wounded animal.

Any one, or even several, of these signals may not indicate another division could be foundering. If three or four of these signs appear, however, then it's time to assess the division's importance to the corporation and what impact a serious problem with that division might have on your own career.

A Nine-Point Plan That Will Help You Get Noticed by Senior Management

One shortcut to advancement is to get noticed as a comer by senior management. They're on the lookout for talent as much as any Hollywood scout is. Many young managers are bright and eager and ambitious. What can you do to get singled out of the crowd?

1. *Work Harder.* This sounds like Horatio Alger stuff, but it's a strategy that still works today. Be there in the morning when the boss arrives and be there grinding away when he or she leaves in the evening. Long hours don't always mean more or better quality output, but it sure looks that way.

2. *Have the right attitude.* That attitude means being cheerful, optimistic, and cooperative. It's hard not to like someone who displays these qualities, and being liked by superiors never hurt anyone's career.

3. *Be honest and direct when asked for an opinion.* It's not necessary to be a yes-person to succeed. In fact, most senior managers have no respect for someone who won't occasionally offer a contrary view. Candor is particularly valuable in meetings that decide the fate of projects.

4. *Be prepared.* "Fortune favors the prepared mind." Anticipate questions. Anticipate problems. Anticipate whatever demands your boss is likely to make.

5. *Show up.* The person who is always there, available and eager for whatever assignment comes along, has a better chance for promotion than the person who occasionally misses work, however valid the reasons.

6. *Don't be a jerk.* That means don't get drunk at office parties, don't make an overt play for members of the opposite sex, don't tell dirty jokes, don't steal office supplies, don't use the office copier to print the odds on the football pool, don't spread rumors, don't use profanity, and don't complain loudly about minor annoyances.

7. *Learn how to communicate in a clear and concise manner.* Time is a valuable commodity to senior managers. Don't waste it with oral and written reports that wander hither and yon before getting to the point. The written report is hard and lasting evidence of a manager's logical thought processes. If you haven't learned how to write well and succinctly, pay special attention to Chapter Two.

8. *Learn the company bureaucracy and how to circumvent it.* A good manager learns how to get things done, no matter the obstacles.

9. *Like your job.* If you enjoy what you do it will show in your performance and your attitude.

How to Change Your Job Description If It Won't Take You Where You Want to Go

What if your current job description doesn't fit into your career plans? What if it doesn't offer enough opportunity to show off your talents? You like the company well enough, but you feel stifled and the next promotion may be at least several years away. Even that move up appears to be more limiting than you would like. What to do? The answer is fairly simple: *Try to take on more responsibility.* That may seem difficult, but it isn't. Actually, it's fairly easy to acquire additional responsibility just as long as you don't demand extra compensation for it.

There are two basic strategies for acquiring additional responsibility:

1. *Find a neglected task and go to your boss with an offer to take it on.* Every company teems with these kinds of opportunities. It's best to have a plan to present to the boss on how the new task can be done without interfering with your current assignment. (Broad strokes only, you won't want the boss to think you've been plotting about this for a long time.) Chances are you'll get an approval and a pat on the back for your enterprise.

2. *Find a neglected task and just take responsibility for it without checking with anyone.* Usually, if you get by the first few weeks without a comment by your superiors, you're home free. The responsibility is yours by right of forfeiture.

With either plan your job description has just been expanded. Congratulations. You were going home too early anyway.

How to Evaluate a Lateral Move—A Worksheet That Tells You If an Organizational Move Is in Your Best Interests

The company wants you to move into another slot. The job grade is the same and so is the pay, but the company needs the job filled immediately. You're asked to take it on. Should you accept for the "good of the organization"? If you refuse the assignment, will you get a reputation for not being a team player? Are you being tossed into a pit filled with hungry lions?

The right attitudes to have when asked to accept a lateral move are caution and skepticism. You'll be told that the new position is much more important, but if that's really true, why isn't it worth more money? Any goodwill gained with the brass by making a personal sacrifice will be forgotten thirty days after the slot has been filled. The question to ask yourself is "What will the move do to enhance my career ambitions?" The following worksheet will help you come up with the answers:

Lateral-move Worksheet

Current title _____ Job grade _____

Proposed title _____ Job grade _____

Size of current staff _____ Size proposed staff _____

Size current budget _____ Size proposed budget _____

Title currently reporting to _____

Relationship with current boss:
Good _____ Fair _____ Poor_____

New reporting structure _____

Reputation of new boss: Good _____ Fair _____ Poor _____

Requires relocation? Yes_____ No_____

Cost to relocate (after company reimbursement) _____

Personal problems, if any, with relocation: _____

_____

_____

_____

Estimated time to promotion with current job _____

Likely title _____

Estimated time to promotion with proposed job _____

Likely title _____

Reasons last job holder left _____

_____

_____

_____

Anticipated problems with proposed position _____

_____

_____

_____

Problems left behind with current position _____

_____

_____

_____

_____

Position offering best chance for limelight:
Current job _____ Proposed position _____
Reasons why one position offers better opportunity to shine: _____

_____

_____

_____

Is career in jeopardy if job is refused?   Yes _____   No _____

Could company be phasing out current position?
Yes _____   No_____   Maybe_____

Filling out this worksheet will help put the proposed move into perspective. Not all the answers carry the same weight. If you suspect your current job may be phased out, accepting the proposed change may represent your only chance to stay with the company. Be particularly cautious about a lateral move that requires geographic relocation.

How to Read the Promotion Timetable within Your Company

Promotions take forever. At least it seems that way to many managers anxious to keep their careers moving. In the armed services, officers must move up in rank or get out. In private industry an individual can rise to a certain level (a level of their incompetence according to Laurence Peter) and go no further. The manager who is passed over once or twice, no matter what the reasons, may be considered to have reached his or her niche and is no longer a candidate when other promotion opportunities become available.

How can managers know if their careers are still skyrocketing or if they are fizzling? One way to tell is by answering the following questions:

1. *How long did the previous manager who held your position stay in the job before he or she was promoted?* (If that person left the company out of frustration, it's a bad sign.)

2. *On the average, how long do persons in your job grade stay in their positions before being promoted?* Has your tenure exceeded the average?

3. *Is there general movement upward for qualified employees, or has the current economic situation frozen everyone in place?*

4. *Is there a logical opening for you upstairs if you were qualified and had paid your dues?*

5. *Do you have the feeling that someone at the senior management level isn't "buying your act" and may be holding you back?* More often than not, these feelings have a factual basis.

6. *Is your boss or some other mentor guiding and promoting your career?*

7. *Has the company recently hired an outsider to fill a higher position that you feel qualified to handle?*

8. *Does the boss put you off when you try to talk about promotion possibilities?*

9. *Are people with less tenure being promoted and leaving you behind?*

10. *Have you inherited a job responsibility where the problems keep multiplying faster than flies on a horse's carcass?*

The answers to these questions will give you a good handle on the promotion possibilities with your particular situation.

How to Develop Your Own Promotion Timetable

Let's say that the average time in your kind of position is three years before you can expect a promotion. Let's also say that this seems like an eternity for someone with your burning ambition. You'd like to move up much faster. Don't despair. The timetable can be accelerated, even in the most structured of companies, if the desire and talent are there. Here's how:

1. *Select the position you're aiming for.* This should be done anyway when drawing your personal career chart.

2. *Go to your boss or mentor.* Tell this person about the position you'd like to have and seek advice on how to go about earning it. Expect one of several reactions. The mentor may suggest a list of accomplishments that must be done before receiving consideration, or may suggest that you choose another goal. If an alternative goal is suggested consider this advice carefully because the mentor knows how the company operates. If a list of accomplishments is offered, write them down. In very few instances will you be completely discouraged. Ambition is admired.

3. *Go on about doing the things the mentor suggested.* Report back on each accomplishment.

4. *Keep on top of your current job responsibility.* Excel.

5. *Let others in the company know about your target and timetable.*

Soon, all of senior management—heck the entire company—will know about your personal promotion timetable. They'll be watching your accomplishments. Most will be rooting for you to succeed. You will have singled yourself out as someone with enough confidence to announce intent. If that position becomes available within a two-year time frame, you'll be the first person management thinks of to fill it.

How to Survive and Thrive When the Company Is Trimming Staff

The 1990s are the decade of corporations running lean and mean. One industry after another is trimming staff. Even spectacular growth industries, such as personal computer manufacturers, are cutting personnel.

The question is, how to survive when the front office is drawing up a plan to trim X percent of all personnel? Here are the answers:

1. *Get an operational rather than a staff position.* The worst kind of title to have is one with the word "support" tied to it. Cutting support people causes a company the least near-term pain so these people are the first to go. Those who are bringing home the bacon last long enough to smell it cooking.

2. *Develop several talents.* People who have knowledge about several different operations are like utility ballplayers who can take many different positions. They're extra valuable during a time when personnel is reduced.

3. *Show up every day and don't bring your problems to work.* In a cutback the company wants to retain those who are most reliable, upbeat, and best fitted to weather any storm.

4. *Get out of the spectacular growth divisions and into the "cash cow" operation.* Most high-growth operations hire too many people too quickly. They are the first to be cut. The old reliable money-makers are more stable during rough times.

5. *Learn some things about the operation very few people in the company know how to do.* ("We have to keep Mary, she's the only one who knows how to process the insurance claim forms.")

6. *Become a can-do person who can slice through company red tape.* When choosing whom to retain, management is least likely to pick those who appear to be stumbling blocks toward getting anything done.

7. *Take the initiative to pick up responsibilities that went unassigned after the cutback.* You become even more valuable to the organization.

8. *Keep alert for operational problems caused by the personnel cutback.* Bring them to the attention of senior management, *with suggested solutions.*

9. *Be candid, but upbeat when questioned about the cutback by prospects and customers.*

10. *Do your best to provide recommendations and job leads to employees who were cut.* If you help them whenever possible maybe they wouldn't mind a call or two when you need to find out where a bone is buried.

11. *Think about doing today's job today.* Tomorrow is for the long-range planners, and long-range planning is one of the first job descriptions to get axed when times are tough.

How to Survive and Thrive When the Company Is on the Wrong End of a Takeover

The takeover mania of the 1980s appears to be over. It was a bad idea whose time had come and many companies are still paying for their cannibalistic appetites with indigestion in the form of debt loads that are almost impossible to manage. (Perhaps there ought to be a Weight Watcher's program for CEOs who feel the urge to gorge on another outfit.)

Merger, takeover, and consolidation are still going on, however, and they will continue. Leveraged buyouts don't have to make business sense, they just have to make money for the bankers, lawyers, and stockbrokers who put the deals together.

If you're working for a company on the wrong end of a takeover you have a problem. That problem is survival. The dilemma is even more acute if the two companies being merged are in the same industry. In this instance the CEO of the dominant company will justify taking on additional debt by announcing that "economies will be realized by the elimination of duplication of effort." This phrase, used to placate the Wall Street bankers who sold junk bonds to their customers to finance the takeover, means *heads will roll*. The senior-management staff of the dominant company will decide which heads. As a manager for the company being acquired, you're among the nominees. Here's how to avoid being elected:

1. *Ignore statements to the effect that no changes are planned in your specific operation.* The takeover team is merely trying to avoid panic and bailouts until they find out where the bones are buried.

2. *Be in an operational position, not in planning.* Managers for the dominant company will do all the planning from now on, thank you.

3. *Be in a position that doesn't have a direct counterpart in the takeover company.* Given a choice between you and an individual the takeover team has known for years, who do you think they'll pick?

4. *Be in a location where the takeover company doesn't have a presence.*

5. *Appear to be cooperative, friendly, and useful with members of the takeover team, but make them see how difficult it would be to replace you.* Don't tell them everything you know. Become indispensable.

6. *If you're in sales make sure the takeover team recognizes just how much of the business you bring in is based on personal relationships.*

7. *Never complain about procedural differences in how the two companies operate.* You'll be perceived as someone who can't adjust to a new situation.

8. *Never reminisce about the good old days before the takeover.* Same reasons as item seven.

9. *Try to find a mentor within the takeover company.* This may be difficult to accomplish, but it's worth trying.

10. *Learn the new reporting structure and always be up to date with reports to the new management.* Show the new management that you'll be a valuable member of the team.

11. *Don't let loyalty to old friends get in the way of your own survival.* If the head of your former boss is on the chopping block there's probably little you can do to save it. Of course, never do anything to survive at the *expense* of a colleague.

Do all these things but keep your resume polished as well.

A Ten-Point Checklist That Reveals If Your Job Is Safe

Are you on solid ground or headed toward quicksand? With so many companies cutting back these days it's important to know. The following ten-point checklist is to help you determine if your job is safe.

1. Is the company/division you're working for losing money?
   Yes _____ No _____

2. Is your company/division in a troubled industry?
   Yes _____ No _____

3. Are company/division projections on sales and profits being met?
   Yes _____ No _____

4. Are sales and profits down from previous years?
   Yes _____ No _____

5. Are you accomplishing the objectives for your operation?
   Yes _____ No _____

6. Are ominous rumors flying of pending changes?
   Yes _____ No _____

7. Have there been any resignations or changes in the executive suite?
   Yes _____ No _____

8. Is your boss on the hotseat?
   Yes _____ No _____

9. Are you making more money than most of your peers?
Yes _____ No _____

10. Could your job easily be handled by someone else?
Yes _____ No _____

Three or more "yes" answers are a sure sign of trouble. However, even a single "yes" answer is a cause for concern. If the company is losing large sums of money, that alone is often enough to trigger personnel reductions.

How to Solidify a Shaky Job

Do you have a feeling that your job sits squarely astride the San Andreas fault line? The ground trembles and what you think you feel may really be occurring. The boss, the organization, your fellow employees, all may be sending out signals that are difficult to miss. If the job is shaky here are several ways to shore up the foundation:

1. *Be sure your performance measures up to others in the company.* Good performance is the best way to nail down a job.

2. *Identify problems that may be preventing you from performing as well as others, and go to your boss with an action plan to resolve those problems.* The boss is probably already aware that these problems exist and is more likely willing to give you time to put things right if you take the first step.

3. *If you're feuding with fellow employees, stop it.* Forget about who is right or wrong, just stop being part of a disruptive situation.

4. *Learn what your boss really wants out of your operation.* Give it to him or her.

5. *Be cheerful, cooperative, and helpful to other personnel and departments.*

6. *If any employees who report to you harbor resentments, clear them up.* You won't get peak performance from anyone who holds a grudge.

7. *Initiative is a wonderful thing; take on more responsibility if you can, but not before your assigned operation is running smoothly.*

8. *Work harder and longer.* Employers recognize industry.

9. *Become informed.* Read industry newsletters, publications such as *The Wall Street Journal* and *Forbes.* Attend industry functions.

10. *Be positive and forthright.* The right attitude is a powerful asset to a career.

What do all these steps demonstrate? *That you want the job!*

Four Job Titles to Avoid in a Down Economy

Which jobs are likely to go first when a company is experiencing tough times? If you were picking what to cut wouldn't you choose those jobs whose loss would have the least near-term impact on the company's ability to perform? Those are the jobs that senior management usually decide are expendable. In particular jeopardy are the following job titles:

1. *Any title with the word "planning" in it.* If you're in market planning, or product planning, or, may the saints protect you, long-range planning, the company may feel they can do without your services until times get better.

2. *Any title with the word "coordinator" in it.* In most companies no one is quite sure what coordinators really do, so management may decide they can do without whatever that is.

3. *Any of the communication arts.* Companies going through a rough spot may decide that in-house advertising, public relations, and art departments are expensive luxuries. They often decide to buy these services, as needed, from outside sources.

4. *Private secretaries and assistants.* These too are luxuries, personnel perks for performing senior-level managers. When the company isn't performing the assistant goes out the door, the senior manager fetches his or her own coffee, and the private secretary now serves three or four people.

The Best Recession-Proof Jobs

Those jobs best situated to survive a night-of-the-long-knives include:

1. *Financial managers.* Watching the pennies, nickels, and dollars is more important than ever.

2. *Performing salespeople.* Anyone who is still bringing in business is relatively safe.

3. *Personnel managers.* If many employees are being shown the door, it's important to have a knowledgeable personnel staff to ensure that the layoffs are handled fairly. If not, the company can anticipate a host of lawsuits.

4. *Production managers.* The goods still need to get out the door.

Why the "Fast Track" Is Turning into a Path of Quicksand

Most large corporations have some kind of fast-track program in place to help attract bright young people with good academic credentials. Company recruiters, saliva barely under control, line up to interview MBAs from Harvard (the West Point of Business Schools) and other fine institutions. What they offer these graduates, in addition to excellent starting salaries, are in-house training programs designed to quickly bring them to the senior-management level.

In many companies the program means giving their prime recruits departmental responsibility on a rotating basis. The fast tracker will spend a year or two running one department, then be shifted to another with slightly more responsibility and still another shift with more responsibility a year or so later. The idea is to groom the fast trackers for senior management by giving them a rounded view of how the company operates.

In lean times the programs are often considered a bit of a luxury. For starters, the company is paying top dollar to hire on young men and women without a bit of experience. There's usually internal resentment of the program among the middle-level managers who don't have the benefit of an MBA and would like to see salaries and promotions based solely on merit.

Moving managers from department to department to "educate" them can be expensive. There's always a learning period when taking on a new responsibility. Efficiency sometimes suffers during these periods. As companies trim back, one of the tendencies is to keep managers in positions for longer times, regardless of their academic credentials. What counts most is current performance. The fast trackers are required to compete for the next step up the ladder, just as everyone else is. In this manner recessions can be said to have a democratic effect on corporations.

Kick-Starting a Stalled Career

There are sure signs that indicate a career has been stalled and likely to go no further. Some of these signs include:

1. *Promotion has passed the manager by more than once.*

2. *The manager is no longer invited to important meetings.*

3. *The manager is left off important project teams.*

4. *The boss no longer consults with or even criticizes the manager.*

5. *The manager learns about the juicy stuff that's going on internally only after everyone else seems to be tired of the story.*

If these signs seem familiar, your career has been stalled, adrift in the sea of despair without a breeze on the horizon.

Getting that stalled career moving again is difficult because senior management no longer considers you a serious candidate for promotion. However, it can be done. Try the following steps:

1. *Review your own performance.* Is it mediocre? What can be done to improve it? Develop an action plan and take it to your boss.

2. *Review your relationship with your boss.* If there's a personality conflict, perhaps you should consider a lateral move. Getting a fresh start in another department has revived many a career.

3. *Scramble to get on those project teams that will bring you to the attention of the senior management.*

4. *Take more risks.* If your career is stalled you don't have much to lose. Most senior management appreciates risk takers if the risks are calculated and well conceived. (Remember the GE informal policy that states no person can rise to the presidency who hasn't had at least a one-million-dollar failure.)

5. *Ask your boss what's holding you back.* You may not get a candid answer, but you may be told where you're lacking. If you are told, act on the advice.

6. *Emulate those in the company who are succeeding.* Obviously, the company likes what they are doing, so why not do the same thing?

7. *Develop listening skills.* One sure path to success is to really listen to and understand what people have to say.

8. *Concentrate on the job.* If your personal life is causing distractions find a way to put them aside while at work.

9. *Take some classes.* Learn something you don't know.

Jumping Ship: Five Distress Flares That Signal When It May Be Time to Bail Out of the Organization

Staying on with a company that's in trouble is admirable. It shows loyalty and dedication. There are, however, signs of financial distress that cannot be ignored by managers interested in their own well being. When these signs are present it may be time to polish up that resume:

1. *Accounts receivable are increasing faster than sales.* This means the company has been so anxious to book business, they haven't been too discreet about issuing credit to marginal credit risks. Once started, it's a losing game. When accounts receivable reach a certain age, a portion of them won't ever be paid. Uncollected receivables have driven more than one company under.

2. *The company warehouses are stocked with dusty boxes of unsold inventory.* This means the company hasn't correctly projected sales and/or that market conditions have changed drastically. Always remember that inventory is another form of money. Stacks of dollar bills are sitting on those skids.

3. *Company checks are being returned marked NSF.* This is a dead-certain sign of a critical cash-flow problem.

4. *Senior management is squabbling about everything under the sun.* Pressure leads to short tempers. If the quarrels are no secret, the problems may be serious.

5. *Short-term debt is increasing.* The company may be borrowing money to stay afloat. One day the banks will refuse to give them any more.

This kind of information may seem difficult to acquire, but it's not. A friend in finance would be useful, but even that connection isn't absolutely necessary. Look around you at every opportunity. Stroll through the warehouse or plant. Are boxes stacked to the ceiling? Are there critical shortages of vital supplies? Is the company running two and three months late paying expense checks? Have suppliers threatened to cut off further shipments?

Does management seem reluctant to solve any problems if the solutions require a cash expenditure? Are doors being slammed in the executive suite, and the voices behind them raised in anger? Does everyone upstairs seem stressed? Does the credit manager have a look of hopeless desperation? Have friends or business acquaintances asked you if anything is wrong at your company?

If the answers to many of these questions are "yes," it may be time to start building that life raft.

❖ 2 ❖

LEARNING HOW TO COMMUNICATE: THE KEY TO SUCCESS IN ANY CAREER

Learn to Present Ideas Simply

Business is a game of ideas, connections, and, most of all, persuasion. Clever ideas are not enough. Effective managers are able to communicate the wonder and glory behind their ideas. The "golden throats" get the corner offices and the keys to the executive bathroom.

An entire library could be filled with books on persuasion techniques. The bottom-line conclusion of most of these works is that it's not so much what is said, but *whether or not the listener buys the message*. Convincing talk beats smooth talk every time.

Here's a short course on how to get an individual or group to buy your "pitch":

1. *Be convinced yourself.* Belief is contagious. Leaders with fixed convictions have infected entire nations.

2. *Present ideas as clearly and simply as possible.* Put them in a context that will make the listener comfortable. In order for the message to be accepted it must be understood.

Imagine two proposals given to the board of directors of a major corporation. One is a brilliant scheme offering a wide range of benefits to the prospect corporation. However, the presentation is muddled, the details of the plan are fuzzy, and the explanation is complicated. As a consequence the board members don't fully understand what is being proposed. Questions to the person making the presentation cause further confusion because the answers are not candid or the explanations seem to bring up further complications.

The second proposal doesn't offer the company nearly the advantages of the first, but the presentation is clear and logical. The ideas are explained simply and smoothly. The board members are made to understand the full benefits of the offer. The presenter is likable, has enthusiasm and passion for the subject matter, uses displays to illustrate the more complex issues, establishes eye contact and rapport with the board members, fields questions easily, and has anticipated most objections.

Which of these two proposals is more likely to be accepted? The answer, of course, is the simpler one. Decision makers want to understand something before they agree to it. So the first rule of communication is to keep the message simple. The more radical the change that is being proposed, the simpler the explanation must be.

Senior management has a distrust for complicated: They believe it is inefficient. That doesn't mean there isn't hope for a complex plan. There is, if the explanation for that plan makes it easy to follow. The more simply and clearly an idea is explained, the more likely it will be accepted by others. Want career success? Learn how to express ideas so others can understand them.

The Art of Persuasion

There are many different styles of persuasion. Watch the Evangelists in action. Many are powerful spellbinders, spilling out a torrent of words and emotion to bring people to religion. If you've ever seen people marching down the aisle to accept Jesus you know how effective these persuaders are. The pitchman selling a kitchen product overwhelms the listener with benefits. It "slices, dices, shreds, and peels." They keep on buying expensive television time to sell in this manner so the system must work. The political candidate uses solution selling, first outlining the severity of the problem the nation faces, then offering the answer in terms of his or her election.

In most business situations, however, managers don't have the luxury of giving an uninterrupted harangue to an audience already half convinced or half-bemused. There is usually a to-and-fro between speaker and some-what skeptical listeners. This requires a different approach, beginning with an apparent appeal to logic. All good persuaders in business situations have several things in common:

1. *They connect ideas to the well being or the benefit of the listener.*

2. *They use emotion to sway judgment, but mask it as logic.*

3. *Through the use of questions they probe for any of the listeners' lingering doubts.*

4. *They make sure that understanding and agreement have been reached on one point before going on to another.*

5. *They give the appearance of being candid and open when questioned.* In fact, they welcome objections.

6. *Their enthusiasm is infectious.* Like the Evangelist, they get the audience involved.

The effective persuader tries to cover these six points when trying to convince one person, or an entire group.

Why Listening Is the Single Most Important Communication Skill a Manager Can Possess

Communication is an interchange of ideas, thoughts, and opinions. There's not much interchange of anything if only one person is doing the talking. You can learn a lot more with your mouth shut and your ears open. Listening is the way to learn what's going on, a way to find out what you don't know. It's the best method ever developed to gather information.

There are many good talkers, but too few good listeners. Some managers and many salespeople believe that "communicating" means en-gaging in a nonstop monologue. What is being communicated is a disregard for the other person's point of view. That leads to resentment and disbelief. Want to be more persuasive? Let the other person do most of the talking.

For those who always seem to be causing hurricane-force winds with their rapid lip movement, here's a simple question to ask before each meeting: *Which is the more important goal for me today, to give information or to obtain it?* If the purpose of the meeting is to obtain information, then shut up and listen. If the other party is also a listener, ask a series of questions to get that information flowing in your direction.

Never consider listening as passive. The good listener is like a counter puncher who steps inside a roundhouse right to punish his opponent's rib cage. Allowing the other person to do most of the talking while you listen helps you evaluate the person, while revealing few cues about yourself.

Listening to your boss and customers is important because it's the way to learn what they expect of you. The surest path to success is to give people what they want. How can you know what they want? Listen and they will tell you. Prospects tell salespeople exactly what they must do to get the business. Women tell men what they must do to win their hearts. Voters tell candidates what they must do to win their votes.

Listening is a simple, sure-fire formula for getting ahead in business. Once you learn how to do it constructively, don't stop with bosses and customers. Listen to everyone—even your wife or husband. Listening to employees is worthwhile because the practice will help you retain the good ones. In return for the use of your ear, employees will warn you about the problems that must be faced to get the job accomplished. Listening to friends helps cement relationships. Listening to the wise can help you gather wisdom.

Ten Steps Toward Good Listening

Those who haven't had much experience listening, and that covers most of the population, need to practice acquiring good listening habits. Here are ten steps in acquiring these habits:

1. *Be more devoted to acquiring information than to imparting it.* Decide that you want to come out of a conversation with more knowledge than you had when the talking began. A desire to learn more is the first step toward acquiring listening skills.

2. *Be prepared to like the person doing the talking.* People sense when they're liked and are more inclined to open up.

3. *Ask for clarifications on any points you don't understand.* Most people don't mind expanding on their explanations. Many are pleased because it's a sign that you're really listening.

4. *Show that you're interested in what the other person has to say.* Maintain eye contact, keep facial features alert, use body language, such leaning slightly forward, to indicate interest.

5. *Being a good listener doesn't mean forcing the other person to conduct a nonstop monologue.* Most people will eventually run

out of gas. Participate in the conversation with comments, questions, observations, reinforcements, laughter, approvals, and so forth. Rather than directing the conversation, let it flow. Ask questions, but never in a manner that seems to cross-examine the speaker. You're not the District Attorney or the Grand Inquisitor.

6. *If you're looking for candor in the other person, be candid yourself when asked questions.* The best way to inspire confidence is to give it.

7. *Be a trustworthy confidante.* Never betray a confidence. Don't be a snitch. Don't use anything you've learned to hurt anyone. Don't indulge in gossip.

8. *Don't use questioning as a method for delaying important decisions.* People will see through this stalling tactic.

9. *Don't ask stupid questions.* People find this habit irritating.

10. *Be careful of asking "why?" when probing through questioning.* This word puts people on the defensive because it is judgmental. It suggests the reason may not be satisfactory to the person doing the questioning.

Ten Clever Questions That Get People Talking

Good listeners prime the pump with provocative questions that get others talking. Here are open questions that can be used in almost any business situation.

1. *What is your personal responsibility in this organization?* Starting any inquiry by recognizing the individual being questioned as a valuable contributor is always a good idea.

2. *Do you like what you're doing?*

3. *How do things really work around here?* What would you change if you could?

4. *What kind of results would you like to see that you're not now getting?*

5. *How do you feel those results could be achieved?*

6. *What's not working well?* Alternate: What's the biggest bottleneck?

7. *What do you think needs to be done to fix things?* What stands in the way of these changes being made?

8. *What are the good things that we should keep or build upon?*

9. *What would you like to see me (my department, my company) do in this situation?*

10. *What are your biggest concerns?* What could go wrong? How can we guard against these things?

Ask those questions and you may get more information than you can assimilate.

How to Read the Hidden Messages Behind What People Tell You: a Guide to Verbal and Nonverbal Clues

There's a famous cartoon in which one psychiatrist says, "Good morning," and a second psychiatrist replies, "I wonder what he meant by that?" The point is that it's difficult to understand human feelings and motivation. People don't always say what they mean. That's one reason the phrase "hidden agenda" has become so popular today. So how can we find out what's really on another person's mind?

Fortunately, people reveal themselves in other ways, such as in the way they dress, gesture, position their bodies, use facial expressions, use tone of voice, and even in the words that are chosen to disguise their true intentions.

The first rule in understanding hidden messages is *don't look for them everywhere.* Usually, the obvious, the face value, is the correct perception of the situation. (The guy who bodily throws you out of his office really doesn't like you.) Adopting the attitude that not everything has a subliminal meaning will save the manager a good deal of time trying to interpret every innocent gesture.

The smile is the single most used nonverbal method of communication. Most people smile many times a day. The principal message the smile is intended to convey is that everything is "okay" on the smiler's end. Another meaning is, "I'm no threat." Bosses use it to show that a criticism is not serious, or that an employee is still in favor. Women smile as a social gesture to indicate friendliness.

Conversely, managers who are skilled nonverbal communicators can use a frown or an irritated look to indicate dissatisfaction with an employee's work without saying a word. Some bosses have so mastered the art that their subordinates would rather endure a dressing down than a single withering look.

In a meeting arms closed over the chest usually means the mind is closed as well. The person with folded arms is fortifying himself against the facts. A listener's frequent eye contact with the speaker means the message may be getting home. The listener leaning slightly forward is another indication that the message is being received. Nodding is another indication of mental agreement with the speaker. Some persuasive techniques call for the speaker to nod frequently, hoping the listener will copy the head movement.

The executive who comes out from behind a desk to greet visitors and seats herself next to the visitor on a sofa or in facing chairs during the entire interview is saying she is open and doesn't need the protection of a barrier. This is a very thoughtful business courtesy.

The person who receives a proposal and throws it, unopened, on a desk with the comment, "I'll look at it later," is saying, "I'll pick my own priorities, thank you. Looking at your stuff right now isn't one of them."

Much has been written about "personal space" and the "territorial imperative." What's meant by those phrases is that nobody wants another person right in his or her face. In business meetings, however, if the others are leaving you too much space they may be symbolically casting you out of the group. It may be time to review recent disagreements with other group members. (Not showering for a month would also explain it.)

Tone of voice and even style of speech communicate certain things. The style of delivery can become more important than the message. Want to develop a reputations as a cool, dispassionate thinker? Start speaking only after everyone else has offered an opinion, then speak slowly, measure every word, hesitate every now and then as if seeking precise meaning, fiddle with something, catch everyone's eye for one brief, significant moment, and finally return to silence as if your remarks covered everything of any possible consequence.

Actors aren't the only ones who use stage props. A pipe used to be a very popular device to indicate the deliberate thinker. The pipe user can scrape the bowl, tamp the tobacco, unscrew the stem, take forever lighting up, let aromatic fumes drift through the room, all the while permitting others to do the talking. When this person finally opens his mouth, it's as if Solomon were voicing an opinion.

Silence is another powerful communicator. It is usually used in a negative manner. *Silence indicates the withholding of approval.* It is a negative vote without actually saying no. Those who are silent will be courted by others who try to change their opinion. The silent ones are considered thoughtful, deliberate, incisive, deep thinkers, careful. In other words, a wonderful reputation can be earned by merely keeping your mouth shut.

In some business organizations the person they'd like to see out the door is often given the silent treatment. This isn't done in the "Sent to Coventry" method of the British Trade Unions, who wouldn't recognize the existence of the person given the treatment. The American method is much more civilized. Other employees still talk to the person, but not about anything that matters to the business. He or she doesn't learn about the important meetings, is left off committees, doesn't get copied on memos, gets crummy service from the steno pool, is sometimes assigned demeaning work, and so forth.

The important thing for managers to learn is that nonverbal signals, smiles, frowns, body positioning, eye contact, closeness, style of speech delivery are all important communication tools that can help get the message across.

How to Use Internal Memos to Get Promotions

The internal memo can be an art form just as creative as the novel or a Shakespearean sonnet. The difference is that, properly used, the internal memo can advance a manager's career.

Memos were originally intended to convey information between company departments and between bosses and their subordinates. Today they are primarily used for either defensive or self-serving reasons. These reasons include:

1. *To take credit for things that go right.*

2. *To avoid blame for things that go wrong.*

3. *To warn about impending disaster and thereby avoid responsibility for the fallout from that disaster.*

4. *To put the manager's interpretation of the facts on the record early in the game in case things go wrong later.*

5. *To appear incisive and resourceful to members of senior management.*

Some managers are "memo happy." They go through enough paper every day to destroy acres of timberland. Their memos usually predict dire circumstances if certain things aren't done. These are just another version of the Protect Your Butt memo. ("Hey, don't look at me, I warned you guys this would happen.")

Neither the taking-credit-/or the avoiding-blame-type memos are likely to advance a career, so forget about them. Both are greeted with yawns in the executive suite.

The kind of memo likely to move you up the ladder a bit ahead of schedule is the "enterprise memo." These memos involve risk because the author suggests real change in the organization. He or she sees something that could be done better or targets an opportunity the company would be advised to pursue. A good idea advanced with enthusiasm and daring shows the kind of enterprise and risk taking that senior management is looking for. However, there is always resistance to genuine change, so the memo writer making this kind of suggestion can expect resentment.

When writing the enterprise memo, keep the following things in mind:

1. *Write only an outline of the idea.* Short memos have a better chance of being read and understood. Have the details available for those who express an interest. This procedure also protects against someone pirating your plan.

2. *Polish the writing until a child could understand what is being proposed.*

3. *Try to suggest evolutionary rather than revolutionary changes.* They are easier for others in the organization to understand and accept. They also have a better chance of working.

4. *Suggest changes related to the manager's particular areas of responsibility and expertise.* Offering suggestions for improvement that relate to the department across the hall will not endear any manager to peers in that department.

5. *Expect criticism.* Be prepared to defend the ideas. Write down any anticipated objections and have brilliant replies ready that overcome them. People resist change, and they attack the messenger who suggests it may be necessary.

6. *Send copies of any recommendations as high up the managerial ladder as is politically prudent.* Don't overreach.

7. *Expect inertia.* There may not be much reaction unless the memo is followed up. Wonderful, innovative ideas clutter the bottom drawer of file cabinets all over America. To get action, take action.

8. *Save the ammunition.* Don't bombard senior management with a series of enterprise memos just to show the brass what a clever person they have on board. Quantity dilutes strength.

9. *Give credit to others who have contributed to the plan.* The idea hasn't yet been accepted. Don't hog the glory until there's some to hog.

10. *Have an implementation plan ready to go just in case the suggested changes are accepted.* The manager who makes any suggestion has a big stake in its success. Make sure the predicted results come true.

Writing the PYB (Protect Your Butt) Memo

Copy-machine manufacturers owe much of the success of their products to the proliferation of the PYB memo. These memos, with copies distributed to everyone listed in the local white-pages directory, are written to avoid blame for things that could go wrong. The writer senses calamity on the horizon. By warning everyone within memo range about the danger, he or she feels righteously absolved of further responsibility.

Of course the PYB memos are entirely self-serving. They usually offer no solutions, just preach impending doom. Others are side-kicks sent along with other material to prove that something was done. (Here's the stuff I promised you by November 1st.) Others complain about things that weren't done. (Your report did not arrive on schedule. That puts this entire project in jeopardy.)

It's easy to be scornful of PYB memos, but many managers feel they are career insurance. Given the bureaucratic climate of most large corporations and the mincemeat that is made of scapegoats, who's to say they're not right? If PYB memos are a survival tool in your outfit, you might as well make sure they are correctly written.

The well-polished PYB memo consists of several elements:

1. *A statement of the potential problem.*

2. *The irreparable harm that will be caused by the problem.*

3. *How the problem affects the manager.* (I can't do my job because _____)

4. *A course of action by others in the company that would resolve the problem.*

Note that the PYB memo writer considers duty to the company is done once the alarm has been raised. He or she has done everything humanly possible to sidestep calamity.

The most important factors when constructing a PYB memo are:

1. *Have the facts straight.*

2. *Don't leave out important parts that someone responding to the memo could use to diffuse the arguments.*

3. *Don't criticize or even imply criticism of anyone more that one level higher on the corporate ladder.*

4. *Don't complain about company procedures that have been in place since The Flood.* You'll just irritate the brass who have learned to love this red tape.

5. *Stash the memo in a desk drawer for at least two days before sending it.* That will provide enough time to see if it's really necessary.

How to Respond When on the Receiving End of a PYB Memo

The morning's internal mail contains a bombshell in the form of a short note from one of your peers complaining about a perceived problem in one of your areas of responsibility. The note is diplomatically worded, but the implication is that you aren't doing your job! It may require two or three readings to understand the intent of the memo if it is written by one who is a master of the style. What to do? This kind of implied criticism cannot go unanswered.

First, look at the bottom of the memo to see who received copies. Some managers may try to sandbag one of their peers by sending off blind copies to everyone in the company who comes to work in a business suit, but this is really dirty pool. You'll need to copy everyone that the sender copied. If no one of importance was copied you may be able to resolve the problem with a phone call.

An early personal contact of the, "Hey, Charley, what's really bothering you?" variety could circumvent a possible memo avalanche. (They don't call it the "white death" for nothing.) Whenever possible, seek intramural solutions without bringing the problem to the attention of others.

Next, examine the contents of the memo to see if the sender's complaint is legitimate. Step outside your own operation for a moment. Would you be complaining too about this matter if you were the other guy? If so, and the problem can be fixed, then fix it. Be sure to let the memo writer know that the problem is being addressed. (Dear Chuck: Thanks for bringing this to my attention.)

If the complaint is just self-serving baloney to make the sender look good at your expense, study the memo for flaws in fact and logic. Don't be surprised if you find them by the carload. Many of these kind of memos omit or deliberately distort details to make the arguments more persuasive.

A reply that includes details that diffuse the arguments makes it appear as if the sender shot from the hip and makes the answer seem well thought out. If the sender's reasoning is sloppy, a little sarcasm may prevent a reoccurrence. (Sarcasm is a powerful weapon when replying to a peer, but extremely risky when answering a superior.)

Remember that the real "audience" for the reply are senior managers who were copied by the sender. Don't do anything to infuriate them. Don't appear to be feuding with the original memo sender.

Whom to Copy on Memos and Whom to Leave Off

There are certain courtesies to be observed when putting that old "CC" at the bottom of the page.

1. *Always send a copy to anyone mentioned in the memo, particularly if that person is criticized.* This gives the person a chance to respond.

2. *When writing a memo critical of another person or department, be sure to have the facts right.* If you're wrong about something, the return memo—and an answer will be coming just as certain as Christmas is coming—may make you look foolish.

3. *Don't ever direct a memo to your boss's boss without clearing it in advance.* End runs won't endear you to anyone. When it is necessary to send your boss a memo, however, it's usually okay to copy the people upstairs.

4. *Keep memos directed to your boss at a minimum.* They are more formal than a chat. Establish the kind of relationship that allows for informal discussion of most issues.

5. *Copy your boss on all memos sent to others so he or she will know what you're up to.*

6. *Sending a copy to the boss of someone you're criticizing is optional.* It all depends on how much you wish to annoy, wound, or make an enemy out of that person.

7. *Don't send copies to people who have no interest in the subject matter.* They get enough memos as is.

8. *Be generous with memos that praise others for a job well done.* Praise memos should outnumber critical memos by a ratio of at least ten to one.

Why You Should Avoid the "Gotcha" Memo Whenever Possible

Some managers can't seem to avoid feuds with their peers. Perhaps they have a need to make the job more interesting. Hostility for those around you does provide another fascinating reason for coming to work. Putting that hostility in writing to "get" someone else, however, is counterproductive. It detracts from the sender perhaps more than it does from the recipient.

If another manager has made an error or neglected a vital portion of the job responsibility, let the managerial chain of command handle the situation, unless it directly affects your own operation. They probably know what's going on. If the problems of another department are interfering with your own performance, bring them to the attention of your direct supervisor. Let your boss write the nasty memo.

The written rebuke by a peer is like a gauntlet thrown down as challenge to a duel. It's bound to get a reaction, most often in the form of a countercharge. At the very least it creates an internal foe, someone who wishes you ill and thinks bad thoughts about you on the bus going home.

If a subordinate is causing a problem, a personal talk may produce better results than will a strong written rebuke, which would become part of that employee's personnel file. The written rebuke will be in the file forever. In fact, don't write any memos that are designed solely to make someone else look bad. It's the best way to avoid being on the receiving end of the same kind of guided missile.

How to Get a Handle on Your Boss's Hidden Agenda

The person you report to is likely have goals and aspirations that you don't know about. Some managers are so focused on their own careers they never bother to find out what their direct superiors want. That's a mistake because one sure way to get ahead is to help the boss get ahead.

Unless you become a confidant, chances are you may never learn what the boss has outlined as a career path. Some goals are fairly easy to guess. For example, the boss probably yearns for the next step up the managerial ladder. However, he or she may hunger for something entirely different. Perhaps the boss wants to take over control of another department. Other goals remain hidden. Perhaps an older boss is maneuvering for an early retirement offer.

Here's a list of fairly common hidden agendas and clues that help identify them:

Hidden Agenda	*Clues*
Wants a promotion	• Tries to outperform other departments. • Grooms a successor. • Plays company politics. • Eagerly accepts additional responsibility. • Drives people hard. • Anxious about performance of peers. • Deeply concerned about day-to-day operation.
Wants power	• Cultivates senior management. • Plays politics. • Writes long-range plan type memos. • Tries to dominate other departments. • Conspires or feuds with other department heads. • Leaves day-to-day operation to subordinates.
Wants to ride out a few year until retirement	• Doesn't make waves. • Won't take chances. • Doesn't work long hours. • Makes subordinates responsible for things that go wrong. • Frequently unavailable. • Nice to everybody.
Wants to be CEO of the company	• Flirts with financial community. • Acquires disciples. • Tries to develop knowledge of all company operations.

	• Spends a lot of time with the balance sheet.
	• Talks about the "Big Picture."
Wants out	• Frequently absent.
	• Usually distracted.
	• Office door frequently closed.
	• Only mildly concerned about department's results.
	• Has temper tantrums.
	• Knocks top management.
Looking for a scapegoat	• Flurry of "gotcha" memos.
	• Focuses on errors, no matter how small.
	• Blames other departments for anything that goes wrong.
	• Loses employees for one reason or another.
	• Won't put directives in writing.
	• Frequently changes mind.

How to Use Your Boss's Hidden Agenda to Get What You Want

Why is it important to know what the boss really wants? Because your own career can be advanced by helping the rascal attain it. In many cases you'll find yourself drafted to help out, but whether conscripted or not, make yourself a willing participant in the achievement of the boss's career ambitions. This policy almost always works to your advantage. If the chief is promoted, someone is needed to take his or her place. Who is more likely to be recommended than the person who contributed most to that promotion?

Loyalty and devotion to a superior are excellent tactics for career success. If the boss is headed for greatness, so much the better. Being carried along in the jet stream of a shooting star makes the rise to the corporate suite much less fatiguing.

What to Avoid Putting into Writing

Some managers like to detail everything. Writing things down does seem to make the work place more open, directions and procedures more precise, and commitments more solid. The problem with being "memo happy" is that a specific detail (euphemism for mistake) will inevitably come back to bite the manager. If one of your recorded blunders is in the file somewhere, count on at least one of your dear buddies in the corporation to make sure it eventually sees the light of day.

Mistakes in verbal directions, conversations, can always be attributed to a "wrong interpretation of what was really meant." This lays the blame on the listener for being too dull-witted to fully understand. The written record, however, is there for all to see and interpret as they will. The commodity buyer's prediction, "corn will go higher," three weeks before the most bountiful grain harvest in history and a disastrous drop in prices is bound to create problems for the Nostradamus who made it, if it's in writing. If said verbally, the speaker can make the claim that he meant that corn would *grow* higher.

What specifically should you avoid committing to paper? Here's a handy little list.

1. *Long-range predictions, unless your job is forecasting.*

2. *Criticism of another operation or person in the company unless that criticism is based on dead certainties.*

3. *Commitments to achievements of goals above and beyond what the company and your superiors expect of the operation.*

4. *Information of a negative nature about another employee's habits outside the work place.* (Never do this unless you have a lawyer in the family who is willing to work for nothing.)

5. *Suggestions that the company engage in any illegal activity, such as bribing an important buyer, hiding a problem with a product, or ignoring a government regulation.*

6. *Acknowledgment that the company has in the past engaged in illegal activity.*

7. *Commitments to employees for special payments on items not covered by the company's standard compensation plan.* (Unless specifically authorized by personnel.)

8. *Plans on how to put a competitor out of business.*

9. *Plans on how to circumvent industry or government standards.*

10. *Suggestions that reports or findings be covered up because the results might embarrass the company.*

Obviously it's best not to engage in these activities at all. To engage in them and commit the details to paper is downright indiscreet.

How to Respond to a Critical Memo from Your Boss

It came without warning in the afternoon interoffice mail, a stinging rebuke from the boss concerning your performance. The memo is several pages long, goes into detail about your alleged transgressions, and everyone in the company phone directory seems to have been copied. There's no doubt about it, you've been stuck in the side by a lance. What do you do now?

The first thing to do is the hardest thing to do, and that is *take your emotions out of the situation*. Forget about being hurt, forget about striking back, for the time being even forget about defending yourself. The immediate goal is damage control.

Next, ask yourself a critical question: How, when, and why did all communication between yourself and the boss break down? You see, if the memo comes as a surprise, if you weren't called into the boss's office and told verbally that your recent performance was causing an odor permeating five floors in either direction, the communication between you two *must* have broken down. Search hard for the answer to that one. because it's the key to fixing things.

Read the memo thoroughly and objectively. Go back and read it again until you almost have it memorized. Make sure that you understand every point the boss makes. More hard questions for yourself come now:

1. *Is the criticism justified?*
2. *If it's not justified, what can be done to set the record straight?*
3. *Is there a possibility the boss knows the criticism is not justified?* If so, what's the motive at work?
4. *If the criticism is justified, what can be done to fix things?*

If the memo makes valid criticisms, *acknowledge them*. The memo was probably the result of your boss's frustration in trying to make you shape up. Write a reply memo, detailing how you plan to do better. Don't send it, but rather take it in to your boss and explain each point. Set timetables for improvement. Obtain agreement that the plan is feasible. Ask for suggestions on how to make it better. Close the meeting by thanking the boss for the "constructive criticism" and for taking the time to set you straight.

If the facts of the memo are in error, now is the time to set the record straight. Reply to each point in detail. Prove your case through reference to records, old memos, outside sources, anything that is difficult to refute. Take the reply into the boss. Don't be confrontational, but go over the details with him. If the boss caves in a bit, settle for an admittance that this was all a "misunderstanding." If he's firm, ask for a written reply that responds to the corrections you've made. Make sure every person copied on the original memo gets a copy of your reply.

If the memo is deliberately misleading, you have a serious problem. The boss doesn't like you, but it's often difficult to prove that malice motivated the memo. Many memos that are deliberately meant to wound contain a little truth, a little fiction, and a lot of exaggeration. It may be difficult to sort out the categories.

Concentrate on what is patently false. If enough details can be presented to convincingly refute a few claims, the rest may be discounted as well. Copy everyone on the reply memo. Review your reply with the highest person you can reach on the executive ladder. Don't worry about alienating your boss; that has happened already. During a quiet moment ask the boss why the attempt to harm your career. You may not get a candid answer, but the boss will know that you recognize what has been going on.

The Report Worksheet: Suggestions for Writing Reports That Get Noticed

Want to write reports that sparkle and bring you to the attention of senior management? Consider these factors before striking the first key on the word processor:

1. *Who gets a copy of the report.* Send copies only to parties interested in the subject. There's nothing more boring than reading about something in which there is no interest. Better to leave someone off who should have a copy than add someone who couldn't care less. Remember the old show-business motto: keep them crying for more.

2. *Tell them what you're going to tell them.* Detail the subject matter early on and detail it succinctly. Let those who aren't interested in this subject file the report, unread, now.

3. *Tell them where you're going with all this.* Define the report's objectives. What do you hope to accomplish with this report?

4. *Tell them how you did it.* Define the methods used to develop the material used in the report. However, don't make this section an epic. There's no point in describing the problems you had in obtaining the material.

5. *Tell them what you're telling them.* Write the body of the report. Keep the sentences short, the words nontechnical, and the language easy to understand. It's the surest method for being original. The way to avoid clichés, hackneyed expressions, and pompous phrases is to write as simply as possible.

6. *Be positive about what you want to say.* State your case with conviction. Avoid equivocation. That means stay away from words such as "however," "usually," "sometimes," "often," "seems," and so forth.

7. *Use displays.* Charts, graphs, tables can often tell a story far more dramatically than prose can.

8. *Reach conclusions.* To make a report come alive, the report writer must have a point of view. Nothing is more unsatisfactory than a report that is only a compilation of facts and figures.

9. *Make recommendations.* Climb out on that shaky limb. Tell the readers what should be done.

10. *Polish the work.* Most novelists rewrite their manuscripts many times before sending them off to a publisher. Do the same with your reports.

Report Worksheet

On pages 54–55 is a report worksheet that covers the basic ingredients found in most reports. Many reports will include additional factors.

Why "Less Is More" in Business Writing

Some creative writing instructors believe that if the plot of a novel can't be described in a single sentence the novelist doesn't have a clear idea of what she wants to say. Use that criterion in business writing. Present only the bare bones of your ideas. Use as few words as possible and choose words that everyone understands. Think of a memo as a guerrilla raid on foreign territory. Get in, do what damage has to be done, and get out quickly.

Report Worksheet

Subject matter_____

_____

Date due _____ Ordered by_____

Copies to_____

_____

_____

Objectives_____

_____

_____

_____

Methodology _____

_____

_____

_____

_____

Body of report (use as many pages as necessary) _____

_____

_____

_____

_____

_____

_____

_____

_____

_____

_____

_____

Displays _____

_____

_____

_____

_____

Conclusions _____

_____

_____

_____

_____

Action recommendations _____

_____

_____

_____

_____

The longer the memo, the less chance of its being read. With today's attention spans, anything longer than a page is on the endangered species list.

How to keep memos short? Here's a short list of do's and don'ts:

1. *Define what you want to get across.* Make sure the message is important.

2. *Don't package too many ideas in a single memo.*

3. *Write simple declarative sentences.*

4. *Avoid clichés and trite phrases.*

5. *Don't qualify every statement.*

6. *Don't confuse formality and stiffness with good writing.* For example, why write "It has been brought to my attention," when, "I heard that," says the same thing in fewer words?

Read your memos over several times before sending them. Be ruthless when editing. Use slash-and-burn tactics on the text. The shorter and clearer the memos, the more the writer will gain the reputation as a "good communicator."

How to Present Boring Details

There's some material, such as technical specifications, that must be included in certain proposals, memos, and reports. This is stuff that is so boring Hemingway couldn't make it interesting. Still, there's good and sufficient reason for the material to be there.

Only lifetime members of the Nitpicker's Association are likely to wade through this section of a report. Recognizing that corporate decision makers are usually not classified as dogged readers (unless perusing the section of the compensation plan that pertains to their bonuses) here's the best way to handle this kind of material.

1. *Put the boring details all the way in the back as an addendum.* When necessary, refer to it in the text of the report.

2. *Advise the reader that the following section is technical or detailed in nature and refer to the point where the memo again becomes "interesting."*

3. *Eliminate the technical language and jargon to present the material in a way that most readers can understand.* (This is easier said than done.)

4. *Provide a one-page synopsis of the technical stuff to the full report.*

5. *Go over the memo verbally with the recipient by passing the boring details, and leave a hard copy for later review.*

6. *Bring along a technical type and let him present the material to the prospect's technical type.*

How to Use Details to Mask the True Agenda

The magician doing sleight-of-hand tricks directs the attention of the audience in one direction with a flurry of gestures while the real "business" is taking place in another. The movements themselves are meaningless, except as a device to catch and deflect the viewer's eye.

Business writing can likewise be sleight of hand, designed to obscure the author's true intentions. For example, a memo that expresses alarm about a situation might be designed to relieve the writer from pressure from a far more serious situation.

One way a memo writer can mask true intent is to bury the recipient in details. The more "evidence" that is presented, the more carefully that both sides of the question are apparently identified and considered. the less the sender's motives are suspected. Somewhere in the body of the report hides the "zinger" the sender wanted to get on record. This tactic is particularly useful when trying to obtain approval for projects. The real cost for the project might be buried in paragraph fourteen on page five.

How to Write Effective Proposals

Writing proposals takes time and money. Here are a set of informal rules that will make them more effective:

1. *The first rule of proposal writing is to be convinced that your company has something to offer that meets the prospect's need.*

2. *Proposals should be in plain writing that nontechnical people can understand.*

3. *Proposals should be specific; like all good sales pitches, they should emphasize the benefits.*

4. *Proposals should be as short as possible.* They should demonstrate logic and organization.

5. *Most of all, proposals should reflect that genuine thought and consideration had been given to the prospect's problems and that inspiration had gone into the solution.*

A typical proposal usually includes the following sections:

1. *The way the prospect does things now.* (An outline of the prospect's problem.)

2. *A new and improved method that the writer is "proposing."*

3. *The steps by which this new method will be delivered.*

4. *A breakdown of the costs associated with the proposed new system.*

5. *A detailing of the savings in money, time, materials, and labor by adopting the new system.*

6. *An implementation schedule that details how long it will take to get the new system up and running.*

7. *The credentials of the company making the proposal to give the prospect confidence that the company can handle the job.*

8. *References, testimonials, and so forth on past successes.*

Many proposal writers also swear by an executive summary that details the results being offered. This is the section that senior executives at the prospect company are likely to read.

Public Speaking: How to Use the Lectern as a Stepping Stone to Career Advancement

Ever study how a good speaker manipulates an audience? Some are marvels. The motivational types send their listeners charging out of their seats to slay dragons. The persuasive ones shape logic to change the most closed minds. The spellbinders use emotion to make the color black appear white. The storytellers rely on humor and example to quickly establish rapport with the wary. These speakers may use different styles to reach their objectives, but what they have in common is the ability to reach out from the lectern and touch their listeners.

This is an ability that would benefit every manager who has been required to "hold the floor" at one time or another. The occasion may be a small meeting of peers, a major project presentation to senior management, or a proposal to a client. Each time behind that lectern should be treated as an opportunity for career advancement.

Verbal communication is still the essence of business. The ability to persuade is highly treasured by senior management. The best (and easiest) time to display this ability is when making some kind of presentation. One reason presentations offer the best opportunity to shine is because there are limited interruptions. The person at the lectern has the chance to present a positive, forceful image. This is the time to show off a variety of talents including:

Verbal skills

Material preparation

Organization

Knowledge of the subject matter

Logical thought processes

Daring as it regards recommendations

Managerial ability

Ability to think fast

The problem is that many people are nervous, and some poor babies are absolutely terrified when speaking before groups. They worry about everything: Will they remember what they want to say? How will the audience receive the message? Is the presentation convincing? Can they handle questions and interruptions? Will everything go right?

Everyone dreads looking the fool, and for the novice speaker there's good reason for the fear. We've all agonized while one of our peers botched a presentation.

The best way to avoid the anxiety is to stop being a novice. Practice speaking before groups at every opportunity. Organizations such as Toastmasters provide excellent vehicles for public speaking.

Here are twenty additional tips:

1. *Have a purpose.* Know what you want to accomplish with the presentation. Convey this purpose as a theme.

2. *Be prepared.* Know what you want to say and how you will present the material.

3. *Practice in front of the mirror, before family members, and before anyone else who will listen.* Be able to give the presentation in your sleep.

4. *Do your homework.* One of the things that can disconcert any speaker is a dispute from the audience over a claim. Avoid stating things that can't be proven. Know you're right.

5. *Don't read the presentation; there's nothing worse; deliver it.*

6. *Use anecdotes and examples to illustrate important points.*

7. *Pause and take a breath before beginning.* Don't speak too quickly. Speak up. If not using a microphone it's almost impossible to talk too loudly.

8. *Look at various people in the audience.* If a senior executive is present, try to establish eye contact.

9. *Personal conviction is the best persuader of others.* If you're convinced, you are more likely to convince the audience.

10. *Use a delivery that is natural to you.* Don't tell jokes if humor is not your natural style. Do tell jokes if you're good at it.

11. *Use language the audience will understand.* No one is there to be impressed by the size of your vocabulary or the extent of your technical knowledge.

12. *By all means use displays, graphs, charts, slides, films, tapes, and so forth, but be sure that the audience can see the displays, that they make the points you want made, and that they are easy to understand.*

13. *Check out the props, such as audio equipment, slide projectors, lighting, and so forth well before the presentation starts.*

14. *If others are involved in the presentation, be the person who apparently "orchestrates" it.* This will make a stronger impression with senior management. (Providing they like what they see.)

15. *Leave time for a question-and-answer period.* Anticipate the questions that are likely to be asked and be prepared for them. One technique to impress management is to make a presentation that almost demands a certain question be asked and wait in the weeds with a powerful answer. If a senior manager asks a question, give the impression that it exposes a provocative side to the issue not before considered. That posture flatters the manager while making your answer appear extemporaneous.

16. *Get the right audience to attend.* If you have something "hot" to deliver, make sure that the managers you want to impress will be there. Postpone, if necessary, until schedules fit.

17. *Make a recommendation.* The presentation of facts alone is unsatisfactory. Go out on a limb and suggest that the company do something. Frighten yourself with your audacity.

18. *Keep to a schedule.* One of the worst things that can happen during a presentation is for a senior manager to leave in the middle because of other commitments.

19. *Try to arrange a site where the presentation won't be disturbed by personnel breaking in with "important" messages.*

20. *Prepare a written summary of the presentation and give it to all attendees at the conclusion.* Make sure that all senior-level managers get copies. See that your name is in a prominent place on the report.

Follow these guidelines, get behind a podium at every opportunity, and you'll soon attract the attention of senior management as someone who is articulate, persuasive, and a "comer."

❖ 3 ❖

HOW TO GET MORE DONE IN LESS TIME

Remember the explanation offered at the beginning of this book on exactly what managers manage? To save you the trouble of going back and looking it up, managers manage resources in the form of money, people, or time. Of these three resources, that old devil time is the most difficult to control because its passage is unrelenting.

Time is the great leveler. The CEO of a company receives no greater allotment of minutes, hours, and days than does the lowest stockroom clerk. Yet, some people seem to get more done with their ration than others do. They have an apparent knack for controlling the clock. This knack can be acquired, and it is the most valuable asset a manager can possess.

The First Rule of Time Management

Don't begin an effort to make better use of time with the wrong expectation of the benefits. You'll be disappointed. Being well organized won't result in less pressure, spending lazy afternoons at the ball game, or a reduction in stress. Managers who become masters of time efficiency are just as rushed as before. Other tasks and responsibilities inevitably creep in to fill up the hours they've gained. The old conundrum, "If you want something done, give it to a busy person," certainly applies in business.

The "bonus" of good time management is not relief from the hectic pace at the office, but rather in gaining the reputation as someone who consistently accomplishes what senior management requires. That's why it's such a key ingredient to success.

Charting What You Do Now—A Baby Step in Better Time Management

Want to make more time available for productive work? Sort out all nonproductive activity and stop doing these things. Just chuck them out. That solution sounds simple enough, but how can anyone tell what is productive and what is not? Everything seems important, right? Other tasks are coated with the patina of tradition. They have been done by one person or another since Noah first noticed the falling barometer.

Start by questioning everything. Examine every hour of the workday for a full week. (You may wish to start from the time you leave the house.) What happens from the minute you get on the train or walk into the office? Make an hourly diary of what you do and the reasons behind that action. Pay special attention to those tasks you've been doing forever. You may find that the main reason you're doing a certain job is because you've always done it. Inertia doesn't have an automatic braking system. You'll have to engage a hand brake if you want to slow it down.

A sample chart for a single day is on page 63. List everything from working on an important project to taking a coffee break. Repeat the exercise for an entire week. If the week is atypical, repeat for a second week.

Now analyze your activity. Be critical. Ask yourself, *why am I doing this*? What's necessary and what is window dressing? Are you spending the first half hour of every day "getting settled"? Do you spend the last half hour tidying up? Are you doing some things because they've always been done? Have you set false priorities? Are the objectives of your tasks worthwhile? Are you doing little jobs that are the responsibility of your subordinates? Are you spending twenty minutes at the copy or fax machine to get something done "right now" that a steno could have for you within an hour? Are you checking over material that others have already verified? Are the results of your efforts useful to others in the company?

Just becoming conscious of your actions will help make more time available. You'll begin to see where the fat can be trimmed.

Current Activity Chart

Hour	Task	Objective
8:00		
9:00		
10:00		
11:00		
12:00		
1:00		
2:00		
3:00		
4:00		
5:00		
6:00		

This exercise is so valuable it should be repeated every six months. We all get into ruts doing certain things almost by rote. Examining what we do and the reason we do it is the first step in climbing out of that rut.

The second step, abandoning useless tasks, is more difficult. It requires a change in mind set, an admission that hard, dedicated work doesn't always result in a contribution.

Meetings: The Great Time Waster

One way to save time is to avoid meetings whenever possible. They are inefficient because they require managers to stop what they're doing, gather at a central place, wait until all have arrived, spend ten minutes or so on pleasantries, and finally talk about whatever. Meanwhile, the real administrative work of the managers remains undone.

Many meetings accomplish nothing except to learn how other people or departments within the company "feel" about some issue. To show team spirit there is an inclination by individuals to defer decisions until the entire group reaches some kind of consensus. That's why so many committees are appointed. They're a way of demonstrating that no one person is trying to steamroll a pet project past the others. Of course steamrolling is exactly what's needed to get certain things done.

Most meetings run past their allotted time. Have you ever been in a fifteen minute meeting that lasted only fifteen minutes?

Our corporate culture being what it is, it's impossible to avoid meetings altogether. There are ways, however, to reduce their drain on your time:

1. *Get there late.* How much time have you spent in meetings waiting for others to arrive? Why not come a few minutes after the scheduled start time and make them wait for you?

2. *Leave early.* Have you ever stayed for an entire meeting just to be polite? Just walk out if the subject matter does not pertain to you or your department.

3. *Create an emergency.* Arrange for a secretary or subordinate to call you out of meetings that you are required to attend. If they whisper a message to you rush out with a worried look, everyone will know there's a fire to be put out somewhere.

4. *Don't come at all.* Claim prior commitments that prevent your attendance.

5. *Show up, leave, and come back.* Come to a meeting, walk out just after it begins, and return just when they're ready to sum up. It will be just as if you were there for the entire time.

6. *Don't come, but keep abreast of the results.* Get on the mailing list for the minutes just in case anything transpired that affected you.

Twelve Time-Saving Secrets of Hands-on Managers

Ever heard of the "Parado 20–80 Rule"? A simplistic explanation of this rule is that 20 percent of resources accounts for 80 percent of the results. For example, 20 percent of the product line will account for 80 percent of income. Twenty percent of the customer list will buy 80 percent of the merchandise. Twenty percent of the sales force will make 80 percent of the sales. The system also works negatively. Twenty percent of the deadbeats will account for 80 percent of the bad-debt losses. Try using this perspective and run figures on your own organization. You'll be surprised at how often the Parado rule applies.

A human corollary is that 20 percent of the managerial staff accomplishes 80 percent of the assigned tasks. Senior management instinctively understands this ratio is at work. They're always on the lookout for middle managers who are among the top 20 percent performers.

The top 20 percent get more done because they've learned certain secrets of time management. Here are twelve of the most important:

1. *They define what's really needed.* The first requisite in time management is to determine what needs to be achieved.

2. *They make decisions when they need to be made.* Good time managers don't defer decisions. They make them and go on to what's next on the agenda.

3. *They set priorities.* Good time managers decide what is most important.

4. *They delegate authority and trust their subordinates.* Good managers don't spend hours at tasks that should be done by staff members.

5. *They set up automatic reviews of projects in process.* Making sure that a project is on schedule and being done correctly is more than a comfort. There's no greater time-wasting effort than trying to put a project back on course.

6. *They take responsibility for mistakes and correct them as soon as possible.* Nothing absorbs more time than trying to hide a mistake or allowing a simple error to grow into a disaster.

7. *They don't demand perfection.* "Wild Bill" Donovan, founder of OSS, said that "perfection is inefficient." What he meant was that nitpicking through a process until everything was absolutely 100 percent accurate is a tremendous time waster.

8. *They'd rather ask for forgiveness than permission.* Good managers don't always wait for approval from someone higher up before wading into a project.

9. *They question precedence.* Just because a thing has always been done a certain way doesn't mean it must continue to be done that way.

10. *They look for bottlenecks and the ways to eliminate them.*

11. *They key on the result and not the process used to reach that result.* This mind set allows them to consider alternatives.

12. *They don't allow themselves or their staffs to be distracted.* It's easy to lose sight of objectives when there are so many interesting things, such as office politics, to consider.

Notice something about these secrets of good time managers? They are the work habits of good managers, period!

Knowing What Responsibilities to Avoid, the Real Secret in Time Saving

The ultimate time-saving secret is to simply avoid those thankless tasks that won't enhance a career, but will consume hours, days, or weeks that could be spent more productively. These tasks are often temporary assignments parceled out at committee meetings simply because someone has to do them. They can do harm to a career if not handled well, ("Kelly really botched the tour arrangements for our foreign visitors, didn't she?") but they won't result in any Brownie points if done well. Run from these assignments as you would the plague. They are a distraction from your primary responsibilities.

Here's how to weasel out of thankless jobs and still be considered a team player:

1. *Consider the wisdom of the average army private and never volunteer for assignments that have no personal payoff.* Stay away from employee entertainment committees. Keep off the Christmas party committee, the picnic planners, the chorale singers. Instead, attend the functions these groups put together and be generous with your compliments.

2. *Resist strong hints from the boss to serve on go-nowhere committees.* If the boss becomes insistent, look at a pocket schedule and shake your head in despair. "I'd love to, boss, but my plate is full right now."

3. *If ordered on a go-nowhere committee, now is the time to recite every single obligation you have for the next six months.* Say that you'll be delighted to serve on this committee as long as senior

management understands that many deadlines you've been given won't be met. Put it in writing.

4. *If absolutely forced to serve do as little as possible.* Don't head up any subcommittees. Choose the easiest tasks. Let others take the glory.

How to Persuade Other Managers to Take a Thankless Job off Your Hands

No matter how you wiggle and squirm, you're sure to be stuck with a thankless assignment sometime. Whenever possible, try to persuade another manager to take it off your hands. There are several approaches that can be used.

1. *Give the boss the "jam-packed-schedule" story and nominate another manager to take your place.* Convince the boss that the suggested replacement has skills that more closely match the committee's aims.

2. *Ask another manager to sit it on several committee meetings for you because of schedule conflicts and just assume that the manager has permanently taken your place.*

3. *Offer to switch committees with another manager.* Obtaining an advantage by swapping a go-nowhere committee for a plum assignment depends on your skill as a trader.

Five Ways to Extract the Most out of Every Hour

The secret to getting more done is to spend less time on each task. Every production manager knows that simple truth. The trick is how to spend less time on tasks without sacrificing quality. Here are five ways that any manager will find useful:

1. *Get rid of the time tyrant on your desk.* What tyrant is that? The telephone! Some managers wouldn't think of seeing someone without an appointment, yet will allow a telephone caller to interrupt the most important projects. Get a voice-mail system that screens calls, or set aside a time of the day when you'll accept phone calls. Make sure your colleagues know when that time is.

2. *Respond to memos and letters by jotting a reply at the bottom or margin of the correspondence sent to you, make a copy, and send*

the original back. This saves your time dictating a reply and the time of a secretary who would type it. Because there's limited space in the margin your reply will necessarily be succinct and to the point.

3. *Work when no one else is in the office.* It's remarkable how much you can get done without interruption. (Incidentally, home is not normally a place where work can get done without interruption.)

4. *Don't allow interruptions.* If someone walks into your office unscheduled to talk about something "important," shoo them right back out with a comment such as, "Sorry, Fred, I'm busy right now. See me about that at lunch."

5. *Know where to find everything.* One of the greatest time wasters is looking for something that must be found right now, but can't be located. Keep the reference material you'll need close at hand. Develop a filing system that will enable you to put your hands on copies of correspondence and reports. That doesn't mean your desk can't be cluttered. Just be sure you know what lies in each pile.

How to Thrive on Deadlines

The efficiency of managers is often measured by their ability to deliver on or before deadlines. A reputation for possessing this ability is invaluable when it's time to pass out promotions. In all large corporations, however, very little work is done in a vacuum. The contribution of many people or departments is required to complete projects. Managers can find themselves criticized for failure to deliver when the reasons for that failure were beyond their control.

The first step in achieving the reputation as someone who delivers is to defer "signing off" on a deadline just because the boss wants a project completed by such a date. A statement such as: "Let me see if that's possible. I'll get back to you tomorrow," will only add to your reputation as someone who is cautious before making a commitment. The things you'll want to investigate before agreeing to a schedule include:

Ten Steps Toward Determining If a Deadline Can Be Met

1. *The reason for the schedule.* Many deadlines are arbitrary dates with little negative results if they're not met.

2. *The contributions other departments will be making to this project.*

3. *The dates by which you need to receive these contributions to hold up your end.*

4. *The relationship you have with heads of contributing departments.* Will they cooperate with you?

5. *The possible bottlenecks that could delay completion dates.* (Never underestimate hostility as a possible bottleneck. If there is someone in a position to influence the results who is deliberately uncooperative for personal reasons, take this factor into consideration.)

6. *The time and resources necessary to complete your end of the project on schedule.*

7. *The availability of needed resources, including personnel, to complete the project.*

8. *The projects for which your department is currently committed, their deadlines, and their demands on your time.*

9. *The day-to-day demands on your time and the time of staff members.*

10. *The interruptions or brush fires that could possibly occur that could affect your ability to deliver.*

After examining these factors, there are several replies that you could give to your superior. These include:

1. *Yes, we can do it.* This project is a piece of cake.

2. *Yes, we can do it providing these other departments deliver their contributions by such and such a time.* Let's set a conference to see if they can commit. (A negative response by another department takes the monkey off your back.)

3. *It doesn't appear as if we can promise to deliver by the deadline you request.* However, we can meet a later schedule.

4. *Yes, we can deliver on schedule if you're prepared to offer relief on the deadlines for other projects already committed.* Which has greater priority?

5. *We can't swallow the whole project right now.* However, we can take the meat of it. Can you get another department to do the rest? (Here's a chance to get rid of the thankless tasks.)

6. *We can do it if you're prepared to give us these additional resources.* (Or increase budgets or authorize overtime.)

Notice that none of these answers is a flat no. Managers who want promotions achieve reputations as "can do" people.

A worksheet can help determine what is needed to complete a project on schedule. It can also be used to keep a project on schedule.

Completion dates for the needed contributions of other departments would come under the benchmark heading.

Project Worksheet

Project Name _____

Team leader _____

Team members_____

_____

_____

Start date _____ Completion date _____

Estimated hours required _____

Resources needed _____

_____

_____

_____

_____

Project Benchmarks

Benchmark   *Date*

_____

_____

_____

_____

_____

_____

How to Work Faster and Smarter than Your Peers

The business world rates everyone on his or her ability to produce. The competition is so keen today that the key to advancement is to produce more than your peers do. Take heart; this doesn't necessarily mean working harder. It does mean working smarter and faster. Here's how to get a few steps ahead of your contemporaries:

1. *Learn how to take advantage of the electronic devices that have changed the office world in the last five years.* Become familiar with personal computers, facsimile machines, voice mail, electronic organizers, and so forth. These tools enable you to work smarter and faster. (However, don't become so fascinated that all your time is spent peering at a CRT screen. The computer is a tool, not a toy.)

2. *The number-crunching ability of the PC is awe-inspiring, but never let electronic circuitry substitute for personal judgment.*

3. *Make friends with the movers and shakers in other departments.* Learn how they get things done and what is possible. Form a mutual-cooperation league. They help you; you help them.

4. *Don't automatically accept every assignment that comes along.* If the boss wants you to do something that devours time and leads nowhere, try to get out of it.

5. *Identify the results required on every assignment.* Deliver these results, no more, no less. Make sure that senior management knows the results have been delivered.

6. *Be lavish with praise.* There's no better way to get people to work hard on your behalf.

7. *Ask for advice from senior executives and peers when unsure about how to proceed with something.* The person asked will be flattered. (That doesn't mean you must follow that advice if it isn't valuable.)

8. *Don't be caught up in internal feuds.* They're a waste of time and take attention away from worthwhile objectives.

9. *On projects with long time frames, key on intermediate results.* Achieving benchmarks helps to keep enthusiasm high.

10. *Enjoy your work.* There's no greater aid to efficiency. If you hate what you do, why are you doing it?

11. *Get enough rest and lead a balanced life.* Rest, good nutrition, and adequate recreation lead to a high energy level, and nothing matches energy for working faster and smarter.

How to Get a Reputation as a Cool Head During Times of Crises

In every corporation the sky comes crashing down every so often. In many outfits it happens periodically and can almost be forecast. One way to be noticed by senior management is to get a reputation as someone who can handle an emergency. The first step toward achieving this reputation is by acquiring the right attitude toward emergencies.

Think of any office crisis as *nothing more than an ordinary business problem with the volume turned up.* Just viewing all emergencies in this manner will help you attain a reputation for having a cool head. That's because you won't be reacting to the crisis, you'll be looking for a solution to the problem.

When confronted with a crisis, openly ask the following questions about it:

1. *Is the crisis real?* (Many are false alarms.)

2. *Who has identified this situation as a crisis?* Someone pulled the alarm bell. Is that person qualified to identify a crisis? (Not all crises are initially identified by senior management. If the company night-shift maintenance man says the pipes have burst and three feet of water cover the factory floor, that's a crisis!)

3. *Is it possible that the crisis might go away if it is ignored?* Judicious neglect should always be one considered course of action. It may be the best solution for this particular problem.

4. *What are the consequences if this crisis is not resolved?* Are these consequences so terrible that all attention should be devoted to solving the problem?

5. *What's the best way to solve the crisis right now?* (Remember, the cost for resolving a problem escalates as time goes by. The first remedy tried should not necessarily be the least-cost solution, but the one most likely to quickly stop the hemorrhaging.)

6. *What side effects are the proposed solution likely to produce?* Like most medicinal treatments, drastic measures to solve business

problems create new sets of symptoms. Make sure the cure isn't worse than the disease.

7. *Don't worry too much about so-called deadlines associated with the crisis.* ("If we don't give them a decision by such-and-such a date, we'll lose the option.") One of the facts of business life is that *deadlines come and go and nothing happens.*

8. *Is there consensus within the organization on the proposed cure?* If management is divided on what should be done, count on recriminations if the solution chosen doesn't work out. The "I told you so" syndrome is alive and thriving in the corporate work place. If there's division in the executive suite on a course of action, perhaps it's wise to stay off the team trying to fix things.

Raising these issues during times of crisis helps place the emergency in perspective and enhances your reputation as a manager with a cool head.

How to Clear Your Desk of Clutter

Is your desk a rat's nest of unanswered correspondence, trade and technical journals, interesting business articles, internal memos, fax messages, computer printouts, reports, requisitions, binders, art work, brochures, resumes, files on work in process, charts, spreadsheets, product literature, advertisements, work orders, and so forth? Is it so crowded there's no room for the picture of the spouse and kiddies? Welcome to the Desk Clutter Club. It is not an exclusive society. You are among several million members.

Getting out of the club may be harder than breaking a narcotics habit, but it can be done. Kicking the clutter habit takes determination. (Like all addictions.) Here's how to achieve that pristine look that the CEO's desk enjoys:

1. *Make more on-the-spot decisions.* A good portion of the stuff on your desk is there because you're "waiting for more information" before reaching a decision. Trust your instincts. Go with the decision you know is right *now* and much of the clutter disappears.

2. *Answer memos anyplace that's handy in the bottom margin and send them back on the same day they arrive.* If something needs clarification, send it back. In fact, practice handling every piece of paper that comes across your desk only once. Pick it up, read it, take an action, dispose of it.

3. *Establish a tickler file for the work that needs input from others.* Put all the pending stuff in it. Keep the file in your desk drawer. (This won't work unless you go through the tickler file every now and again.)

4. *If the completion of a report or project is the mutual responsibility of several departments, send the material off to one of these departments.* Let them complete their end first.

5. *Review everything that's still on your desk at the end of every business day.* It's remarkable how much you can simply throw away.

6. *Do you delegate responsibility to members of your staff?* Delegate the paperwork as well. Pass along that correspondence the moment it comes in.

7. *Are you clipping interesting articles on the competition or business trends or new product developments and passing them up the line to senior management?* Stop kissing up! You're not accumulating any Brownie points with this practice. Meanwhile, your desk is cluttered with copies of magazines, journals, and newspapers.

8. *Learn to have confidence in the company's filing system.* (Or revise the system.) One of the reasons material stays on your desk is that you're afraid you won't be able to find it once filed.

9. *Throw stuff away.* Most of the junk on your office desk belongs in that circular file the cleaning people empty out each night.

10. *Don't copy and hang on to material merely because you want to protect your backside.* (If managers would stop this practice, Xerox stock would plummet like a stone.)

Put these suggestions into practice and you'll soon uncover the mystery of whether there's wood grain or metal trim on the surface of your desk.

One warning: There's a high recidivism (backsliding) rate among reformed desk clutterers. Unless vigilance is exercised, those clean desks somehow get messy again by themselves.

A Tracking System Worksheet for Projects in Progress

One of the worst surprises a manager can spring on her boss is a last-minute announcement that a project has been delayed and target dates won't be met. The question always asked is, "Why didn't you tell me sooner?" Very few answers to that question will be acceptable to the boss. That's because the delay often comes as a surprise to the project manager. Delays are often unavoidable. Being ignorant of these delays until they occur is the sign of an incompetent manager.

The way to avoid surprises on important projects is to keep track of the work in progress. This is particularly important on long-term projects. Set intermediate goals to ensure that schedules are being met. Here's a worksheet that tells the tale at a glance:

Work-in-Progress Worksheet

Project _____

Start date _____ Completion date _____

Project's goals _____

_____

_____

_____

_____

Staff Responsibility
Name   Responsible for

_____

_____

_____

_____

Intermediate Goals
Goal   Due Date   Date Completed

_____

_____

_____

_____ *continued*

Important Benchmarks
Benchmark   *Completion Date*

_____

_____

_____

_____

_____

This is a simplistic worksheet, but it tells the project leader at a glance if intermediate goals are being met, which staff members have responsibility for meeting those goals, and when important benchmarks are met.

How to "Lose" Inconvenient Information

Some managers like to leave a paper trail that provides a complete record of what has transpired. They consider it necessary to have every correspondence, every report, every memo, everything really, duly recorded and on file.

In the number-crunching end of the business—such things as inventory status, orders processed, goods purchased, accounts payable and receivable, payroll and tax records, and so forth—a meticulous recording system is absolutely vital to the health of the organization. Companies could not exist unless this information is carefully maintained.

However, much of the correspondence and many of the memos that fill file cabinets to overflowing have no critical business use that requires their preservation. This material is stored and kept for years solely so certain individuals can be "on the record." In some organizations keeping every scrap of paper, if not in the original then on microfilm, for five or seven years is company policy.

The problem with filing everything is that mistakes as well as triumphs are recorded where anyone with a nasty turn of mind can dig them up. It's a good idea to keep track of victories, but keeping a record of defeats doesn't help a manager's career ambitions. We're not suggesting revising history or destroying company records, but putting the embarrassing stuff, those nagging mistakes, where no one can find them just might be the prudent thing to do.

The question is, how can that inconvenient memo, the one that predicted a Communist Europe and a collapse of the Common Market by 1992, be hidden? The proliferation of personal computers with their incredibly large storage capacities makes that question difficult to answer.

The obvious solution is to simply misfile. Put the Europe file under the letter "W" where no one is likely to look for it. However, what about the copies that were proudly sent hither and yon when the prediction was still fresh? Here's a more complete solution:

1. *When going out on a limb, copy as few people as possible.* This means there are fewer copies to retrieve if the limb breaks off.

2. *When a prediction or project appears to be headed south call the people who have the copies.* Ask for their return on the pretext that they "need more work." Secretaries of senior managers are often sympathetic to this plea.

3. *If copies can't be retrieved, send addenda that essentially modify the position taken in the original.*

4. *Search your own records for the data or reports that caused the wrong conclusion or the error.* Make this data part of the file on the subject.

5. *Send the file out to be microfilmed.* Assign a low priority to the project so it will be in process for a long time.

6. *Put the file in computer memory and encourage a power surge that wipes everything out.*

Another answer, of course, is not to worry about past mistakes and get on with the business at hand. This is the situation we endorse.

ACQUIRING AND MASTERING MANAGERIAL SKILLS

❖ 4 ❖

THE MANAGER'S ROLE IN A CHANGING WORK PLACE

How the Work Place Is Changing

The automated plants are here. Some, with double and even triple the capacities of counterpart manual operations don't require a single worker on the production floor. The raw material goes in one end, the finished product, unsullied by human hands, pops out the other. Sounds absolutely divine for reducing production costs, doesn't it? But what happens when *everyone* automates? The answer, of course, is a massive displacement of the labor force.

Not to worry, say the economists; there have been many large-scale labor displacements in the past. While they may have caused individual pain, most didn't really do permanent injury to the economy because emerging industries soon absorbed the labor surplus. The people who lost their jobs in the buggy-whip factories went to work making horseless carriages. In fact, traditional wisdom maintains that lowering costs improves economic conditions by making more goods available to greater numbers.

Today's factory automation, however, is reducing the need for the skilled production worker. The loss of jobs this time is permanent. The emerging industries of the Nineties will be automated too. They will make money for their backers and offer new goods to the public, but they will not provide enough job opportunities to replace those that have been lost.

Many of those jobs that can't be automated have already been packed in a crate and shipped offshore. Companies are on a global prowl, seeking low-wage workers in Sri Lanka, Mexico, India, Eastern Europe, and other places. Today Fortune 1000 companies in the United States employ more than 11 million workers. (Down from 16 million in the early Seventies.) By the year 2000 the number will be reduced to 8 million.

The questions, still unanswered, are just who will buy the products produced by the automated plants? Who will have the money to buy the goods produced by the Sri Lankan peasant?

Over the past ten years an entire economic class in the United States has been decimated. The carnage continues, and it means a long-term impact on our country's economy. The skilled production worker who earned good wages represented an important market for all kinds of goods. This market won't be replaced by people working for minimum wages at fast-food franchises.

(Long before his company was unionized, Henry Ford raised the pay of his workers to $5 a day and urged other industries to do the same. At the time this was more than double the going rate for factory workers. Ford wasn't being a philanthropist; he just wanted to create customers who could afford to buy his automobiles. Perhaps modern business executives could learn something from Old Henry's example.)

Office automation hasn't had the same effect as factory automation has. Up to a few years ago the ranks of the office worker and the middle manager were largely untouched by the improved efficiencies provided by the personal computer, new communication techniques, and other developments. These products just helped middle managers and their staffs get more work done. After enough labor-saving devices were installed, however, management wanted to see results in the form of tangible savings. Men with Long Knives began to prowl the administrative halls. *What happened on the factory floor a few years ago to skilled production workers is happening in the corporate office to white-collar employees today.*

The emphasis of many corporations over the next decade will be to continue on cutting back middle-management staff. The labor reductions of the Eighties will seem like boom times in retrospect. The senior corporate managers who control major companies are convinced there are still layers of fat marbled throughout their organizations. They mean to remove this fat. The operative words today are "lean and mean." (Considering the outplacement policies of many companies, the emphasis is on the *mean*.)

A story that emphasizes this point is told about Robert Crandall, chairman of American Airlines. In an economy move he replaced a night watchman with a guard dog. Later, he fired the dog and replaced it with the taped sound of an animal barking. Even that may not be the ultimate efficiency. Perhaps American is looking at further savings through ways to phone in the barking noise on an as-needed basis.

In many industries middle-management jobs have already gone south. There are more ex-bankers on the street today than there are street-walkers. (Any comparison between their professions, outside of similar ethical standards, is unintentional.) Banking is a particularly troubled industry, but other industries are also experiencing mass layoffs.

Here's what these changes mean for the corporate manager:

1. *More competition for every job and every promotion.*

2. *No long-term job security.* The corporation isn't a surrogate parent anymore.

3. *More freedom to move to something else if the current position doesn't suit the manager.*

4. *More emphasis on results.* The corporate manager will be weighed as a unit of production, just as an automated punch press is.

5. *No room for yesterday's stars.* Like a baseball team, the corporation will evaluate personnel on what they can accomplish this coming season.

6. *Less loyalty to the cause.* The corporation lost its right to demand complete loyalty when they abandoned the promise of security.

Yesterday's Skills Won't Cut the Mustard in Today's Marketplace

The conventional wisdom is that the safe managerial jobs of the next decade will be the ones that require special skills. However, special skills didn't save the production worker. No matter what he or she did, management decided it wasn't worth nineteen dollars an hour when they could get it done for a buck and a half in Korea. Skills won't save the middle manager either, unless they're the right skills. Pay close attention to what comes next: *The skills in hot demand over the next decade won't be the same specialties that guaranteed success in the past.* Many specialized professions of today will go the way of the elevator operator.

Skills on the endangered species list include any number-crunching job that can be handled by a computer. For example, a credit analyst used to be an invaluable asset to any organization that granted credit terms to its customers. A good analyst could take a single glance at a credit application and invariably separate the prime risks from the deadbeats. They didn't produce profits, but they prevented loss.

Today, many companies use point-scoring systems to make credit decisions. These systems bring uniformity to the credit-granting process, and they can also be automated. The computer makes the credit decision based on predetermined criteria. The skilled credit analyst is replaced (at a lower wage) by a data-entry clerk who punches in the numbers, and the data-entry clerk is eventually replaced (at zero salary) by an optical scanner that "reads" the information from the application into the computer. Progress marches on.

The moral is that if a computer can do your job expect to see a microchip in the personnel office filling out a job-application form.

The corporation planners will also come under pressure. "Wait one cotton-picking minute," you say, "planning is always needed. We planners determine the direction of the organization. We steer the damn ship!" Sure, but the method is changing fast.

The traditional corporate planning cycle consists of:

Of course the planning is reworked based on what actually happens during the action phase. Each step is meticulously documented. Managers are evaluated based on minimizing changes to the plan. They try to get it right the first time. It is a rigid, careful process designed to reduce the risk involved in any new venture. In short, it is a paper shuffler's dream.

Unfortunately, this planning process is so careful, so thoughtful, so deliberate it won't be responsive to the next decade's market conditions. Maybe it never was a good method. Nothing comes out in reality the way it is planned on paper. Things will change too fast. Computers help shorten the planning cycle, but they will never replace intuition and experience.

More companies eager to get in on the ground floor with new products will be willing to experiment and take risks based on "incomplete data." Corporate America has taken note of the examples set by brash new companies such as Compaq Computer, which went from zero sales to one hundred million dollars in shipment in a single year. They did it by taking chances. Of course, it's always easier for young companies to take risks. They have everything to gain and very little to lose.

Large corporations are dividing their business operations into smaller units to give them entrepreneurial zing. Even that monolith, IBM, is segmenting its divisions, giving each more autonomy.

The desired result is fewer controls, less interference from above, less bureaucracy, more decision-making responsibility at the operational level, faster response times, less paperwork and, it is hoped, a quicker response to the needs of the marketplace.

Which workers will suffer in this Brave, New, Less Compartmentalized World? The incessant memo writers, the chronic detailers, the dotters of i's and the crossers of t's, the meticulous ones, all will hear the whisper of the ax. They'll be left by the wayside. If your skill is the beautifully crafted, carefully documented, every-contingency-considered operational plan, watch out. The next memo you write may be your farewell message to fellow workers. (Carefully edited to take out the bitterness.)

Any manager whose skills are not transferable is also in jeopardy. Be wary of devoting all your time to mastering a skill so arcane it is useful only to one employer. Don't learn too much about very little. Proprietary is out. Interchangeability is in. Corporate careers in the Nineties will require a series of positions, passages if you like, with different companies. Lifetime jobs with a single company are quaint remnants of the past, like men on subway cars who rise to give their seats to pregnant women.

Skills That Will Help Managers Find Employment in the Next Decade

If the demand for many traditional management functions are declining, just which skills will corporate employers be clamoring for in the next ten years? Glad you asked. They include:

1. *Communication skills.* Our high schools, and now our colleges, are turning out students who read and write at fifth-grade levels. And these are the high achievers! The ability to write a simple

declarative sentence and the ability to understand one in the context in which it is presented will make the holder of this "skill" a valuable employee to any organization.

2. *Technical skills.* Master a technical discipline to go along with your managerial know-how. Many senior managers have problems managing professionals and technical types. If you have enough knowledge so technical staff members can't intimidate you, companies will be lined up for your services.

3. *Flexibility skills.* I'm not sure if this is a skill or an attitude. The important point is that market, financial, economic, and political conditions will change quickly in the Nineties. The managers who advance will be those who see the changes coming and adjust for them. This time around no medals will be awarded to the rearguard defenders who defend the old ways.

4. *Marketing skills.* Every manager, no matter the responsibility or job title, will have to learn to take marketing seriously. That means assisting in the development of the product's value to the customer. In some cases it may mean getting out into the street and moving product.

5. *Learning skills.* The Nineties' manager must be like a sponge, soaking up new things and retaining them until squeezed. He or she must be alert and, above all, receptive. The next decade will be one of continual education for corporate managers. The "good students," those who learn quickly and adapt to changing conditions, will get ahead.

The Seven Basic Personality Traits of a Good Manager, Including One That's Money in the Bank

Corporations buy managerial ability. They're willing to pay a premium for it when the ability comes wrapped in an attractive package. That package is the manager's on-the-job personality. In some cases the right kind of personality can overcome indifferent performance. In many cases it will give the manager a second chance. Here are the managerial personality traits that will be sought by corporations in the Nineties:

1. *Mental toughness.* The marketplace will be so competitive in the next decade, the Eighties will look like a cake walk. The managers

who succeed in this rough-and-tumble market are those tough hombres who don't panic, who are willing and able to be as tough as the competition.

2. *Cooperative attitude.* The days of the old curmudgeon who ran his department like an isolated fiefdom, responsible to no one except the CEO, are over. There's too much at stake to indulge this kind of Lone Ranger. The successful manager of the Nineties will assist, not obstruct, enlighten, not obscure, contribute, not detract.

3. *Openness.* The secretiveness and "protecting your turf" managerial styles won't cut the mustard in the next decade. Want to surprise, dismay, and get a leg up on your contemporaries? Practice being candid every now and again. You'll be a bit ahead of your time, but not by much.

4. *Likable personality.* This is an old, but reliable standard. It won't change over the next ten years. People will still encourage, counsel, root for, and promote those they like. Being likable is one of the easiest roads to the top. So lighten up. Practice humility. Don't be a jerk. Smile at your peers every now and again. Don't turn every encounter with another department into a contest.

5. *Loyalty.* Another tried-and-true standard. Want loyalty from your superiors? Give it to them. That includes being loyal to the programs your superiors develop. Give loyalty to your staff members as well. Who knows? They may reciprocate and be loyal to you.

6. *Positive outlook.* The job will be difficult enough without a Calamity Jane on board who claims it can't be done. When necessary, voice concern about projects, but once a decision is made, commit yourself thoroughly to the program.

7. *Honesty and a strong ethical code.* This is the character trait that will be money in the bank for the manager who has it. American management finally understands that unethical conduct costs the corporation large sums of money when it is uncovered. The profit potential of illegal deals is not worth the risk from possible law suits, a tarnished public image, and government fines.

Aside from moral considerations, dishonesty is just poor corporate policy. Senior management can't be everywhere, so they'll seek out company employees with the right instincts who are not likely to behave in a manner that puts the company in jeopardy. Honesty will be very much in demand over the next decade. You can bet that a few companies will lay claim to inventing it.

A Surefire Schedule to Develop Needed Skills You Don't Currently Possess

Worried that you don't have the right skills to succeed in the Nineties? Just the fact that you're concerned makes your fears legitimate. You can wring your hands over the perceived shortcomings or you can do something to correct them.

The first step in skill enhancement is to take inventory of current capabilities and compare them against perceived need. What skills that you currently lack do you feel are desirable? Make a list. You'll feel silly, but make it anyway. This list will become your stated goals. Be hard on yourself when making the list, but be realistic too. If you're forty-five with a high-school education and look upon the invention of the pocket calculator as a miracle from the gods, acquiring an advanced degree in nuclear science is not a realistic goal.

Have someone you trust check over the list. Review it with your boss or spouse or even with both parties. If they make suggestions for additions or deletions to the list, don't argue. These suggestions needn't be accepted. If several people offer similar ideas, they should be carefully considered.

After editing the list, develop a plan for how these skills can be acquired. For example, for improving written communication skills, consider a course in business writing at the local junior college. For greater ease in speaking before groups, think about joining Toastmasters. Read trade journals and attend seminars to acquire product or industry knowledge. For other skills ask for your company's support in attending special management courses.

The next step in skill development is to set up an implementation schedule. Just when are you going to start the long, tiring march toward all these worthy goals? Realism has to come into play once again. Set too heavy a schedule and you're likely to be overwhelmed and abandon everything. To keep on track, put the entire plan on paper. Include benchmark dates. Take it out and look at it every so often. Here's a worksheet that will help.

```
┌─────────────────────────────────────────────────────────────┐
│                   Needed Skills Worksheet                   │
│                                                             │
│ Skill              Method to Acquire              Timetable │
│ ──────────────────────────────────────────────────────────  │
│ ──────────────────────────────────────────────────────────  │
│ ──────────────────────────────────────────────────────────  │
│ ──────────────────────────────────────────────────────────  │
│ ──────────────────────────────────────────────────────────  │
│ ──────────────────────────────────────────────────────────  │
│ ──────────────────────────────────────────────────────────  │
│ ──────────────────────────────────────────────────────────  │
│ ──────────────────────────────────────────────────────────  │
│ ──────────────────────────────────────────────────────────  │
│ ──────────────────────────────────────────────────────────  │
│ ──────────────────────────────────────────────────────────  │
│ ──────────────────────────────────────────────────────────  │
└─────────────────────────────────────────────────────────────┘
```

Eleven Management Tips for Mid-level and Senior Managers

One of the keys to success in a large organization environment is learning the facts of corporate life. The player who knows all the rules has a better chance of winning the game. The facts differ from company to company, but the following tips will serve the manager well in most organizations.

1. *Understand the character of the company.* Every organization has a distinct personality and certain rules of behavior. Corporate manners and protocol are important. Learn what behavior in your company is acceptable and what is prohibited. You'll soon know what behavior is valued, and therefore rewarded, and what actions are likely to get you shown the front door.

2. *Don't keep repeating yesterday's triumphs.* Just because something worked in the past doesn't mean it will succeed in the future. At some time the old formula is bound to fail. Revise and improve

the ingredients of success yourself before someone else does the job for you.

3. *When trying to correct problems, don't mistake symptoms for causes.* A high temperature may be a symptom of a fever. Infection is the cause. High overtime expense is a symptom of absenteeism. Low employee morale may be the cause.

4. *Don't trust in simple solutions to complex problems.* They are always appealing and they are almost always wrong.

5. *Work with good people.* Make a point to become friendly with the most able and brightest people in your organization. Form a mutual assistance league that cuts across departmental lines. Seek their advice and give them the benefit of your counsel. Combine the group's skills and imagination for the common good. You'll have more fun because you'll be working with people you like.

6. *Make decisions and take risks.* If you're a manager that's what they're paying you to do. Don't go upstairs for approval on every risky situation. Earn your salary.

7. *Nurture your staff members.* Be a friend, confidant, coach, and teacher to your staff members as well as to their supervisor. Learn their goals and help them to attain these goals. Groom a successor. Become known as someone who develops winners.

8. *Break the rules once in a while.* Sometimes shattering some glass is the only way to get things done. When you do break a few panes, be sure that you're acting in the best interest of the company.

9. *Develop a sense of personal integrity that exceeds the ethical standards of the organization that employs you.* Don't flaunt a halo; saints may be above reproach, but they are also tedious. If your personal standards are high you won't have any hard decisions to make if anyone in the company asks you to do something that isn't "kosher."

10. *Be willing to cause friction and confront others in the organization, even your superiors, if you feel strongly about something.* Don't nitpick; make sure the principal is worth fighting for. When you do choose a battlefield, fight hard.

11. *Don't be a one-trick pony.* The modern manager must possess multiple skills and be versatile to be successful.

Why Performance Reviews Are Seldom Fair

The annual performance review became a corporate rite of passage about the same time the Personnel Department began calling itself Human Resources. Perhaps there's a correlation because there's something pompous and overbearing about the process.

There's nothing wrong with the idea of the boss sitting down with a staff member and assessing that employee's performance over the past twelve months. If the employee has been given a specific set of goals at the beginning of the year, theoretically it should be fairly easy to determine at the end of the period if those goals have been reached. The employee can be praised if objectives were met and improvements can be suggested if they were not.

Anyway, that's the general theory behind performance reviews. In practice something far different usually occurs. For one thing, the goals set at the beginning of the year are often nebulous. An example might be something such as, "improve internal communication skills." How can anyone determine, with any objectivity, if that goal was reached? Faced with this problem, the manager responsible for the review will often arbitrarily assign a percentage factor such as "achieved 80 percent success rate with this objective." What a statement such as that actually means is anybody's guess.

Another problem is that both parties to the review realize that raises and even careers ride on a positive evaluation. An employee who receives an indifferent report is likely to be stuck at the same salary for another twelve months. It's a confirmation to the employee that management holds him or her in small regard. That means a disgruntled worker. Perhaps the manager will have to explain to superiors why certain staff members who performed poorly have been retained.

A poor review may also cause an unpleasant on-the-spot confrontation between manager and employee, a scene the manager may choose to avoid. As a consequence, many managers moderate the performance evaluation of their ineffective employees by giving them better reviews than they deserve. They do it for the sake of "morale." Really poor reviews are reserved for those unfortunate few whom senior management wishes to nudge out of the organization.

On the opposite end of the scale the truly excellent performer is often not praised in direct proportion to his or her degree of accomplishment. The excuse given is that there must be room for improvement in the next reporting period. For many managers it is unthinkable to give any employee, no matter how efficient or productive, the highest score possible.

As a result, the reviews become homogenized. As with homogenized milk the cream doesn't get a chance to rise to the top. There are only subtle shadings of difference between those who performed well and those who failed to do the job. Because they don't truly rate actual accomplishment, performance reviews are unfair.

As this book is being written, IBM announced a policy to rate all employees in every department from best to worst. That means if there are 100 people in a department, one of them will be "number one" (Now why do I suspect that the top spot will almost always go to the person running the department?) and one poor soul will be holding up the totem pole as "number 100." As long as they're going that far, I have something for the suggestion box in Armonk: How about requiring the employees to sew badges on their sleeves that display their ranking?

How to Guarantee Yourself a Good Performance Review

The easiest way to guarantee a good performance review is to perform well, but let's get past that obvious point to more practical advice. Here are some steps that will get a good review every time.

1. *Make sure your goals are difficult to quantify.* The more nebulous the objectives, the more difficult they are to measure, the more positive the review is likely to be.

2. *Get your boss to like you.* The reviewing process is supposed to be dispassionate, but it's impossible to keep personal considerations out of the picture. If the boss really likes you it will be difficult for him or her to give you a bad review.

3. *Be prepared for the review.* If you know a negative topic will be discussed, have ammunition to prove you did all that you could in that particular matter. If possible, stress the boss's involvement in any disasters.

4. *React in a positive manner to any advice for improvement.* Agree to take steps to make these suggested improvements. Take the attitude that criticism is for your own good.

5. *Increase your activity in the time period immediately preceding the review.* Become such a dynamo the boss won't want to discourage your zeal with a negative review.

Company policy may be to offer employees an opportunity to file rebuttals to poor reviews. It's a waste of paper. Yes, the rebuttal becomes part of the personnel record along with the review, but it still does no good. Senior management reads the review and ignores the rebuttal.

How to Deal with Prejudice in a Performance Review

If managers play favorites when handing out positive reviews, their dislikes and prejudices often come into play in negative reviews. What can an employee do when given an undeserved poor review by a manager? If written rebuttals won't work, what will?

Preparation works. Most employees can sense if a bad review is likely. (Never dismiss the possibility that it is deserved.) They also have a pretty good idea if the negative report is based on personal dislike on the part of the manager.

If the reasons for a negative review appear to be racial, sexual, or age discrimination, most large corporations have specific policies in place to deal with these kinds of prejudices. Contact the Human Resources department and file an official complaint about the treatment you've received. No one openly admits to prejudice these days so be specific and detailed when giving information about the circumstance of your complaint.

If the problem is that the boss just doesn't like you and detests your taste in neckties, dealing with a poor review is a bit more difficult. The best opportunity to get the review changed is during the meeting on the subject. Here are several arguments that might help persuade the boss that the judgment was unjustified:

1. *The goals set for you this year were entirely unreasonable.* Achieving as much as you did was close to a miracle.

2. *The measurements used to judge your success or failure were entirely unfair.* Others in the company were judged by a different standard. (As most performance reviews are subjective, this charge is difficult to disprove.)

3. *You believe the boss has let personal feelings influence judgment.* If there's animosity, why not bring it into the open?

These arguments must be given during the review process. Fight the evaluation on a point-by-point basis. If you're successful a few times it could have the effect of upgrading the review from poor to mediocre. Don't expect miracles. Contest hardest those really subjective categories, such as "works well with others." Even if you've turned your office into a hermit's cave, emerging only when it's time to go home and once a year for the Christmas party, a reviewer may concede that you're a team player if you keep insisting you are.

A Four Point Program That Identifies the Job Management Really Wants Done

The servant employers treasure most, and if you're working for someone else in any capacity you're a servant, is the one who anticipates his or her master's wishes. (The servant who anticipates them often enough usually finds something extra in the Christmas stocking.)

The best corporate managers are those who anticipate what their employers really want out of the operation for which they have responsibility. It may be something quite different from the goal objective for the department or the job description stated for that position. In some cases it may just be tranquillity. The brass may want a department that doesn't require constant attention. Here are a few tips that will help you find out what management really wants.

1. *Ask the person who previously held the position.* If he or she is not available, review the correspondence. Ask staff members.

2. *Learn which actions illuminate the faces of the brass upstairs.*

3. *Ask the boss if there's something "extra" he or she would like to see from your department.*

4. *Start serving up various extra dishes (services) and take note of those the brass gobbles down.*

How to Manage Managers

The first rule in seeking to manage the manager who is your direct superior is to *approach this endeavor carefully.* Bosses aren't stupid. Experienced managers will recognize, and usually resent, all efforts by staff members to manipulate them.

The second rule is to concentrate attempts to manage your manager for things that benefit your operation and, therefore, the company. In fact, managing the manager is part of your overall responsibility because it helps you do the job better. In every company a certain degree of management manipulation is absolutely necessary to get the job done, so don't feel guilty about a little chicanery.

How can a middle manager manipulate a senior-level executive? It isn't difficult. Servants have been managing their masters and mistresses for centuries. English man-servants are considered experts at the process. Their technique works so well it's worth recounting.

1. *The servant uses a nonconfronting approach, seldom disagreeing with the master.* (Usually agreeing with the boss is not a bad strategy in the business world either.)

2. *Objections by the servant to imprudent actions on the part of the master are offered in the form of suggested difficulties if that action were to occur.* (Reciting the possible dangers of a course of action are part of a staff member's responsibilities.)

3. *Things that happen downstairs in the servant's quarters are generally not brought to the master's attention.* (The boss doesn't have to know everything that happens within the department.)

4. *The servant tries to anticipate what the master requires.* (There's no easier path to success. Find out what the boss wants and give it to him or her.)

5. *The servant modifies or influences the master's behavior in indirect ways, such as bringing the car out front and polishing it if the servant needs a ride to market.* (Indirect methods such as suggesting the boss read magazine articles that support your point of view are often the most persuasive.)

We are usually more direct today, but the English man-servant's methods can often be adapted to many situations in which the boss must be managed.

The Decade of the Fall Guy

In tough economic times companies frequently look for scapegoats so blame can be assessed for poor performance. The companies in trouble pick someone near the top to sacrifice. Throwing appointed victims into active volcanos has fallen into disfavor. Today they are stripped of all responsibility, publicly fired and humiliated. The sacrifices occur at the highest levels in the organization. They are extremely visible so everyone can see that something is being done. They usually accomplish little in correcting problems. In other words, the sacrifices are tribal ceremonies meant to appease the gods (who take the shape of the financial community).

Of course, the practice is reaction to crisis as opposed to genuine planning, but it is likely to continue throughout the next decade. Ways to avoid hearing the whisper of the ax include:

1. *Don't volunteer to clean up a hopeless situation.* The circumstances that made it hopeless will be forgotten after you take over.

2. *Don't hide bad news.* Henry Kissinger said, "What must be revealed eventually should be revealed immediately." There's nothing worse for job tenure than concealing a negative situation until it bubbles to the surface on its own.

3. *If you've been given the job of wielding the ax, don't appear as if you enjoy it.* If you make life miserable for others, they'll find a way to make life miserable for you.

4. *Don't think problems can't happen to you.* If the company really is in trouble, no one person is indispensable.

Seven Telltale Signs That Forecast Downsizing

Open any paper in any major city, turn to the business page and expect to find an article on a local or national company cutting back on the number of employees. Even IBM, a company that brags it has never had layoffs in its business history, is reducing its work force by tens of thousands.

The financial gurus tell us the cutbacks are necessary for corporate survival. "Fat must be trimmed," pontificate the CEOs, many with multi-million-dollar bonuses riding on improving the price of their companies' stock. (The practice will continue because it works! After a company announces a major layoff its stock inevitably goes up.)

The skilled production jobs have long since been automated or shipped offshore, so the fat that is being today is sliced from the ranks of administrative personnel. Middle managers are particularly vulnerable.

The question today isn't whether your company will downsize, it's *when.* Here are seven clues that help determine if such a move is near.

1. *The company is in a highly competitive, capital-intensive industry, and most outfits in it are losing money.* A typical example is the airline industry. Airlines borrow heavily to buy airplanes. They

cut ticket prices to keep those airplanes full. Their competitors cut prices again, this time below realistic profit margins. The planes run half full. The airlines can't meet the debt payments for the aircraft. The financial gurus have the answer: Cancel the future orders for planes and lay off a few thousand people.

2. *The company's products are losing market share.* Have the competitors come out with products that work better, look more attractive, and cost less? There's no surer sign of mass layoffs than being noncompetitive. Perhaps your company will fire a few thousand bodies and put more cash into R & D.

3. *The company's stock is headed toward the basement.* The people in Wall Street seem to sense that something's wrong with a company long before its employees do. If the company's stock is moving south, perhaps there's a good reason.

4. *The company has announced several cost-cutting procedures, but they aren't reducing losses.* The next cost-cutting move may be to reduce staff.

5. *There's a sudden reduction in internal activity.* There seem to be few directives from above, no long range plans, not even complaints from the boss about mistakes. It's the calm before the storm.

6. *No senior manager is available to talk about anything.* No decisions get made. Calls to the executive suite are not returned. Rumors fly. The rumors are probably right.

7. *People from Human Resources seem to be everywhere.* They also seem to be asking a lot of questions.

If these signs are all around you polish up the old resumé. Mail out a few thousand copies just to "test the market." You'll be a few weeks ahead of your fellow employees.

❖ 5 ❖

DEALING WITH THE
NINETIES

Why There's a Stampede to Downsize Companies

Until a little more than 100 years ago, bleeding the patient was a popular treatment for almost any malady. The graver the poor fellow's condition, the more blood the doctor drew away. Of course, the practice killed many people who might have otherwise recovered, but it was a drastic remedy that caused a lot of pain and suffering. This proved to one and all that the attending physician took the illness seriously.

A modern equivalent to the practice of siphoning blood from the sick and dying is the current rush to downsize no matter what the corporate woe. This reckless staff reduction is a bad idea whose time has come. No matter what the problem—declining markets, poor competitive position, crummy products, heavy debt loads, management blunders, or plain stupidity—corporations are determined to trim fat.

In many cases, the staff-trimming operations will be butchery rather than surgery. That means that where there is no fat, management will slice away lean. In other words, some organizations will be eliminating those basic functions and subtle differences that separated them from their competitors.

Methods to reduce the number of employees on the company payroll will preoccupy the CEOs and planning-study committees of most major corporations throughout the next decade. Cutting staff is the number-one item on a great many business agendas. For example, General Motors plans to trim more than 74,000 people from its ranks by 1995. The "new and improved" GM will be only half the size it was just ten years earlier. In the last quarter of 1991, announced staff reductions by major corporations eliminated 2,600 jobs every day.

Even the young, growing companies, who typically created the new job opportunities in this country, are thinking about scaling back. One of the reasons for this caution is a spotty recovery that evokes no faith in the future. Another is the realization that in an uneven economy costs must be contained. Still another reason is that a great number of senior executives are plain running scared.

Now that everyone understands "downsizing" really means "mass layoffs," the spin doctors are starting to call the action "rightsizing." Some outfits downsize through attrition. When people quit or retire the company doesn't hire replacements. Others offer early retirement to induce older employees to leave. Still others grudgingly parcel out two weeks pay and show employees the door. The result is the same no matter which method is used. More people are out of work, and they're chasing fewer jobs.

Outside of the fear induced by hard times, what prompts a chief executive officer whose power and prestige is directly related to the number of bodies on the payroll to downsize a company? There are three typical reasons:

1. *Everyone else is doing it and the CEOs of large companies have been known to play Follow-the-Leader.* The operating wisdom right now is that the corporation of the future must be smaller and "more focused."

2. *Wall Street loves to hear news of cost reductions.* A massive layoff at a major corporation usually has a positive effect on the company's stock. The CEO, whose seven-figure bonus may be riding on improving the value of the company shares, pleases the financial community and makes herself richer when staffs are cut.

3. *The work force reductions may really be necessary.* Many companies became much too large. They hired people because they could afford to do so, not because the people were needed.

Corporate survival for these companies over the next ten years depends on trimming all unnecessary expenses. "Focusing," that is, paying close attention to the things a company does best, is not a bad idea.

What Downsizing Means to Middle Managers

When downsizing becomes a national phenomenon the natural result is that fewer jobs are available. A look at the planning charts of most major corporations reveals that these jobs won't come back soon. Companies won't ramp up again if things improve. The one growing market segment, the service industry, offers jobs at much lower pay scales. In any case, the service industry has limited potential. We can't all thrive by waiting on one another. As a result, the country is going through what society watchers call a "lessening of expectation." The good life appears more remote to the younger generation.

The middle manager is particularly vulnerable. Who is most in jeopardy? Senior management regards paper shufflers, long-range planners, mid-level administrators, and so forth, as the least painful job categories to cut. One reason they're expendable is because the productivity of these kinds of jobs is difficult to measure.

Those managers who do survive the shakeouts will face the following changes in the "right-sized" corporate environment:

1. *Fewer people-management responsibilities.* Fewer Indians require fewer chiefs to lead them.

2. *More "hands-on" tasks of the sort they assumed had been left behind when they vaulted into management.*

3. *More accountability.* When something goes wrong, the managers responsible for the problem will be identified. There will be less patience with mistakes.

4. *Increased demand for immediate performance.* There'll be less time to learn the craft of management.

5. *More cynicism on the part of workers.* They won't be giving the old college try for the sake of alma mater.

6. *Fewer opportunities for advancement.* The smaller organization just won't have the same number of managerial jobs available.

How to Cope with Morale Problems in an Organization That Is Downsizing

There's a line in Rudyard Kipling's poem "If" that goes, "If you can keep your head when all about you are losing theirs and blaming it on you . . ." We won't take you through all the verses, but the poem concludes that the person who maintains calm and integrity through times of crisis can gain the earth.

The problem is that it's difficult to stay calm in a period of downsizing when everyone knows careers are on the line. Morale falls to pieces. If you're a manager charged with the responsibility of getting a job done when everyone about you, including staff members, are panicked or depressed because of rumors concerning the imminent loss of jobs, how best to handle the situation?

1. *Reduce the number of rumors and eliminate hearsay.* This can be accomplished by being candid and forthright with staff members. Share with them everything you know about the situation. Don't conceal information from a group who have been loyal employees just to get a few weeks' extra dedicated work out of them. Sharing information will also result in fewer hard feelings toward you and the organization in the event that any employees are let go.

2. *Point out to staff members that downsizing for most organizations usually means the loss of only a small percentage of jobs.* Not only are most people retained, but their jobs are generally "safe" for the foreseeable future.

3. *Play it straight.* Some staff member whom you'd like to retain may panic and accept a lesser job with another organization. Unless you know for sure that this employee is on the "safe" list, don't discourage her too strongly from accepting the offer.

4. *Be available to your staff members as much as possible to answer questions and diffuse rumors.* Right now you're the anchor that keeps the ship from drifting.

5. *Concentrate on near-term tasks.* Staff members may adopt a "what's the use?" attitude if asked to participate in long-range plans or projects when the immediate future is uncertain. Getting today's job done today can help boost morale.

6. *Develop the camaraderie of survivors, the defenders of the besieged fortress.* A shared trial can bring a group closer together.

7. *Point out to staff members that times of turmoil are also times of opportunity.* Those who survive may find themselves with more responsibility, more interesting tasks, and perhaps better compensation.

How Management Decides Whom to Keep and Whom to Dump When Downsizing

Are they sharpening the long knives in your organization? What are the chances that your neck will feel the blade? When the organization is forced to let people go, what you do for the company and where you are physically located are often more important than how competent you are. Here are the factors that determine if you're likely to survive:

1. *Line jobs are more likely to escape the ax than are staff jobs.* That's because it's easier to measure the contributions that line position managers make.

2. *Field jobs are more likely to survive than are home-office positions.* That's because national organizations recognize they'll always need a presence in the hinterlands. The finance people are likeiy to tell management that there are too many people cluttering up the home office.

3. *Younger employees are more likely to survive than are veterans.* That's because the people who have been with the company the longest are drawing the highest salaries. Getting them off the payroll has the greatest immediate impact on labor savings. Is this attitude blatant age discrimination? Of course it is!

4. *Politically connected employees are more likely to survive than are those with no pipeline to the executive suite.* Want real job security? Be related to a senior company executive.

5. *Senior executives are more likely to survive than are middle managers.* This is true in every large company. As a class, corporate middle managers are in more danger today than was the czar's family during the Russian revolution.

6. *Managers with special skills are more likely to survive than are generalists.* Knowing stuff nobody else knows is an excellent survival tactic.

7. *Sales people who enjoy special relationships with major customers are more likely to survive than are those who are doing business with a large number of smaller customers.*

8. *Employees who "play ball" are more likely to survive than are those who raise legitimate concerns about company direction and policy.* Downsizing is a wonderful time to get rid of the mavericks who bring new (unwanted) ideas to the corporation.

Why Being on the Committee Wielding the Ax Is No Guarantee You Won't Feel the Blade Severing Your Neck

Senior management has asked you to participate in the management of a large staff reduction. They want you to decide whom to let go, whom to keep in a certain department, branch, or operation. It's all very hush-hush and a heavy responsibility. You weigh the choices carefully, trying to retain those employees who have made the largest past contribution and whose loss would be felt most severely. The decisions are difficult, but you make them.

Perhaps you try to ease the pain for those who will be laid off by offering them job placement counseling, explaining their rights under the company's personnel policies, providing references, giving them desk space for job hunts, and so forth.

This is the sort of project that fully absorbs a manager's time and attention. Some managers become so caught up in the responsibility they never stop to consider that they, too, may be on the *adios!* list. In many cases the manager who so carefully supervised the cuts in a department is the one last one to be let go. He or she is somewhat like the gravedigger who is killed after the grave is dug so no one is left alive who knows the location of the sacred bones.

Sometimes the evidence that the manager is on the expendable list is obvious. When everyone in the manager's department is slaughtered, who does he or she think will be left alive to manage? Still, it does seem to come as a surprise to managers when it happens to them.

The important thing to understand is that just being a member of the long knife brigade doesn't offer any immunity when those knives are unsheathed and begin to flash. If asked to serve on the outplacement team, ask that your position in the new organization be defined. If there's no clear-cut answer, Prepare, Brother, Prepare!

How to Identify Companies That Are Ripe
for a Takeover

This section is not written for the enlightenment of the financial barracudas who cruise the waters sniffing for traces of blood. Their ability to sense a potential victim is keen enough as it is. These words may be useful, however, to a corporate employee who wonders if his employer is secure from the barbarians at the gate.

The informal rules for corporate takeovers have changed over the past several years. In the early Eighties, the ideal takeover candidate was a large company making a reasonable profit, often the dominant force in its industry. (Wall Street likes industry leaders because they set the market agenda.) When this kind of target was identified, a corporate raider would swoop in, buy a large, but minority stock position and use junk bond financing to offer existing stockholders a premium for their shares.

Banking and investment houses, who made huge paper profits on these deals, would underwrite the transaction. (Later, as the value of junk bonds declined, these profits evaporated, but that's another story.) Stockholders anxiously tendered their shares because they received an immediate profit. Wall Street was reassured by the takeover team's promise of "better management" of the acquired company. It was a promise made by the arrogant and swallowed by the ignorant.

As this decade approached, these wonderfully incisive, gifted, and efficient managers often discovered they couldn't meet the enormous debt loads contracted when they took over the target companies. Many good organizations, some leaders in their fields, went belly-up because they couldn't make the payments on the junk-bond issues.

There were, and still are, enough defaults on large loans to make unfriendly buy-outs at premium prices unlikely in the immediate future. Of course, the boys on Wall Street have short memories, and many senior bank lending officers have minds that don't emit discernible brain waves. They can be counted on to repeat their mistakes in a few years.

The kind of takeovers that will occur in the next decade will be different. For the most part, they will occur when a troubled company puts itself on the block looking for a savior. (It's like damsels in distress asking a traveling gang of Hell's Angels for assistance.) The ways to identify likely candidates are:

> **1.** *Look for companies with heavy debt loads.* Those companies who are having trouble servicing their debts may become desperate enough to seek "white knights."

2. *Companies with leading edge technologies are attractive to potential buyers.* If your company is loaded with debt *and* possesses a technological edge, the sharks may be circling.

3. *Companies with long-lasting labor problems are often good takeover candidates.* The trenches where management faces labor may be dug so deeply that a new management team, willing to flank the barricades, must be brought in.

4. *Family-owned companies are good takeover candidates when the Old Guard dies or retires.* (Selling out and splitting the proceeds is one way to stop the squabbling among the heirs.)

5. *Companies with brand-name identification who have recently lost market share are good takeover candidates.* Good marketers can revive a sagging brand, and every takeover artist considers himself a good marketer.

If you're a manager with a company that fits one of the preceding profiles, be careful!

What Side to Be on in a Takeover and How to Cross Over to That Side

It's far better to be part of the company taking over another outfit than to be on the side that is being acquired. That news is hardly a revelation. The management team of the takeover company gets to set the agenda. They generally make all the judgment calls. They decide who stays and who goes when two managers have similar responsibilities. They decide which operations will be eliminated, which will be transferred to another location. They make all the choices, and they've known your counterpart at the takeover company for twenty years while they wouldn't recognize you from a load of coal.

Just as we can't pick our parents, however, managers can't choose which side they'll be on when one company takes over another. What managers can do is to position themselves to survive.

If you're a manager with a company that has been acquired, the path to survival is through cooperation with the managers from the acquiring company. In the beginning, what they want most is information. They want to know how your company does business, its administrative policies, what markets it serves, how the products are sold, who are the major customers, what products enjoy an edge, and just about everything under the sun.

They are entitled to this information so give it freely. Become an unofficial part of the takeover team. The way to do that is to be the person who is the first one asked about anything related to the company's policies and procedures. Never be hesitant about supplying data concerning an operational matter. Volunteer more than is required.

Everything you do, everything the company does, is being evaluated. Don't be surprised if the takeover team comes to the conclusion that they do most everything better back home. Listen with wonderment when they explain how terrific their management system is. By being an information source, and apparently sympathetic, you become part of the evaluation process.

You may also be asked to make judgments or offer opinions on the personnel with your company, including senior level executives. In this area be more circumspect. Don't rush to criticize your co-workers and managers. Instead, stress their value to the organization. The takeover team will appreciate your loyalty to the individuals in the company. This loyalty plus cooperation in making changes will help you to survive.

What They Always Tell the Managers Who Work for Companies That Have Been Taken Over and Why You Should Never Believe It

When one company has taken over another there is one disgraceful line that is invariably used at the first joint managers' meetings. Some senior-level executive from the takeover company will go to the podium and say, "No changes are anticipated. We're not going to interfere in the operation just as long as you keep on doing your jobs." Don't believe a word of this rubbish. It's a blatant lie. A more candid statement by the new management would be, "No changes will be made until we find out where the bones are buried."

No management team that ever existed can resist putting its personal stamp on an operation once they've gained control. The only thing in doubt is the timing. The management of the company that has been taken over can expect alterations to every aspect of how they do business. That includes changes in procedure, perhaps a different marketing philosophy, a new focus, and substantial changes in personnel. Take it as a given that *the company roster will carry a long deceased list a year from now.*

For the Survivors: How to Handle More Responsibility with Fewer Staff Members

The first reaction managers usually have after surviving a visit from the Long Knives is relief to be among the living. This euphoria lasts until the realization that the same amount of work must be completed as before, but the staff has been decimated.

Sometimes the workload is even heavier. The takeover company adds new tasks, new reporting procedures, and new responsibilities. Valuable support services may no longer be available. The challenge the managers face is how to turn out as much quality work as before with fewer resources.

The first step toward producing more with less is to question what has been done in the past. Why is a certain report needed? Why does the system work a certain way? Why is a certain manager's signature and approval needed before processing can begin? Ask questions such as these without hesitation. *There is no time when it is safer to question the time-honored way of doing things than immediately after a major bloodletting.* The executive suite is looking for improvements. They've cut out the dead wood, and they're willing to revise ineffective procedures.

The second step is to attend to the morale of the survivors. This is like giving battlefield aid to the wounded. Some staff members will be ineffective for a time because they're waiting for the other shoe to drop. Convince them that they were retained because they are valued and productive employees. Let them know, without making promises, that their jobs are probably safe for a time. Companies rarely schedule two major staff reductions in a single year. Try to establish a castle-under-siege mentality. People become more willing to sacrifice.

The third step is to document the responsibilities and duties of those employees who were severed. It's best to do this early when the ex-employees may still be available for consultation. (Try to stay on good terms with these old hands. They may give you information about the operation out of friendship that they would probably deny another official of the company because of rancor for the way they were treated.)

The fourth step is to calculate the time necessary to do every assigned task. If there aren't enough hours in the day it's time to ask senior management for relief. Be able to prove your case. (Don't be surprised if the relief comes in the form of new people being added to the payroll. Firms that have just been through major staff reductions frequently reverse the process and add bodies when it can be proven that the cuts were too drastic.)

The fifth and most important step is to be positive and cheerful and convinced that the job can be done. This kind of attitude will help your staff members and help yourself as well.

Evaluating an Early-Retirement Offer

Early retirement offers are often used by companies that wish to reduce their number of employees without wholesale blood letting. They're popular with organizations who wish to maintain a positive image. They usually don't have a negative impact on morale because acceptance of the offer is voluntary. In most cases employees must have a certain tenure with the company to be eligible. There are several types of offers. The most popular are:

1. *A lump-sum payout.* (Usually a certain number of weeks' pay for every year with the company.)

2. *An advance-pension payout schedule.* In many cases the company will offer to continue to maintain for a time whatever obligation it had for hospital and medical insurance.

The offers generally hold the most appeal for those employees who are:

1. *Very close to retirement.*

2. *Looking for a lump-sum payout to finance a business, or some other use.*

3. *Fed up with the company and just about ready to bail out.*

4. *Convinced that the company is headed down a rocky road and not keen on experiencing the bumps.*

The company's dilemma is making the offer attractive enough so that the desired number of employees accept without making it so tempting that the ranks are decimated. That's why the offers are designed to appeal most to those employees who have been with the company the longest.

The lure for the older employees is the immediate lump-sum payout, which can be a substantial sum, or the advanced schedule pension benefit. The contemplation of leaving the problems of the work world behind is never more appealing than when considering an early-retirement offer.

Before accepting any offer, evaluate it thoroughly. Here's a worksheet that will help.

Early Retirement Offer Worksheet

Number of years to retirement _____

Estimated lost wages for those years $_____

Lump-sum payout offer $_____

Net loss or gain $_____

Years to company pension benefits if offer
not accepted. _____

Total sum of pension payments over those years
if advanced program is accepted $_____

Net loss or gain versus lost wages $_____

Does company have a 401k plan?
Yes_____ No_____

Company's annual contribution to 401k $_____

Estimated sum lost in 401k benefits to retirement $_____

Will company continue hospital and medical
insurance coverage?
Yes_____ No_____

For how long? _____years

Increased cost for medical coverage $_____

Are further job cutbacks likely?
Yes_____ No_____

Am I in jeopardy next year?
Yes_____ No_____

Other company perks that will be lost_____

_____

_____

_____

_____

_____

Note: This worksheet is intended only to evaluate the financial advantages or disadvantages of an early-retirement offer from a company. It is not designed to determine if someone should or should not actually retire. This is a much more complicated financial issue. That's why there's no place in the worksheet to calculate social security benefits, income from investments, IRAs and 401k plans, estimated expenses, equity in property and the possibility of "cashing out," and so forth. All these factors, and many others, should be included when contemplating retirement.

Why the First Early Retirement Offer Is Often the Best Offer

One of the factors that must be considered when a company offers early retirement is that this first offer is usually the best deal the employee can expect. Companies offer early retirement because they're hurting financially. They hope that trimming the number of employees will stop the pain. If the initial staff reductions don't work and the company feels the need to make further cuts, the terms the next time around may be far less appealing, and acceptance may not be voluntary. So examine the offer closely. It's probably the best deal you can get.

How to Negotiate a Better Outplacement Deal

Early retirement offers aren't usually subject to individual negotiation because all employees must be treated the same. The company develops a formula that applies to everyone. Any attempt to "custom-tailor" deals for a selected few will bring the attention of the state labor board and could result in legal action by terminated employees who didn't receive the same package as others.

In individual outplacement situations, some negotiation is possible. We'll start with the assumption that the reason for the outplacement is that the company is trimming staff, but by only a few bodies. If the employee is being terminated for inefficiency, absenteeism, insubordination, or other reasons related to performance, these suggestions won't apply.

The first step after being told that the company is letting you go because of tough economic times is to take your ego off the playing field. A natural reaction is: *Why me instead of the person at the desk across the way or in the next office?* I'm sure most of the managers could develop a long list of reasons why others are better candidates for outplacement than themselves. The reasons may be valid, but they don't matter. This kind of thinking will help you nurse a set of grievances, but it won't help get a better package than the one offered. The tactics that may work depend upon the situation. Here are several alternatives:

The Adversarial Approach (Number One)

This is the approach to take when you're told about the termination at 4:00 P.M. on a Friday afternoon, handed a white envelope from as assistant manager in personnel, given fifteen minutes to clear your desk, and are marched off the premises (holding a box with your personal belongings) by a uniformed guard without a chance to say good-bye to your friends. If you weren't terminated for cause, the company is playing hardball and you'll have to play hardball to get a better deal.

1. *Evaluate the outplacement package as explained by the letter in the white envelope.* What is the company offering in terms of notice, severance pay, extended medical coverage, job-placement services, use of company facilities in job search activity, and so forth?

2. *Compare notes with others who were let go in the same bloodletting.* Was everyone treated the same?

3. *Contact ex-employees who had been terminated in the past.* Was the deal offered them the same as the one offered you?

4. *If senior-level executives were terminated in the same bloodletting, check on the outplacement package they received.* If you don't know anyone who will give you any details, this kind of information is often available through the grapevine. A contact in personnel is invaluable. The reason for comparing packages is to determine if the company has been arbitrary and subjective in deciding who gets what.

5. *In a letter, present evidence of any unfairness in the outplacement packages.* Direct this letter to your former supervisor, the head of Human Resources, and the CEO of the company. Be specific and detailed. Request equal treatment with the best package you've uncovered.

6. *If you don't receive a response, send a second letter, this time copying your state's Labor Relations or Fair Employment Practice Board.*

7. *If no answer is forthcoming, request a hearing with your state's Fair Employment Practice Office.* Copy your former employer on the request. Make sure the company knows when a hearing date is set. This is the point when a settlement is most likely. The company is about to incur a legal expense in defending itself. A settlement now may be its most cost-effective option.

8. *If there's still no response go before the state's Fair Employment Practice Board and present your case.*

(We advise making your own presentation rather than using a lawyer. Legal fees are sky-high, particularly for someone out of work, and Labor Board members are often more impressed by a worker making his or her own case. Of course, the company is very likely to use an attorney, but this can work to your advantage. To the board the two of you positioned against each other seem like David versus Goliath.)

The Friendly Puppy Dog Approach (Number Two)

This is the tactic to use when the boss tells you that letting you go was the toughest decision she ever had to make, there's a farewell luncheon during which a decent ball-point pen is presented along with a few speeches, and your peers, who are keeping their jobs and their salaries, take you aside to confide how lucky you are to be getting out of "this zoo."

1. *As before, evaluate the outplacement package thoroughly.* Make sure it is at least equal to what others will be receiving who are in the same situation.

2. *Be cooperative during the phase-out period by giving management all the information they request about your operation. Do not attempt to negotiate a better deal by withholding data.* This appears to be blackmail. Provide the boss with a summary of your activity and a list of things that need to be done. Have a friendly meeting with the person assuming your responsibilities. In other words, accumulate a few IOUs.

3. *Focus on one or two areas in which you would like to see the outplacement package improved.* For example, how long will the company be picking up medical insurance coverage? This cost for an individual can be substantial.

4. *Request that the company up the ante in the areas on which you've focused.* For example, request that the company extend the insur-

ance coverage for a longer period. Ask your boss to go to bat for you. Stress your personal hardship if the package isn't improved.

5. *In exchange for an improved outplacement package, offer to serve as an unpaid consultant on any unresolved problems that crop up after you leave.*

6. *Stop by the office once or twice to say hello to the old gang.* (Don't do it often. You'll be considered a nuisance.)

If nothing else, this approach will ensure that your old boss gives you a good recommendation to a prospective employer. She'll be desperate to get you hired on somewhere else and out of her hair.

What to Do When Being Forced out of the Company When You Don't Want to Go

Sometimes it appears as if companies that are forced to lay off large numbers of employees use the same method for making personnel decisions as armies do when selecting rifle men for the dreaded firing squad assignment: Every tenth man is chosen.

The decisions on whom to keep and whom to let go are often arbitrary. The boss may have a favorite he'd like to keep. Most companies generally prefer retaining young employees over older veterans because the younger people earn lower salaries, have more energy, and are less jaded. When making large scale layoffs, however, companies are supposed to use specific guidelines so the keep-or-let-go decisions on all company personnel are based on the same standards.

When companies ignore their own guidelines, when senior management plays favorites, when older employees are forced out merely because of their age, some employees who were terminated but wish to retain their positions may have a case for possible reinstatement. Here's how to try to get your job back:

1. *Demand to see a copy of the criteria the company used to determine who would be cut and who would be retained.*

2. *Ask for supporting data as to why you were one of those chosen to be let go.*

3. *Ask to see a copy of any negative information on job performance in your personnel file.* Also ask for copies of your annual perfor-

mance review. (Employees should always retain and file copies of their performance reviews when they are received.)

4. *If there's no evidence of poor performance in the file, claim that the company engaged in discriminatory practices by letting you go while retaining others.* Your claim will receive particular attention if:

   a. You're a member of a minority.

   b. You're female.

   c. You're approaching senior-citizen status.

   d. You're an American working for a foreign-owned company.

   e. You have more tenure than many of the employees who were retained.

5. *In writing, ask for your old job back.* Make sure that senior-level executives and the head of Human Resources receive copies of the letter. If the request is denied, or if you receive no reply, petition for a hearing with the state's Fair Employment Practice Board based on the charge of discrimination.

6. *The board will set a hearing date.* (If your case has merit, shortly before the hearing the company may contact you with a settlement offer.) If possible, conduct your own case. (Until a few years ago many terminated employees were afraid to cause any kind of row with their old employers because it might result in negative references, making it difficult to land another job. Today, so many former employees have won large judgments because of unwarranted derogatory reports that many large companies are reluctant to pass along anything "bad" about a former worker.)

Four Steps to Take When Outplaced by a Foreign-Owned Company

Many foreign-owned companies. particularly the Japanese, use American workers to market, and sometimes manufacture, their products in the United States. They set up American subsidiaries staffed mostly by Americans, but controlled by the foreign ownership. Senior management, and often the engineering staff, are usually the same nationality as the foreign owner.

(Incidentally, most of these subsidiaries are structured to make little or no profit so they pay few U.S. taxes compared to their American-owned competitors. The profits are made based on the price the parent company charges the American subsidiary when the products leave the foreign docks. It's a lovely little tax dodge that allows foreign companies to operate here without contributing to the cost of government.)

Even these foreign-owned companies are taking the downsizing theory seriously by cutting back on the number of employees. However, most of them are eliminating American workers while leaving their national staffs intact. This is outright discrimination and a point of attack if you are included in a layoff by a foreign-owned corporation. Here's a four-step program that might get you additional compensation.

1. *Obtain a copy of the complete company roster before the layoffs.* Calculate the percentage of American to foreign national employees.

2. *Review the payroll roster after the layoffs.* Is the percentage of American to foreign national workers the same as before? Many cases have revealed wholesale layoffs of Americans while not a single foreign national was terminated.

3. *If the percentage of foreign nationals to American workers has changed drastically as a result of layoffs, bring the matter to the attention of the state's Fair Employment Practice Board.*

4. *Contact other employees who were terminated at the same time.* As a group, contact a good labor lawyer. There may be grounds for a class-action suit. (After losing a few legal battles on this point, many foreign-owned companies are getting cagier. Terminations will seem to affect just as many foreign national staff members as Americans. In most cases, however, when their own people are eliminated from the subsidiary's payroll they are sent back to the parent company where they resume their careers. This is still discriminatory treatment.)

Chapter Summary

❖ In the next decade corporate trimming will reduce the number of available management jobs.

❖ Staff jobs are more vulnerable than operational responsibilities.

❖ To maintain employee morale during a period of downsizing, be open and candid with them. Don't keep secrets.

❖ Those most likely to survive downsizing are younger employees who possess special skills.

❖ Being part of the downsizing committee is no guarantee that a manager isn't on the list to be let go.

❖ Companies that are ripe for a takeover are those experiencing some financial woes or other problems.

❖ The management staff on a company that has been taken over by another can expect some rough times.

❖ A new management team coming into a company almost always makes many changes.

❖ An ideal time to make needed changes is just after a takeover or downsizing.

❖ The first early-retirement offer is usually the company's best offer.

❖ It's possible to negotiate a better outplacement deal by comparing your offer to what others have received.

❖ It's possible to fight and win if the company attempts to force you out against your will.

❖ Foreign companies operating in the United States almost always give special consideration to their national citizens when reducing staff levels.

❖ 6 ❖

HOW TO MANAGE
A PROJECT

Why Projects Are the Best Place to Make a Reputation as a Skillful Manager

Doing a really terrific job for your company? So what? Don't expect senior management to notice. Middle managers are supposed to handle their daily routine work with efficiency and dispatch. By themselves, dedication and responsibility are not enough to move a manager up a few notches on the promotion chart. That's not to say the nose-to-the-grindstone approach to career advancement doesn't work. It just takes time—a very long time.

One shortcut to becoming noticed, and therefore a shortcut to promotion, is through heading up special projects. These projects include the studies, the reports, the marketing trials, the business experiments, the items beyond the daily routine that major corporations are always engaged in to investigate new opportunities.

Why can these assignments provide a quicker road to the top? Because special projects attract the attention of senior managers. They are more interested in things out of the ordinary that they are in the humdrum of daily business. Management is always looking for more profits. They place a high value on the scouts who are able to blaze a trail to these profits.

The special project is like an audition. It's a chance for middle managers to show off their talent. When heading up the right kind of project, managers have the opportunity to demonstrate all their administrative and managerial skills. They can show off their abilities to put things in logical sequence and reach the right conclusions. They can exercise their persuasive powers. Through their recommendations they can prove their willingness to accept risks. The project team leader often gets the chance to showcase these skills before members of senior management, people he or she might not otherwise meet, except perhaps at the office Christmas party.

Never consider a special project as just another chore. This is one time when it may pay to volunteer. A project that is handled well and is observed by the right audience will do more to enhance a manager's reputation than a year of cranking out assigned tasks on schedule. The key is choosing exactly the right projects.

How to Handpick Projects That Could Enhance Your Career

Just as important as doing a good job with assigned projects is selecting the right projects to take on. Not every project has the potential to advance a career. Some could even be damaging. Much depends on the scope of the project and who is interested in the results.

A project that investigates new market opportunities for the company's products will likely attract the attention of senior management. An exercise whose aim is to hold down the cost of consumable office supplies will draw yawns in the executive suite. That's because expansion and growth are more exciting than conserving and saving. During a time when most companies are interested in trimming costs, however, gaining the reputation as a conservator of resources can be useful.

Projects with intracompany political implications can be dangerous. If a segment of senior management has an "investment" in a certain conclusion, they may harbor resentment against a project leader who reaches another. Projects begun to find the causes of internal problems can also be dangerous for the project leader. If the project team finds a certain department or departmental procedures responsible for the problem, the involved department head is not going to be happy with the result.

However, most projects do offer the opportunity for the project leader to strut his or her stuff. When asked to take on a project, give it the following litmus test:

1. *Does this project have the interest of senior management?* (Obviously, you hope for a "yes" answer to this one.)

2. *Will the project leader be given the resources and time to do justice to the project?* (Another "yes" is required here. Don't accept a responsibility unless you are also offered the authority and resources to fulfill it.)

3. *Is there controversy connected with this project that could attach itself to the person in charge?* If the answer to this one is "yes" think hard before taking on the project. If there are different points of view within the company on a controversial subject each faction is hoping to be vindicated or to have its power enhanced by the results of the study. In this instance it might be best to gracefully decline the offer and walk away.)

Avoid those projects that are dull and time-consuming and small-minded. That means stay away from the study on maximizing the parking spaces in the company parking lot. Don't get involved with the plan to put meters on the copy machines so each copy made can be charged to an individual department. Also avoid extracurricular projects. Plead a killer schedule when asked to serve on the office picnic committee or the Christmas party planners or the glee club. There are no Brownie points for these kinds of assignments. In fact, committee members on these kinds of projects are often indulged as harmless fools.

The Project Worksheet: How to Plan Projects That Are Completed on Time and Within Budget

After accepting responsibility for a project it's absolutely vital to produce. Failure can be career damaging. Remember that the right kind of project puts the project leader under a spotlight. The glare of that light becomes awfully harsh when things aren't going right. (That's why it's a good idea to walk away from those projects for which you wouldn't be given sufficient resources.) When starting a project, use a worksheet such as the following to help determine if targets are being met.

Project Worksheet

Project Name _____

Start date _____   Completion date _____

Who is interested _____

_____

Why the interest _____

_____

Goals

1._____

_____

2._____

_____

3._____

_____

4._____

_____

5._____

_____

6._____

_____

7._____

_____

8._____

_____

Preconceived notions _____

_____

_____

_____

Team Members
Name   *Department*   *Responsibility*

_____

_____

_____

_____

_____

_____

Project's Budget Estimated Expenses
Item   *Est. Cost*   *Actual Cost*

_____

_____

_____

_____

_____

_____

Total Est. Cost _____ Tot. Act. Cost _____

Benchmarks
Benchmark   *Completion date*

_____

_____

_____

_____

_____

_____

Who receives copy of results _____

_____

_____

_____

This kind of worksheet is valuable because:

1. *The goals of the project have been clearly identified.* (Always confirm the defined goals for an assignment with senior management. There's nothing worse than working for months on a project, coming in with a final report, and then being faced with an after-the-fact complaint that the brass was looking for something else.)

2. *The responsibilities of team members have been defined.*

3. *A crude budget has determined that the project can be brought in with the amount allotted.*

4. *Benchmarks have been established to assist in determining if the project is on schedule.*

5. *The preconceived notions associated with the project have been identified.* This is important if the results don't agree with the preconceptions. You'll want to get the word out as soon as possible.

6. *Timetables have been set.*

How to Focus on Project Results

Three of the most important characteristics of projects are:

1. *They have relatively short life spans.*

2. *They have a very narrow franchise; that is, they are usually begun to find an answer to something.* Any attempt to widen their horizons is usually met with hostility.

3. *They are activities conducted outside the normal flow of company business.*

The "juggling act" for the project leader is to produce the desired result within the deadline while allowing team members to handle their other assigned responsibilities. The limitations on time to complete everything required and time available from team members makes focusing on the project's results mandatory. This focus can be maintained if the project leader will conduct a simple exercise before beginning the endeavor. Gather team members together and, in an open discussion, ask these questions:

1. *What is the primary goal of this project?*

2. *What, if any, are secondary goals?*

3. *How can we accomplish these goals in the allotted time?*

4. *What do you perceive as your specific role in helping the team achieve these goals?*

5. *What problems do you foresee for yourself and the team?*

6. *What could possibly delay us?*

7. *How can we guard against these delays?*

The open discussion is helpful because all team members should have a clear understanding of the project's goals and their individual roles in achieving those goals by the time the talks are concluded. (Believe it or not, in many projects team members are working toward different goals.)

It's also a good idea to have a member of senior management present as an observer at this discussion to be sure that the objectives have been "cleared" by the brass. A member of senior management may also be able to help with a perceived roadblock.

How to Build the Project Team and Win Over Unwilling Members

Running a project is like any other management responsibility: To ensure good results, recruit good people. When taking on responsibility for a special assignment, the manager should first determine just what special skills or experience would be useful for the completion of that assignment and recruit team members accordingly. Would a marketer be helpful? A numbers person? A distribution expert? A production specialist? Select team members carefully. You'll be held responsible for the sum of their results.

The worksheet on the following page might make the selection process a bit easier.

Personality is another factor that should be considered when selecting project team members. The operative word here is *team*. It's best to recruit people who recognize that a group of people will be embarking on what will be a joint effort. If forced to choose between the cooperative and the brilliant, pick the cooperative. Stay away from prima donnas, avoid the cantankerous, pass up the unreliable, and race past the hair splitters.

One problem with recruiting team members is that they may not be willing to be drafted. It's extra work, and except for the project leader, little glory. Expect to hear a number of alibis. The most popular excuses are:

Project Team Selection Worksheet

Area of Investigation   Skill Needed   Candidates

---

1. *It's impossible.* This is our department's busy time of year. I'm absolutely swamped!

2. *I've got my own problems whipping my department into shape.* The brass just doubled our work load.

3. *I'm shorthanded myself because I'm missing a few staff members.* (Or, I'm training new people.)

4. *We're right in the middle of installing new equipment, or a new system, or we're moving to a new location.*

5. *I'd love to help you, but this is outside my area of expertise.* Why don't you ask Fred? He knows this stuff inside and out.

6. *I'll ask my boss, but I don't think he'll go for the idea.*

There are dozens of variations to these cop-outs. In essence, they all carry the same message: "Don't bother me, boy, I'm busy."

The real reason, however, is often because those asked feel they will gain no glory being mere members of a project team being headed up by somebody else.

The way around these perfectly valid reasons is to offer the following arguments to the reluctant team member:

1. *This is an important subject that has the attention of senior management.* It's worth the extra demands on your time. (Don't get involved with trivial projects and this argument will be valid every time.)

2. *You bring special knowledge or experience that is absolutely vital to the success of the project.* We'll limit your involvement by calling on you only when necessary.

3. *This will be a true team effort, and credit will accrue to every member of the team.*

4. *Hey, you may be heading up a project sometime soon.* If you cooperate with me now, I'll cooperate with you later.

How to Obtain Support for Your Project from Other Departments and Managers

Project leaders soon learn that not everyone in the organization is thrilled and delighted about cooperating in helping the leaders reach their assigned goals. Reactions from department heads can range all the way from indifference to actual sabotage. The degree of resistance to a project is in direct relationship to the fundamental changes that project could create.

The more bureaucratic an organization, the more it will resist change. Information may not be supplied when it is requested; facility support, such as computer time or working space, may be withheld; personnel loaned to the project may be withdrawn; and not-so-subtle roadblocks may be erected to stop the project dead in its tracks.

The way to gain cooperation from wary department heads is through early-on meetings with each manager who could be affected by the project or whose help you need. At these meetings be prepared to discuss:

1. *The goals of the project.*

2. *The senior management level that is sponsoring the project or is interested in the results.* Be sure to let the managers know exactly which senior managers will be receiving report copies.

3. *The impact the goals are likely to have on involved departments.* (Focus on the positive things.)

4. *The kind of cooperation you'll need from the department heads to achieve the assigned goals.* Be very specific as to what you expect.

5. *The time frame in which you need to get things done.*

6. *The manner in which information concerning the project will be shared with the various departments.*

Be candid.

Be receptive to suggestions.

Answer questions fully.

This kind of open discussion will eliminate any misconceptions about the purpose of the project and who wants the work done. Offering to share the results is important because this shows that everything will be done in the open.

Expect to receive a vague commitment to assist. Even if a department head is vehemently opposed to the goals of a project he or she is not likely to openly reveal this opposition. This is particularly true if the project has the blessing of senior management.

Accept the reluctant commitments as if they indicated unbridled enthusiasm. Write memos to the department heads thanking them for their cooperation. It's okay to gush a bit. In the memos detail the "promises" the department heads have given you. Copy senior management on the memos. Following these steps will gain you the cooperation you need to get the project completed.

This procedure suggests that no one is ever willing to cooperate with a project leader. Obviously, this is far from true. It is true, however, that department heads have their own priorities and, in most cases, your project isn't one of them. The struggle is against indifference, not intransigence.)

One other useful tactic to gain internal support for a project is to get the reputation as someone who is cooperative in supporting the projects headed up by others. They're honor bound to reciprocate. In fact, accumulate IOUs whenever possible. You never know when you'll have the need to cash them in.

How to Anticipate and Deal with Problems Related to Your Project

Organize a brainstorming session shortly after a project team has been assembled. The subject of the session? *What can go wrong?* Let fancies range as far as they will and write down every imaginable thing that could prevent the project team from reaching the assigned goal on schedule. Help the team along by suggesting problem categories. These could include:

1. *Possible breakdowns in equipment, communications, systems, and so forth.*

2. *Potential bottlenecks.* Where does the information flow get squeezed?

3. *Potential roadblocks.* (Not the same as a bottleneck. A roadblock is a deliberate attempt to sabotage a project.)

4. *Possible personality conflicts among project team members.* (Yes, get this problem out in the open. It almost eliminates the possibility that you'll have them.)

5. *Internal opposition.* Who has a vested interest in the status quo?

6. *Labor problems.*

7. *Access to resources needed to do the job.* Is there needed information that will be difficult to obtain?

In the second half of the session develop contingency plans to deal with these potential problems should they arise. For example, if someone suggests that the company's Management Information Service (MIS) department may not be willing or able to give the project team needed access to the mainframe computer, perhaps now is the time to investigate buying computer time from a local service bureau.

No project manager will be able to anticipate everything that could go wrong. The gods enjoy hurling their thunderbolts at the self-satisfied. Taking the time to think about and planning around potential problems, however, helps the project leader to be prepared for those problems that inevitably occur.

How to Ensure Getting Credit for Project Results

Getting proper credit and recognition for the good things in a project takes a bit more effort than merely signing off on the final report as team leader.

Yes, senior management will note the name when they read the report. (That is, assuming the report is read. We're not a generation of readers. It's very likely a staff member will give the senior manager a written or verbal summary.)

However, your name on the title page doesn't indicate your level of involvement or commitment. That still must be proven. The proving process is through conviction concerning the conclusions reached by the project team. Does the project leader stand behind these conclusions? Here's what senior management wants to know when a project is completed:

1. *What were the findings?*
2. *What changes do these findings suggest?*
3. *How should these changes be implemented?*
4. *What will these changes mean to the company?*
5. *Is the project leader ready to put his or her reputation on the line concerning the recommended changes?*

The project manager who wants "credit" answers these questions for the senior-management staff. It's better to answer them in personal meetings, preferably one-on-one, because in these kinds of meetings personal commitment and conviction shine through. The leader becomes an advocate of the conclusions reached by the entire team. By carrying the banner, he or she becomes so identified with the project that any good stuff that results is naturally credited to the project leader.

Writing the Project Report

The shorter the report the more likely it is that senior management will actually read it. Here's what goes into most project reports:

1. *A summary of the problem or area being investigated.*
2. *The method used for that investigation.*
3. *What the investigation revealed.*
4. *Conclusions reached by the revelations.*
5. *Recommendations in detail for action based on the conclusions.*
6. *A summary of the recommendations.*
7. *An index that tells just where the summary information can be found in case that's all the senior manager chooses to read.*

Use short sentences and simple language. Graphs and charts are nice if they're easy to understand; otherwise, they're a disaster. Here's what to keep out of reports:

1. *A recitation of the problems encountered in gathering the data or completing the project.* If management wanted epics, they'd read Homer.

2. *Equivocation.* Don't build a report with too many escape hatches. Have a point of view and state it plainly. Remember that the point of any study is to reach conclusions.

3. *Misleading data.* Don't slant the evidence to make a stronger case. If you can't sell the product based on the facts, then it is career threatening to try to sell it based on falsehoods.

4. *Telling the audience what you think they want to hear.* Don't write a project report to please a senior manager with a vested interest. If you have no faith in the recommendation, don't make it.

What to Do When the News Is Bad

One theory of project management is to pronounce that the results are a success no matter what happens. It takes reading between the lines to pick out the failures. ("We found out exactly what we needed to know so there's no point in going further.") This is the philosophy of the Power of Positive Thinking bunch. Rose-colored glasses are okay, but the real world can be seen better without them.

Managers assigned responsibility for projects should recognize that some will inevitably fail to achieve their objectives. It's best to be candid and admit failure when it happens. Senior management is likely to recognize it anyway.

A report that analyzes what went wrong and how these problems can be corrected is what management would really prefer from a project leader. Valuable information can be gleaned from failure.

A self-serving report, one that is enthusiastic about reaching vague goals, or achieving certain bench marks, when in fact the exercise was a flop, is likely to be treated with impatience by senior management. So, in the words of a former sports announcer with an insufferable personality, "tell it like it is."

How to Guarantee Good Results

Success is always better than failure. For one thing, success creates possibilities; failure eliminates them. To "guarantee" good results, or success, with a project, keep several things in mind.

1. *Make sure the desired goals of the project are achievable.* If you have reservations about the goals, make those reservations known. Negotiate for realistic objectives you believe can be met.

2. *Recruit a project team of people you trust whose abilities you respect.*

3. *Create a team spirit by sharing credit and responsibility.*

4. *Obtain the cooperation of other involved departments in the company.*

5. *Develop contingency plans that deal with foreseeable problems.*

6. *Establish benchmarks to make sure the project stays on schedule.*

7. *Present the results to senior management verbally and in written summary form.* These presentations not only give you the chance to explain the project, they provide the exposure that could lead to promotion.

8. *Work like the dickens.*

❖ 7 ❖

HOW TO MANAGE
UNDER PRESSURE

Why Management Applies Pressure

If there is one constant in today's business world it is unrelenting pressure. There is the pressure of deadlines, the pressure of impossible quotas, the pressure from management always demanding more, the pressure of the competition, the pressure of falling profits, the pressure of a weak market, the pressure of bosses who are jerks or idiots, the pressure of incompetent co-workers and subordinates, the pressure of inefficiency, the pressure of the company bureaucracy, the pressure of self-doubt, the pressure of changing market conditions, the pressure of killer schedules, the pressure of not enough resources to do the job properly, and the Nineties' contribution to the job-stress Hall of Fame: pressure from the realization that the position itself may not be there tomorrow.

There is no escape from these work-place pressures so don't look for relief in these pages. Management believes all kinds of good things happen through applying pressure, and they're not about to abandon a philosophy they embrace with more enthusiasm each passing year.

There are a significant number of senior managers who truly believe that pressure improves performance. Quotas are deliberately set too high, deadlines are purposely short, praise is parceled out by eye droppers, the scent of fear is wafted through the air conditioning ducts, "voluntary" unpaid overtime is expected, all because a pressure atmosphere "keeps the staff on their toes."

It's difficult to quarrel against the tactic because it probably works. At least, applying the screws works on some members of the labor force. Pressure will weed out those employees who are incompetent or unwilling. They'll move on rather than "take the crap." It also improves the performance of those employees who don't have strong motivation and those anxious to hold onto their jobs at all costs. These two groups will work harder out of fear.

Applying pressure also comforts senior management because they get to feel that they're really doing their jobs by putting the fear of God into those shiftless employees.

No one is exempt from pressure. The line employees get it from their supervisors who get it from their bosses all the way up the line to the CEO who gets it from the stockholders and the financial wizards. The message is the same at every level: Do more, do it better, do it faster, do it cheaper.

Why Pressure Kills Motivation

Where a deliberate policy of unrelenting management pressure fails is among those employees who came into the organization strongly motivated to do well. These are the enthusiastic, young, energetic employees with the ability to become the most valuable members of the work force.

It doesn't work on them because pressure kills that wonderful enthusiasm that all employers seek in their employees.

The realization that management is unreasonable in its demands kills enthusiasm.

The lack of praise and recognition kills enthusiasm.

The feeling that one's efforts are not appreciated kills enthusiasm.

The feeling of being exploited—and pressure exploits—kills enthusiasm.

The endless stretch of artificial deadlines kills enthusiasm.

The placing of goals deliberately out of reach kills enthusiasm.

The demand that the job be done without adequate resources kills enthusiasm.

The result is that pressure is a great leveler, lumping the motivated with the malingerers. Unrelenting pressure places all employees in a single category, a category that management feels must be threatened or tricked, or both to do a proper job.

One of the biggest destroyers of motivation is an inefficient or bureaucratic organization. Workers in these kinds of companies "survive" the pressure by becoming fatalistic. They treat each new foul-up, each new senseless regulation with a shrug or even a smirk. They won't fight the system; they laugh at it.

The solution for the manager who wants a dedicated, enthusiastic, motivated work force is to throw away the thumb screws. Sure, assign quotas, pronounce deadlines, set tough standards, make people responsible for their work, but don't make the burden unbearable or the job unrewarding. Praise the people responsible for the things that are done right and hold your tongue about the things that go wrong. The quality employees will assign their own pressures and set their own goals. These will be standards of performance that benefit themselves and the company.

Five Telltale Signs of Pressure from Above

Here are some of the typical advance warnings that indicate senior management is tuning up the rack, sharpening the needles in the iron maiden and oiling the other torture equipment.

1. *Managers are asked to prepare a detailed description of their department's functions, the staff levels, job descriptions of staff members, and why each person is necessary.* This could be a prelude to a staff reduction, essentially requiring you to turn out the same work with fewer bodies.

2. *Lately, nothing's good enough for management.* No matter how well the work is being done, it isn't satisfactory. There are complaints from above about everything, every decision is second guessed, praise is as elusive as quarks, a smile rare as a ten-carat diamond. Senior management is setting the stage for new pressure tactics.

3. *There's a change in operational management near the top.* The new person in charge has the reputation for being a martinet. He has an office right next to the CEO, and he says it's time to get

tough. There are frequent memos from the new guy concerning "sloppy performance."

4. *Budgets are cut, but the work output is expected to remain the same.* Other changes are instituted at the same time. Deadlines are shortened from unreasonable to impossible. The company does an audit on the office telephone calls. Meters are installed on the copy machines. An employee is fired for leaving fifteen minutes early without permission. It takes a written requisition with three approval signatures to get a dozen pencils.

5. *Nobody's word is trusted anymore.* Everything must be put in writing, then it's all checked and verified. Work is closely monitored. Autonomy flies out the window. Yesterday's accomplishments aren't worth spit.

These are all signs that point to a forthcoming pressure-cooker environment. Of course, senior management may be reacting to pressure from the board of directors or from Wall Street to improve performance. *Pressure begun at the top trickles down until it reaches the lowest point in the organization.*

Five Signs That Point to You as the Culprit Responsible for the High-Pressure Atmosphere

Air pressure at sea level is rated at fifteen pounds per square inch. In some companies the pressure placed by management on the workers has to be rated at least at a few thousand pounds per square inch, enough to give everyone on the staff a bad case of the bends. What's amazing is that many managers will deplore the pressure placed on employees, agree that it's bad for morale, yet react with surprise when someone suggests they themselves may be the cause of that pressure. They never realized that their actions caused employees stress. Here's how to determine if you may be the culprit.

1. *Are you receiving unmerciful pressure from above?* You may be acting as a conduit for that pressure from senior management. Unless you're a saint, you're probably passing it along to members of your staff. That's what senior management intends for you to do, but you must do it judiciously, putting less pressure on your star performers.

2. *Have the people in the office stopped kidding around?* Do workers hush up when you walk by? Have the jokes disappeared? If everything is suddenly deadly serious, chances are you've created a high-pressure environment. (Pressure punctures humor's balloon.)

3. *Have some of your best, most enthusiastic workers become sullen and morose?* Have one or two recently "told you off"? Have a couple of your people walked out? Are there frequent office arguments over relatively trivial issues? The staff is reacting to a high-pressure environment created by, guess who?

4. *Do you dread going into work in the morning?* Do you feel crummy by the end of the business day? Is the job drudgery? Are you thinking about getting out of this zoo? That's because you don't like what you've been doing.

5. *Do you have the feeling that the quality of the staff's work is deteriorating?* Do you find it necessary to check everything? Must the workers be kept "in line"? You've put so much pressure on your staff that you've lost confidence in them.

How to Cut Your Staff Members Some Slack and Still Get Needed Results

If you plead guilty as charged to the preceding indictments there is a way to make amends. The work place doesn't have to be purgatory. Some people actually find fulfillment through work. It's possible to reduce the pressure in a highly charged situation, even if that pressure radiates from the very top of the company. Here's how:

Use candor and openness. Get the work group together in an informal meeting. Expect sullen faces if the pressure has been of long duration. You're going to have to win them over.

First, what's the root cause of the pressure? *Most pressure situations are created by management's demand that the job be done with insufficient resources.* Start with that admission. "We've got an impossible task on our hands; now let's discuss how we're going to get it done."

Watch the sullen faces disappear. Using such an approach changes the management-induced pressure into a challenge. Every person at the meeting is part of that challenge. You'll get moaning and groaning, but you'll also get suggestions, volunteers, good and bad ideas, and a spirit of cooperation you thought had flown the company long ago. You'll get griping too. Allow it to go on for fifteen minutes or so, then cut it off. "This isn't a bitching session. We're here to find remedies. Who's got some ideas?"

Let your staff members pick their own assignments. Pick one dirty job for yourself that no one else wants just to show that you're willing to pitch in with the grunt work. Let staff members trade assignments if they choose.

The amount of work that needs to get out the door is still the same. The deadlines haven't been erased. There are no staff additions to help out. So what's different? The one thing that has changed is that your staff members have now assigned their own pressure to themselves. Somehow this make the job much more bearable.

Three Steps to Take When Senior Management Puts Your Feet to the Fire

Middle managers are the ideal victims of a senior-management pressure campaign. After all, middle managers have titles and responsibilities, so it isn't as if the men and women in the executive suite are picking on the little guys. Middle managers also have no union and no clout and they identify with senior executives, which means they have neither the ability nor the desire to retaliate. In other words, they're perfect targets!

The practical reason middle managers are selected for the treatment is that they are the perfect conduit for passing pressure along to the general population of employees. Putting pressure on middle managers is a good way of putting pressure on everyone in the organization.

If your feet are being put to the fire and the reason seems to be that management has decided hysteria is an excellent operating policy, there are several steps you can take to protect yourself:

1. *Don't let your boss get away with making vague complaints such as "recent sloppy work."* Make her recite chapter and verse regarding any complaint. Also, don't allow any meeting where you're being criticized to deteriorate into an anecdotal recitation of a few errors. Stand by your overall record. Be prepared to defend it with facts and figures.

2. *If management is really after you to turn up the pressure in your department, they'll ease up once you've agreed to do so.* That's the easy way out. A better course of action is ask for new departmental objectives in writing. Make senior management quantify their demands.

3. *Take your own notes as the meeting progresses.* In many of these sessions where stress is used as a weapon, many of the complaints and demands upon the manager contradict one another. Hold your ammunition to near the end of the meeting and reveal the contradictions.

4. *Don't react to threats that you can be replaced by someone "who is willing to take a firmer stand."* If your job is really that shaky getting tough with your staff members won't save it.

5. *Concentrate on the job management wants done and not on the method.* Stress results and not the means to those results.

6. *Remember that the boss applying the pressure has probably been given a turn or two on the rack herself.* Find out what really needs to be done to relieve the pressure on your supervisor.

How to Reduce or Eliminate the Pressure of Deadlines

If the entire concept of time is an artificial creation of man, then what are deadlines? In most cases deadlines are nothing more than lines drawn in the water. They are fabricated by management to create a sense of urgency. There's nothing sacred or final about the end of the month or the next quarter or the coming end if the fiscal period, except that management has decreed them holy.

Still, every manager must learn to operate under deadlines. It's the way the game is played. That means managers must learn how to deal with the pressure to produce a certain amount of work or accomplish a set of tasks or reach a specific decision within an identified time frame.

Managers who feel bothered by the pressure of deadlines can take actions to eliminate or reduce their discomfort. These actions include:

1. *Find out who set the deadline and if it's a "drop dead" date, or just an accomplishment that's desirable to reach at a particular point in time.*

2. *Break down the job to be done into a series of components.* As each component is completed, you're closer to the goal, and some of the deadline pressure is eliminated.

3. *Read chapter three of this book again on time management and thriving on deadlines.*

4. *Make your staff members aware of the deadlines and the effort you'll need from each of them to make these schedules.* There's no reason to tackle a deadline problem by yourself.

5. *Follow up frequently on the progress of any activity that has a short-term deadline.* One of the biggest job "pressure cookers" is suddenly discovering you're far behind schedule. Make the discovery when you're only *slightly* behind schedule and still able to take action to catch up.

6. *Have contingency plans for corrective action when things go wrong.*

7. *If a deadline can't be met, let senior management know immediately.* It won't be pleasant, but it's better than a last-minute thunderbolt. Getting senior management involved when the problem is perceived spreads the burden.

Early Warning: A Surefire Way to Relieve a Pressure Situation

Former Secretary of State Henry Kissinger said, "What must revealed eventually should be revealed immediately." Mr. Kissinger has the ability to state the obvious with elegance. There's no point in concealing something that's bound to come out in the end. Unfortunately, managers do it all the time. In concealing bad news they build pressure for themselves, their staff members, and even their companies.

The odd thing is that the act to conceal unpleasant information is often committed to avoid pressure. It works in just the opposite manner. The manager who conceals information now has the added pressure of worrying about being found out,

A surefire way to avoid pressure is to give the top brass early warning about any pending problems. ("Mr. Jones, it appears we won't be able to make our next deadline because of _____") The brass now warned can take corrective action or develop a new schedule. They can also come to a new mind set as to when the work will be finished. (Remember, most deadlines are artificial anyway.) The important thing is that pressure is now off the manager in charge of the project and onto the backs of the brass where it belongs.

How to Cope with Mistakes, Both Yours and Those of Your Staff Members

There are managers who enjoy nothing more than discovering an employee's mistake. It gives them the opportunity to be self-righteous, critical, indignant, sarcastic, parental, vindictive, tolerant, "helpful," and/or patronizing. There's no other business situation that offers a more satisfying emotional run for the money. In other words, for some managers finding mistakes is a cheap thrill.

Let us hope those managers are willing to turn a new leaf. The way to look at mistakes is that they are an inevitable part of business. They aren't terrible. They don't signal the end of western civilization. Most of them don't even do much harm to the organization. Almost all mistakes can be corrected. Life would be far less interesting without them.

The easiest way to deal with mistakes is to acknowledge and correct them as soon as possible. ("Hey, we screwed up. Let's fix it.") Keep using the word, "we" whenever possible. That kind of attitude goes a long way toward relieving the pressure. The manager who acknowledges his or her mistakes is giving staff members "permission" to do the same.

Once your staff members learn they won't be pilloried for mistakes, they'll be more willing to come forward when one is made. The manager's responsibility is to give absolution while making sure the same kinds of mistakes aren't being repeated. Tolerating occasional mistakes is not the same as license to make the same ones over and over.

How to Plan for Crises

My dictionary says a crisis is "a crucial time," or "a turning point." That definition sounds right, but some companies seem to have a crisis every half hour. So the first step in planning for crises is to determine if you're working for the kind of outfit where crises come spinning off the production line faster than the finished product. If you are, decide if you enjoy this kind of environment because you aren't likely to change it.

Planning for crises means first setting up criteria that define what a crisis is for your company. Is a specific situation a "crucial time," or just another run-of-the-mill emergency? The reason the distinction is important is because an emergency will be dealt with through normal company policy, while a crisis may require extraordinary measures.

After the crisis criteria have been determined, the next step is to set up a reporting structure so the burden can be shared. Who is to be told about the crisis? How are they to be told? When? (It may be a good idea to develop a report form so no essential information is omitted.)

Contingency plans are also a good idea—though the crisis that comes along is seldom the crisis that's been planned for.

There should be a chain of command to determine what corrective action is necessary. The bigger the crisis, the higher the problem is taken up the chain. It's better if decisions on any corrective action are under the direction of any one person rather than a committee because it's easier for one person to make decisions.

Keep the final decisions under one person, but consult with others; pick a plan and stick with it.

If the plan picked is not yours, don't second-guess the decision. Get behind the program.

Don't abandon ethical standards just because there's a crisis. This will only lead to a larger crisis down the road.

Don't change your personality and become a screaming maniac just because things are going wrong. Hemingway enjoyed a rich career writing about heroes who exhibited grace under pressure.

Attend to the crisis, but don't allow it to dominate every other phase of business activity.

How to Work and Prosper in a Competitive Environment

In the next decade, competition for middle-management positions will become a blood sport. The reason, of course, is that there will be far too many bodies to fill far too few positions. There won't be as many management jobs, and there won't be as many advancement rungs on the ladder.

Promotions will require more dedication, more enterprise, more risk taking, more knowing the right people, more being in the right place at the right time, and more plain luck. The corporate office will become an evolutionary proving ground, a modern equivalent to the Galápagos islands, for Darwinian theory (survival of the fittest).

The middle manager who wishes to prosper in this environment should:

1. *Recognize just how carnivorous the competition will become and act accordingly.*

2. *Learn something from Darwin.* He proved the species that survived and even dominated were those who were able to adapt to their environment and to changing conditions. Things will move at a faster pace in the next decade. The modern executive must be adaptable to change.

3. *Abandon hostile environments for friendlier ones.* In most cases, the corporate manager of the Nineties can't afford to be tied to a single company for an entire career. It's an outmoded survival strategy, like the armor-thick skin on some species of dinosaurs. Look upon tenure with an employer as a career phase.

4. *Be prepared to prove your worth to the organization every day.* It will be required every day.

❖ 8 ❖

A BLUEPRINT FOR THE WOMAN MANAGER

Why the Nineties Will Be the Decade
of the Female Manager

Female executives working for major companies have complained about the "glass ceiling," an invisible barrier that allows them to rise so high in the corporate hierarchy and no higher. The barrier may not be visible, but it is certainly real. The Eighties saw a marked increase in the number of female middle-management executives, but women never got the key to the private elevator that stopped at the top floor. Women executives tend to be specialists, which in itself is a handicap to rising above middle-management levels. The women claim that the system tends to work against them. They rightly feel that corporations are dominated by a male culture and that males set the rules.

Women managers have been accused of being their own worst enemies. "They're afraid of success," is one frequent charge. "They won't learn how the game is played so they want to change the rules," is another. "They're not really committed to full-time careers," is still another.

There's just the smallest kernel of truth in these charges so that it makes them difficult to refute. As children, women don't play the same kinds of games men do so many don't understand the team concept. Women want to juggle careers and family, which makes them appear less dedicated. Some doubt their own abilities, which makes them adopt a tentative management style.

Prejudice is assuredly one of the major reasons women haven't advanced faster, but there are others. Women executives who focus on the prejudice and ignore the other reasons do themselves and their careers a disservice.

For one thing, even though we're well into the third decade of the women's movement most female corporate managers don't have the tenure of their male counterparts. Harvard Business School did not even accept female candidates into its famous MBA program until 1963. Sure, the argument can be made that females were held back by a male-dominated corporate culture until government regulations forced more equitable treatment. Even now, males are the "insiders" who control the show.

The fact that women were denied equal opportunity is a valid argument, but it doesn't change the fact that, as a group, female corporate managers don't have the same years of experience as male managers do. When it's time for any company to choose a chief executive officer there's not a big pool of qualified female candidates. And right now corporations are picking their leaders based on experience. In the 1950s, Chuck Percy was chosen head of Bell & Howell at age twenty-nine. Choosing so young a person to head a Fortune 1000 company would be unthinkable today.

Long tenure with a company creates the friendships and alliances so valuable when moving up the ladder. It's what some female managers derisively call the "Old Boy network." If it seems closed to women that's because the Old Boy network is nothing more than trust and confidence that's been built up over years and years. It's mutual back scratching and returning favors and understanding idiosyncrasies and learning from experience whose word is money in the bank and whose word is worthless. Like all closed networks it resists outsiders. The way to get in is to cease being considered an outsider. Women can be members too—once they've put in the time.

That's not soon enough for many female managers who want that top-floor elevator key right now. For these women there's good news: The key is at the locksmith right now being cut. The Nineties will see female executives rise to the top ranks of major corporations. In the Eighties women became department heads, middle managers, low-level vice presidents, but they are still not among the real movers and shakers in most companies.

They virtually took over some job responsibilities, with a heavy emphasis on marketing management, human resources, communications managers, and so forth.

In the Nineties women will break out of the specialists category to advance to become division heads with billion-dollar budgets. They'll be executive vice presidents at companies where the title means something. They'll be on the board of directors. You'll even see a few heading major corporations. As they do a credible job as CEOs and make investors more comfortable, their ranks will increase. The business world is interested in the bottom line, and when women managers prove they can deliver the right numbers, they'll be accepted. No, they'll be welcomed with open arms.

What will make the difference? Mostly time and familiarity. The corporate world will have had the time to recognize the worth of female executives, to evaluate them as individuals, and to appreciate their contributions. They'll notice that the sky didn't fall when females were given real authority.

On their part, female executives will have enough time on the job to recognize how the game is played and just how competitive that game is. (They've been a bit naive in believing that advancement depended solely on merit, ability, and dedication.) Getting to the top of a major company requires the ability to excel at in-fighting. The Nineties will bring us the female scrappers.

The Essential Difference Between "Male" and "Female" Management Styles: How to Extract the Best from Both Styles

Ever hear anyone complain about reporting to a female manager? Let's face facts. There is a large portion of the work force that still feels uncomfortable about reporting to a woman. They offer many different reasons, none of which we'll dignify by listing here. I've seen no statistics on the matter, but there seem to be just as many female employees unhappy about their women bosses as there are males.

No one complains about reporting to a man. There is plenty of grousing about the particular SOB in charge, but few workers appear upset just because the person in the corner office has a zipper sewn into the front of his trousers.

Why does this low-level prejudice against the female manager still exist? Perhaps the reason people complain about female managers goes back to what is considered a familiar authority figure. If people assign that role to a man, then a woman in charge seems to be a usurper. What she does and how she does it comes under closer scrutiny. *The important thing the female given her first managerial assignment must remember is that she isn't automatically conceded authority merely by virtue of having a title. She must earn it.*

One of the problems women managers face is the perceived differences in the male-female personalities. Here are some typical assumptions:

❖ Males are active; women are passive.

❖ Males are aggressive; women are conciliatory.

❖ Males risk; women want security.

❖ Males take; women give.

❖ Males are creative; women are "artsy-craftsy."

❖ Males are outgoing; women are self-centered.

❖ Males are strong; women are weak.

❖ Males value friendship; women can't be trusted.

❖ Males are logical; women are emotional.

❖ Males dominate; women submit.

❖ Males value achievement; women want to fit in.

❖ Males are team players; women are loners.

❖ Males are committed to their careers; women place marriage and children first.

❖ Males can keep a secret; women gossip.

The comparison could go on for several pages, but notice that every male "characteristic" listed is considered desirable for a corporate manager and every female trait would represent a serious handicap. Perhaps that is why women complain about a male corporate culture. The corporate culture isn't going to change. That means the first order of business for female managers is to rid themselves of these stereotypes.

Why Women Can't Be Men

The fact that female managers must continually prove themselves and are in effect always "on trial" both from above and below affects their managerial style. Some female managers think they must "out-testosterone" men.

They assume masculine "qualities" and at the same time submerge their femininity.

The problem is that the imitation of a male executive is rarely convincing. Women's actions as managers seem to follow a familiar pattern:

- ❖ They use efficiency as an excuse for a brusque, overbearing manner when dealing with staff members.

- ❖ They seldom offer explanations when giving orders. (They don't give directions.)

- ❖ They are not candid about company operations or their own goals.

- ❖ They don't delegate responsibility.

- ❖ They are so detail minded they drive staff members crazy.

- ❖ They are impersonal in their business dealings and keep all fellow employees at arms' length.

- ❖ They trust no one.

- ❖ They form few friendships inside the company.

- ❖ They don't cooperate with their peers.

- ❖ They are not good motivators, nor are they respected by their subordinates.

- ❖ They're exactly the type of boss employees have in mind when they say they don't want to report to a woman.

Of course good male managers don't behave in this manner at all, but there's a bit of parody in every imitation.

The first rule of management, for both male and female, is to be yourself. A female manager who tries to behave the way she thinks her male counterpart might behave isn't being true to herself, nor is she being a good manager.

What women managers can bring to the table are not the stereotypes listed earlier, but the essential differences between the sexes, the female willingness to bend rather than break, the ability to use tact and diplomacy rather than confrontation to achieve objectives, the greater sensitivity and the empathy that seems to come naturally to a woman.

1. *She can be more sensitive to the feelings and aspirations of her staff members and thus in a better position to motivate them.*

2. *She can follow senior management's directions more precisely to attain specific goals.*

3. *She can be more tactful when dealing with staff members, important customers, other departments, and senior management.*

4. *She can cooperate more fully with other departments to get the job done.*

5. *She can demonstrate the skill, experience, and dedication that any good manager must possess to succeed.*

A Six-Point Program That Will Ensure the Female Manager Is Taken Seriously in Her Leadership Role

Almost every woman appointed to her first managerial position worries that her staff members, her peers, and her superiors will take her seriously. Will her directions be followed? Will other managers treat her as an equal? Will her boss value her contributions or merely patronize her? Will anyone listen to her? Men don't have this concern. They merely worry about being up to the job.

Probably the worst strategy for a first-time female manager is to deliberately set out to "establish authority." The woman who issues a flurry of directives the first day on the job or calls a meeting to sternly tell staff members what's what, or finds a reason to publicly chew out a subordinate is losing credibility, not gaining it.

Respect is something that must be earned. Sometimes it's a bit more difficult for a woman manager to earn it because of the preconceived notions of others, but that just means she must try harder. A six-point program that will work is:

1. *She must learn what's required of her as a manager in that specific position.* The first step to be taken seriously is to do a good job in any managerial assignment.

2. *She should meet with staff members individually to find out about their individual goals and aspirations.* She can show them how these goals can be met through their participation in the achievement of the department's goals. She should gain their trust by engaging them in the decision-making process. (This is what is called motivation. It works on men and women alike.)

3. *She should treat everyone according to the same standard.* That's not the same as treating everyone equally. Of course it's okay for her to have favorites among those who perform particularly well or who are more cooperative than others.

4. *She should not expect perfection, but should uncover the strengths and weaknesses of staff members.* She should build on the strengths and try to correct the weaknesses.

5. *She should cooperate with her peers.* Of course she competes with them on the basis of trying to do a better job, but she should try to avoid intraoffice feuds.

6. *She shouldn't concentrate on individual work habits, but rather on the work itself.* That's another way of saying she should key on the results. This is the surest way of gaining the reputation as a good manager.

How the Female Manager Can Use the "Good Old Boy" Network to Her Advantage

Female managers complain that they don't have access to the "Good Old Boy" network that is a part of every large organization. The Good Old Boys are the insiders who really get things done in the company. Female managers feel excluded from the network and thus excluded from opportunity.

The Good Old Boy network is aptly named because its rules of behavior are based on male culture. The Good Old Boys are people who know, understand, and cooperate with one another. What some female managers don't realize is that there's nothing sinister or conspiratorial about them. They did not evolve because a few males deliberately sought advantage at the expense of others, but rather because people with similar career paths formed friendships and alliances that worked. Most members would be aghast at the suggestion that some managers are being systematically excluded. If they had a motto it would be to "Trust the devil you know."

At most companies becoming a member of this informal club isn't a matter of being voted in, buying a place from someone who has left, or paying annual dues. It is something that happens naturally with time. It's difficult for any newcomer to be accepted and almost impossible for a new female manager to be.

How then can a female manager possibly use the Good Old Boy network in her organization to advantage?

1. *First, recognize that the network exists.* It can be a very useful vehicle for getting things done in the company.

2. *Cultivate the members.* Don't try to push into the club. Just establish yourself as someone who can be trusted to do what she

says she will do. Word will get around. Trust is the entry fee that will eventually get you accepted.

3. *Every young manager's career can benefit from a "rabbi," a member of senior management who takes a personal interest in the manager's career and serves as an adviser.* When looking for candidates for your mentor try to choose someone who is a member of the network and who may be willing to act as your sponsor.

4. *Don't feud with members of the club.* You will gain more than one enemy. In fact, don't feud with anyone inside the company. Office politics takes up far too much energy,

5. *Do favors for the Good Old Boys whenever possible.* Don't ask for favors in return. It isn't necessary.

6. *Don't try to be one of the guys.* You will be resented and viewed as being "pushy."

The idea us to establish yourself as someone reliable who can be trusted. It may take years to become a fully vested insider, but you can become an auxiliary member, someone who is "all right."

How the Female Manager Can Use Her Special Skills to Create a Valuable Role on the Management Team

Women managers tend to "get into" their current job responsibility more heavily than do their male counterparts. It's been suggested that this is because a woman's focus is on the present while men are more concerned about the future. Others say it's because women concentrate on task, skill, and performance. Still others claim female managers, concerned about how they will be perceived by their peers, have a preoccupation with establishing the right credentials. Whatever the reason, most female middle managers who have held a position of responsibility for some time are extremely competent.

It is this ability and willingness to learn the job inside and out that female middle managers can bring to the management team. It offers senior management two distinct advantages. The first is the comfort from knowing that someone competent and reliable is in place in a particular department. Attention to potential problems can be diverted somewhere else.

The second is that the female manager who really "knows her job" is in the best position to offer suggestions on how to improve it, or to react to suggestions from others concerning change.

Competency is a very valuable skill indeed. Female managers who have mastered their responsibilities are creating a special and irreplaceable role on the management team.

The Danger of Being Too Competent

The female manager who has learned her job too well risks the possibility she may be stuck in it for her entire career. Superiors will recognize her value in her current position, but will not regard her as a candidate for promotion. She'll be considered "one dimensional" without the ability to master new skills. Appreciated as a specialist, she will be regarded as too limited for a more senior management role.

To guard against this stereotyping, female managers must consciously strive to learn more about the organization and how it functions. (If you like, women must master the "Big Picture.") Here's a short move-up-the-ladder strategy:

1. *Set career goals.* Where do you want to go from your current position? What title would you like to hold ten years from now?

2. *Learn what goes on in the other departments.* What are the people across the hall up to? How does it impact what you do?

3. *Learn who are the movers and shakers inside the company.* Learn what they want and how you can help them get it.

4. *Form mutual-help alliances with your peers.* Twenty years from now you'll all make up the Old Boy/Girl network.

5. *Be open and less guarded.* Make friends for friendship's sake with people in the organization. If you don't like anyone in the company, why are you working there?

6. *Promote the careers of your subordinates.* One of the surest ways to advance is by gaining the reputation as someone who can develop talent.

7. *Be flexible.* It always was an advantage. In the next decade's pared-down corporation flexibility is mandatory.

Five Ways to Deal with Stereotyping

❖ Everyone knows that women are emotional and illogical.

❖ If you're a tough boss, you're a "bitch" or an "iron maiden."

❖ If you're easygoing, you "can't get control of your people."

❖ You're so detail minded you can't see the big picture.

❖ You're secretive and won't delegate responsibility.

❖ You embrace bureaucracy for bureaucracy's sake.

❖ You're interested in a career only until you have babies.

❖ You're behaving the way you do today because it's the "wrong time of the month."

❖ As a manager, you're self-centered, out only for yourself, and not interested in advancing the careers of your staff members.

Enough? There are literally hundreds more, but we'll spare you the rest. How can female managers fight these stereotypes? Over the short term they can't. People have their prejudices, and they won't be changed by the announcement that, "Hey, these charges are simply not true."

What female managers can do is to demonstrate by example that the stereotypes are invalid. Here are several long-term strategies.

1. *When you obtain your first managerial position, behave in a manner that is natural for you.* Don't imitate the managerial style of others or suddenly assume a different personality. Artificial behavior is strained and easily recognized.

2. *Be candid with superiors about your long-term career ambitions.* Seek their help and advice on how these ambitions can be achieved. Sharing your career goals demonstrates your long-term commitment.

3. *Don't be jealous of your responsibilities, but freely delegate them to subordinates.* This has the dual advantage of freeing your time for other managerial tasks and providing valuable experience to staff members.

4. *Be open and seek the advice of your peers.* There's nothing like discussions of common problems to make you an integral part of the group.

5. *Don't be secretive.* The people who report to you *can't have too much information.*

If you do all these things will there still be those within the organization who label you with stereotypes? Of course there will! It takes a long time to change attitudes. But their numbers will diminish with each passing year. More important, you will have demonstrated to those willing to pay attention that the stereotypes aren't true.

How to Say "No" So Others Will Believe It

Somehow men don't regard a negative response from a woman with the same finality as one from a man. Perhaps that's because of the assumption that "women can't make up their minds" or the paternalistic view that women have the "right" to change their minds as they wish.

The concept of women being unable to act decisively or make business commitments is both indulgent and patronizing. It assumes that women are frivolous creatures who act on whim. That means they don't have to be taken seriously. This attitude can be infuriating for the female manager who simply wants to get on with the job at hand without every decision being second-guessed. Here's a course of action for the woman who wants her decisions to "take" the first time.

1. *Don't make hasty pronouncements.* Wait until all the facts are in. The withholding of a decision gives the manager enormous power while staff members cool their heels and wonder.

2. *Know why you said yes or no.* Be better informed about the facts of a situation than are members of your staff. A better-informed decision is a better decision, period.

3. *Listen to all arguments before making a commitment.* Allow staff members to argue the merits of various positions, but be persuaded by logic, not passion.

4. *Explain your reasons.* Staff members, peers, and superiors, and others within the organization have a right to know why you acted as you did. If you can't defend your position perhaps you're standing in the wrong place.

5. *Be open to revision.* If someone can offer a better solution to a problem be prepared to adopt it. Never allow yourself to fall into the NIH (Not Invented Here) trap.

The idea of all the preceding suggestions is to appear wise and deliberate, never stubborn.

How a Female Manager Who Never Threw a Ball in Her Life Can Learn to Be a Team Player

There's much more than hormones and anatomy and even upbringing that separates men and women. As several pop-psychologists have observed, "men and women occupy separate planets." In most contexts the planets are a lovely place for tourists to visit and the differences between men and women are delicious. In the workplace the differences can be a disaster.

One difference between the sexes is that men have more experience in participating as part of a team. They play team games from an early age, which makes them more prepared to cooperate to achieve a common goal. The female manager, when asked to participate as a team member, may feel that she is being used by the group. As a consequence, other team members may complain that she doesn't have "the right attitude."

As long as males determine the corporate culture, and that will be for a very long time, being regarded as a team player will be an important factor in career success. It's too bad that more females aren't encouraged to participate in team sports as young girls. (Even that is changing as more high schools institute girls' basketball, volleyball, field hockey, and other athletic team programs.)

If "wars are won on the playing fields of Eton," then corporate promotions are won in high school gymnasiums. The female manager who wants to learn the team concept can:

1. *Focus on the goals of the group rather than on individual goals.*

2. *Decide what contribution she can make that will best ensure the group's success, even though that contribution may not position her as a "star."*

3. *Refrain from any bickering and squabbles that deflect from the group's purpose.*

4. *Encourage the efforts of others in the group.*

5. *Argue differences of opinion or procedural methods when necessary, but in the end defer to the group's decision.*

6. *Decide that she really wants the group to win whatever it is they're going after.*

7. *If she still refers to "they" when talking about the team, she hasn't got it right yet.* She must start thinking "us."

How to Distinguish Kidding Around from Sexual Harassment

The charges of Anita Hill against Clarence Thomas and the subsequent Senate hearings brought the matter of workplace sexual harassment into sharp focus. Over the next several years companies, and even the courts, are going to have a great deal of difficulty defining what exactly constitutes sexual harassment.

We're not after a legal definition here, for that won't be easily found. However, our seat-of-the-pants definition is that sexual harassment in the workplace means using managerial clout to try to extract sexual favors from a subordinate or using sexual references to intimidate another employee.

The definition is easy; it's the particulars that are tough. For example, asking a subordinate for a date might not be the smartest thing to do, but it would not normally be considered sexual harassment. If, however, a manager asked that same employee out fifty or sixty times, that probably would be construed as harassment. So where's the dividing line? Is it okay for a manager to ask a subordinate for a date five or six times? A dozen times? Exactly when does a suitor become an intolerable pest? Office romance is still going strong, which means that attention from the opposite sex isn't always unwanted.

An off-color joke or remark might be tasteless and idiotic, but it would be difficult to make a case for harassment based on a single incident. Turning the air blue would be another matter. Remarks about anatomy are generally off limits, but what about comments concerning a "sexy figure"? Most women are uncomfortable if a man stares at a part of her body for an extended period of time. If the boss stares at a woman's chest, is it harassment? What if she's wearing something very revealing? There is a difference between a glance and a leer, but how can it be defined? What about gestures? Using "Honey" or "Cutie" or "Babe," denigrates women, but do these words in themselves constitute harassment?

These are the questions that vex even enlightened management who want to make the workplace comfortable for all employees. The answers aren't easy to find.

For our purpose, we'll focus on intent. Here's how we distinguish sexual harassment from kidding around. (We're focusing on the possibility of men sexually harassing women. While it is technically possible for a female manager to sexually harass a male subordinate, it won't happen often enough to be significant.)

1. *Are sexual remarks continually being made in your presence?* Is there no relief from the tasteless barrage? Are references frequently made to anatomical parts, both male and female? This is an attempt at domination through embarrassment. It is harassment.

2. *In spite of all the recent publicity on sexual harassment, there's still the occasional male idiot who will offer a female subordinate a promotion or raise in exchange for sexual favors.* A guy who behaves in this manner is too stupid to work for and too stupid to keep his job. Report the jerk to your company. If they won't act, see the appropriate government agency.

3. *Does accidental touching of your anatomy happen so frequently it can't be any accident?* Your body is off limits. This is harassment. A single incident, however, may be difficult to prove. Give the jerk a warning. (He'll say you misinterpreted, but he'll also probably stop.)

4. *Does the boss say you look terrific today in that sexy dress, then follow you into the parking lot after work to ask for date? Does he insist several times?* Maybe his advances aren't wanted, but if he finally drops it when you say no dice, this isn't harassment.

5. *Does a male in the office describe in detail an explicit sex scene from a recent movie?* Unless it's done repeatedly, this is crude, but it isn't harassment.

6. *Does a male worker follow you around the office with his eyes?* This may be embarrassing and uncomfortable, but unless he goes further, it isn't harassment.

7. *Does the boss ask you about your sex life?* It's none of his business, and repetition could constitute harassment.

8. *Does the boss show you explicit pictures of a sexual nature?* This is harassment.

As you can see, repetition is an important factor in determining harassment. So is going further than mere conversation. If your interest is in career advancement and not a crusade for absolute sexual equality, let the occasional remark pass unacknowledged. Give the jerks and idiots in the office a little rope before making a formal complaint. Be less forgiving with superiors. They're supposed to know better, and they've certainly had enough warnings about proper behavior.

HOW TO WORK
AND THRIVE WITHIN
YOUR COMPANY'S
ORGANIZATIONAL AND
POLITICAL STRUCTURE

A Primer for Innocents: Why It's Important for
Managers to Understand the Political Realities at Work
within Their Organizations

There's a myth about a business career that suggests if you work hard, are loyal, don't make dumb mistakes, kiss the right rings, and achieve more merit than your peers you will certainly be rewarded by a grateful management with money, prestige, and promotion. It's a myth that goes back to the sweet age of innocence. No one believes it anymore than they believe Arabian Nights' tales about crafty thieves winning the hands of beautiful princesses.

A career in business is partially a political process. Success depends as much on aligning oneself with the "right" people and the right factions as it does on ability and hard work. Promotions are based as much on loyalty to superiors and being politically astute as they are on performance. That's because every big company is a hotbed of intrigue and conspiracy. Companies are made up of people, and people seek advantage over one another.

Actually, corporate political intrigue isn't limited to large organizations. If your company has more than two employees there are differences of opinion on how things should be done. There are rivals, there is struggle, there is the pursuit of power, there is the effort to dominate, and there is the desire to control. Internal conflict is an inevitable part of corporate life.

For beginning managers, it's important to know that the struggle exists. There's a game going on, and its purpose is to acquire prestige and power. It goes on at many different levels. Different departments are fighting to set the company's agenda. Senior executives, with egos the size of the *Titanic,* clash with one another to acquire more turf, to acquire more bodies to supervise, to administer a bigger budget, *to play a bigger role in events.* Near the top of the organization, courtiers beg for bones like so many lap dogs. The CEO struggles with the board of directors and stockholders.

To many of the players, the corporation's fate is less important than the game. It matters not if the company prospers, just as long as certain individuals in that company acquire power and prosper. That's why top executive salaries are going through the roof just as corporate profits for most companies bore a hole through the basement floor. That's why takeover bids that would be in the best interests of stockholders are routinely rejected until the current management team is bought off.

What does all this mean for the middle manager? For starters, the new manager must recognize that every decision that comes down the pike isn't based on what's in the best interest of the corporation. Many are made on the criterion of whether a particular course of action will help someone gain or consolidate power. Some are made to embarrass a rival. Still others are defensive, made to protect turf or countermoves made by others.

In many cases the political intrigue boils so furiously the manager must choose one side or the other. Neutrality won't be respected by either faction. It's important to pick the right side because promotions are based on loyalty as much as on anything else. So the first rule of conduct when forced to pick sides is to *choose the winning side.* You'll never be sorry. If your choice will determine which side wins, *negotiate.* Get something in return for your support. When there is no clear-cut advantage in choosing one side or the other, do what's in the best interest of the company. (Notice that this is offered as a last-resort option.)

What is power anyway? Some feel it is the authority to assign other people or organizations *obligations.* The manager entering a corporation must determine where the power resides. Who has the authority to obligate others? This can be deduced by which department head exercises the most control. Is your outfit a marketing company? Then, aside from the CEO, the power probably resides with the company's top marketing person. Is it an old-line manufacturing company? Manufacturing may pipe the tune while others dance. (One of the wonderful things about corporate politics is that power can shift rapidly. In tough times, such as we're going through now, finance will frequently call the shots, regardless of who called them in the past. Power is wired to the purse strings.)

Once the power center has been identified, the next step is to get close to that warm, cheery glow. If possible, become a part of it. If marketing is the dominant force in your company, try to get into the marketing department. If another department dominates the company, get in there and play with the big boys. If you're part of the first team, recognition and promotions will come much faster.

If you're a manager in a remote outpost, or can't get close to the power center, then the least you can do is not antagonize anyone within the power structure. Instead, be the person who cooperates. Of course it's important to follow the directions of your direct supervisor. Busting your butt to meet the request of someone in the power center, however, may help advance your career a bit faster.

In his book, *Power!*, Michael Korda stated that people tend to shun power areas out of fear. He felt that this was a mistake, that power seekers should learn to identify these areas *and learn to live there.* That is exactly the right advice. Learn the power areas in your company. Be drawn to them as a bee is drawn to pretty flowers. That's where the sweet nectar of success can be gathered.

The Organization Chart: The Company Scorecard That Identifies Players by Position

The organization chart of a company is like a scorecard at a ball game. It tells the bystander which executive is playing which position.

The chart is a diagram that shows the division of responsibilities within a company. It shows exactly who is leading the charge against the enemy and who reports to whom.

Most charts are made up of little boxes with job titles inside. The position of the boxes is important. The closer they are to the top of the page, the grander the title, the more responsibility, the greater the power of the person whose name is inside that box. The number of lines leading down from one box to other boxes is also a grave issue. The more boxes that are linked to your box (as long as your box is elevated above theirs), the more people you can obligate.

How to Behave Toward Your Peers

The rules of behavior toward superiors and subordinates are fairly cut and dried, We take direction from superiors and give it to subordinates. For many middle managers the problems occur when dealing with peers. Direct orders can't be given to equals, and few managers are willing to take them from those who aren't higher up in the pecking order. That sometimes leads to difficulty when interdepartmental cooperation is required.

The important thing to remember is that every business organization is a team (of sorts) and all team members have the potential to affect one another's performance.

The first rule of organizational behavior is to be aware that you're dealing with real people and not just job titles. The titles are held by people who come with their own personalities and idiosyncrasies. There's no such thing as a generic "credit manager." There's only Martha Kotter, who would insist on looking up the Dun & Bradstreet rating for the federal government if your company should be lucky enough to attract that entity as a customer.

Get beyond the job function and recognize the personalities that come with the titles. Cater to the idiosyncrasies. Treat your peers with respect. They report to someone else so they don't really care that your boss "needs this right now." Make requests, not demands. Cast your bread upon the waters in the form of favors. It will come back tenfold.

The Truth Behind the Organization Chart

Every organization chart is part fact and part fancy. That's because some people in the company are more competent than others. There are a few special people inside every company who make things happen. They are at the center of power and they usually enjoy wielding it. Many of the others are just along for the ride. Your company may have a particularly effective department head who can help resolve a problem, no matter whose bailiwick it's in.

As an exercise, look over the organization chart in your company. Put a check mark in front of the names of the people who get things done. These are the men and women you want to cultivate. These are the people who can help your career.

How to Cut Across Lines of Authority to Get What You Want

Sometimes during every career a manager finds it necessary to cut across traditional lines of authority to get something accomplished. This procedure, if used judiciously, is okay. Occasionally cutting corners is part of being a successful manager. The manager should not become so intent on the desired result, however, that he or she completely ignores protocol or the seniority of the people involved.

Making the wrong demand on the wrong person could cost the manager much more than the advantage sought. Sometimes corporate survival depends on understanding the authority level and explosion point of the person on the other end of the telephone. Follow this suggested routine when cutting across established lines of authority.

1. *First, try getting your task accomplished in the traditional manner.* Try to solve your own problem or go to your supervisor for help. You don't want a reputation as a maverick.

2. *Don't use extraordinary measures unless you have an extraordinary circumstance.* Is this situation worth the risk you face by circumventing the system?

3. *Find out if the task can be accomplished by going outside established lines of authority.* Be sure your information is correct. There's nothing worse than risking a scolding when your actions wouldn't have gotten the job done anyway.

4. *Have a heck of a story ready about the urgency of your situation.* Be right in every detail.

5. *Approach the people, managers, or department you feel may be able to help you.* Tell them your very sad story.

6. *Always exercise courtesy and diplomacy when speaking to people in other departments.* Be particularly polite to another manager when making an unorthodox request.

7. *Never make demands or threats unless you have the authority to back them up.* If you're cutting corners, it's unlikely you have that authority.

8. *Call in any markers you may have accumulated because of past favors rendered.* (You are putting other managers in your debt, aren't you?)

9. *Let your boss know what you've done.* She'll find out anyway.

10. *Follow up on the request if there's no action, but don't be a pest.*

11. *If the thing gets done, show the proper parties how grateful you are.*

12. *Realize that you've signed IOUs that may come due sometime in the future.*

How Office Politics Affect the Ambitious Manager

The biggest squabble in any company is over power. At the very top the fight is over who gets to decide where the company is going. At the next level the struggle is over who gets to offer an opinion and thereby *influence* the decision on where the company is going. Below these rarefied strata the power fight is over people responsibility (the more bodies on your staff, the more important and powerful you are), the size of departmental budgets, the pecking order in the company hierarchy, and the other trappings of authority, such as size and location of an office, the right accent on a private secretary, and the use of the company jet. One recent addition to the symbols of power is just how much gold there is in the manager's golden parachute.

The power struggle is not just between individuals, but often between entire departments. At some companies, the barbed wire marking the war zone between departments is almost visible.

What the ambitious manager must know is that it's impossible not to become involved in office politics. Trying to be Switzerland just doesn't work. If the boss is active in office politics, staying neutral instead of rallying to his side would be regarded as an act of disloyalty.

Loyalty to one's supervisor is a valued trait. Give it even if you feel your boss is on the losing end of a squabble. At a lower-management level it won't be held against you personally if your boss is a loser in a power struggle. His defeat won't be attached to you.

Disloyalty, on the other hand, will create suspicion and distrust. So the first rule of office politics is to be loyal to your superior. If you believe he is ill advised in a course of action, say so; you owe your boss wise counsel, but maintain your loyalty.

The second white-collar power rule is to join a faction. *Middle managers can't survive as loners.* They must become part of a larger group for protection if for no other reason. Become part of the Young Turks out to change the direction of the organization. If that doesn't suit, be a member of the conservatives who are trying to preserve the traditional values that made the company great. Still not your cup of tea? Be one of the technocrats who want to automate everything including the toilet flushes. Blend in with the MBAs who want to apply modern management theory to the typing pool. Join your voice to those who want to sell off all the unprofitable divisions. Make common cause with the fast guns who are willing to assume the debt load the size of Brazil's in order to acquire another company. Just be a member of some group. It's easier and safer and more likely to move your career forward than is standing alone.

Why Company Politics Are an Energy Drain

Company politics are as inevitable as the next sunrise, but that doesn't make participating in them an enjoyable pastime. When the company hired you it was to accomplish a specific set of tasks, not to see if you could outscheme Machiavelli. Political intrigue requires time and attention. It inevitably detracts from your performance. The "politician" worries more about gaining a particular advantage than about getting the job done. That can be a fatal mistake.

It's important to recognize the existence of company politics and to participate as a matter of survival, but keep a proper perspective. Job performance comes first. Before worrying about power and factions and who's in and who's out, do a bang-up job in your area of responsibility. Accomplishment and dedication and a reputation as a super performer are the best shields against political adversaries.

Why It's Naive to Assume You Can Remain Aloof from Political Situations

The only companies immune from political strife are the one-person outfits. Even those organizations may be affected when that one person suffers from mood swings. That means the rest of us working stiffs wield our picks in an atmosphere of conflict, maneuvering for advantages, power plays, feuds, hidden agendas, favoritism, and so forth.

The worst strategy is to try to stay aloof and "just do your job." The neutrals in this war don't get to wear red crosses on their sleeves. They are out there on the battlefield being sniped at by all sides. You're going to have to play anyway so you may as well play to win.

A Survival Strategy for Political Infighting

1. *Decide early-on that you'll have to become involved in company politics.*

2. *Survey the situation at your company before making any commitments.*

3. *Be competent at what you do.*

4. *Join a group or faction that has an agenda you find appealing.*

5. *At the least, be sympathetic to the political goals of your direct supervisor.* (Never join a group or faction that is politically aligned against your boss; it's disloyal.)

6. *Never become involved in political intrigue that works against the best interests of the company.*

7. *Keep your activities in perspective.* Don't let your job performance suffer by the time or attention devoted to company politics.

8. *Be loyal to your boss and members of your faction or group.* Don't switch sides.

9. *Let one and all know where you stand.* The secret stuff is for spy novels.

10. *Fight hard for your faction's agenda, but don't do anything underhanded or unscrupulous.*

This strategy will help ensure your survival even if your faction doesn't succeed. (Of course, promotions may be based on the success of your group, or your boss's success.)

What Departmental Skirmishes Are All About

If you've been in business for any length of time you've probably worked for an outfit in which one department head despised another. In some cases the mere mention of a manager's name is enough to send another manager into a white rage. There is so much anger, so much hostility these managers feel toward one another that it seems apparent the company must suffer by this intramural war. Yet, the corporation survives. Lower-level managers of the two departments cooperate with one another when necessary, and the work gets out the door. Often there are smiles and jokes by the workers in the two departments about the situation.

What's going on is a lot more than personality conflict between two strong-willed people, although this is frequently a contributing factor. The two department heads are engaged in that old reliable instigator of political strife, the quest for influence and power. Each department head feels the other stands in the way of his or her having a bigger say in the company's direction. Each feels the other is the reason his or her department isn't bigger. Each feels the other's budget is more ridiculous than the national debt. Each feels the other isn't pulling his or her weight. Each feels the other is an obstacle to personal goals. Perhaps both are on the same rung of the ladder vying for a single promotion.

Both managers are usually clever enough not to let their animosity toward each other interfere with company operations. That's the path to personal disaster. They permit lower-level managers within each department to work together for common purpose and so keep the situation "controlled." That's why the feud is often something of a company joke.

For someone on the outside, the two department heads should be considered as sovereign countries occupying neighboring borders. They exist in a state just short of total war. Even though the border clashes are frequent, they cooperate when necessary because it is politically expedient to do so.

Of course, a manager reporting to one of the "dueling" department heads must enlist in the services of his or her boss.

What to Do When the Boss Is Out of Favor or Out to Pasture

If your direct superior appears to be losing a power struggle, you must continue to offer him or her complete loyalty. Never jump ship while it is still afloat. A senior executive who is out of favor can still be a mentor and sponsor who can help you move up in the company.

If you're stuck with an older boss who's merely grazing on rich grass until retirement, some showcasing of your talent may be necessary. In this circumstance get involved with high-profile projects, make in-house presentations before senior management; do all you can to show off your skills, personality, and knowledge.

The manager working for a boss who has, in effect, retired without announcing it to the company must reach out and establish recognition among other managers and departments in the company.

One of the biggest problems any manager can face is working for a supervisor who is currently out of favor. The stigma attached to the supervisor could become glued to the subordinate. In some cases when senior managers are dismissed their subordinates are fired along with them.

The best tactic when faced with this situation is to establish a network of friends and allies outside of the boss's immediate line of authority. Establish relationships with others, but never make an attempt to make the out-of-favor superior look bad and never undercut his or her efforts. Doing so will make you appear untrustworthy. Never forget that a senior manager, even one in trouble, may still have a powerful network of friends and allies inside the company. Many survive their wounds and live to triumph.

The Importance of Loyalty

Loyalty is one of the most important attributes any manager can bring to the job. It's the one thing any leader cannot do without. If you as a manager want loyalty from your subordinates, then give freely to your superiors. Managers who hope to advance their careers never knock their superiors to staff members. Disparaging remarks about one's superior to another member of senior management is career suicide.

Certainly, there will be differences of opinion regarding decisions and courses of action. These should be discussed freely and argued fully. When the discussion is finished, the disagreement should be left between the two individuals. There's nothing worse than announcing a new company program, then privately confiding to a few staff members that you don't agree with its objectives.

Is there reward for loyalty? You bet there is. The loyal person gains the respect of senior management. They are suspicious of those who don't display this quality. There are countless opportunities for the loyal person. Perhaps you're lucky enough to be working for a boss whose star is rising in the company. Many managers take their loyal people with them on the rocket ride.

What to Do If You've Backed the Wrong Horse

Earlier we suggested joining a group or faction in the company because the loner seldom advances far on his or her own. What if this faction is the loser in a political battle? There you are, exposed as a member of the losing side!

To risk stating the obvious, it's better to be associated with the winners than with the losers. Near-term advancement and promotions will come from this group. To the victors belong the spoils and all of that. All is not lost, however, just because your team lost. Here's a survival strategy for a member of a losing team:

1. *When it's obvious that your faction has lost the game, gracefully accept the inevitable.* Never become a last-ditch defender against overwhelming odds. The guerrilla fighters only serve to irritate the winners. They are usually put up against the wall and shot.

2. *Now, it's more important than ever to be competent at what you do.* Display that competence every way you can. Demonstrate to the winning side that you're a valuable member of the organization.

3. *Don't sulk or bear grudges.* Make a conscious effort to see what you can do to fit in. Let the winning faction know that you are prepared to cooperate.

4. *Study the results.* Learn what happened and why your faction lost. The winners played the game better than your team did. There's no reason to make the same mistake twice.

Why Superior Performance Is Always the Best Defense Against Any Political Situation

This book has stressed over and over the importance of competence and superior performance as a survival strategy against any political situation. It's possible to recover from being on the wrong side or reporting to a boss who is out of favor if you're very good at what you do. There is safety in being invaluable.

Senior managers recognize that man is a political animal and that every large corporate organization is political in nature. They smile at the political dance and often cut in to waltz with a favorite partner. Being on the wrong side of a political squabble isn't a disaster if you're an important part of the team. The marginal worker, however, may not be able to survive throwing in with the wrong gang. Combining poor judgment with poor work habits is usually fatal.

❖ 10 ❖

LIFE IN THE
BOARDROOM

Just Who Are the Directors in a Large, Publicly Held Company and What Do They Do?

The board of directors for most major companies serve at the pleasure of management. They are usually the cronies of the company president, one perhaps an old schoolmate, another a tennis partner. Many are the presidents of large corporations themselves. Some are prominent lawyers, others bankers, still others large stockholders in the company. In some instances they are political figures. Henry Kissinger sits on the board of American Express.

Executives accept board positions for the prestige because there's little money in the job. Most often a board member is paid only an honorarium for each sitting. The amounts vary from company to company, but they are minuscule compared to the salaries and perks these high-powered people command through their normal endeavors. (This is changing slightly as a few companies pay board members high fees for special expertise. Mr. Kissinger gets $200,000 a year from Amex.)

The theoretical function of a board of directors is to serve as wise counsel to the president of the corporation, give their advice on major moves, suggest caution when caution is warranted, and generally offer the benefit of their experience. In reality they are most often rubber stamps for the decisions of the CEO. As being a board member is primarily an honorary position (it looks good on an executive resumé), most are not anxious to second-guess or criticize a peer, and frequently a close friend. Instead they go along with the suggested agendas of the CEO, offer a bland suggestion or two, and sit down to a swell lunch.

So to the question, "What do board members actually do?" the answer is: absolutely nothing. They are figureheads who seldom are willing to take a position opposing the CEO and hence aren't worth their honoraria.

Why the Agendas of Individual Board Members May Not Be in the Best Interest of the Corporation

The people who sit on the boards of major corporations are themselves captains of industry, prominent financial figures, and legal experts. They are the cream of the business world, and they rose to the top because of their ability to focus on self-interest. If there's one thing they know it's what is good for themselves and for their companies.

When they're at a board meeting and routine business is discussed, they smile and nod whenever the CEO wants them to smile and nod. Something else happens when a subject is discussed that involves their own interests. For example, let's say that the CEO advises the board that the company is contemplating a major merger. One board member happens to be the president of a major bank. He's no dummy, so he immediately recognizes that the company will require huge loans to finance the merger. That means tens of millions in financing profits for his bank if the merger deal is done. The deal also means that the company would be taking on a very large debt-load. Do you think he'll advise caution because of the debt load problem or suggest full steam ahead because of the profit potential for his institution? (In case any of you guessed wrong, one of the major reasons for the bankruptcies of today is the heavy debt loads assumed by companies during the merger-and-takeover madness of the Eighties. If the fees and rates were high enough, no banker ever saw a merger or takeover loan he didn't like.)

Is a lawyer on the board, who sees the potential of enough legal fees in the deal to finance that summer home in the Hamptons, likely to say that the merger is a bad idea?

In other circumstances, a board member who is a large stockholder may suggest expenditure cuts detrimental to the long-range goals of the corporation simply to build the price of the shares over the short term.

The important thing to remember is that board members aren't an integral part of the corporation. In fact, they're supposed to be outsiders with special knowledge, contacts, and experience useful to the CEO. Their distance from the operation of the company is intended to allow them to view situations dispassionately. In many instances, however, they may have a vested interest in the company's specific course of action. In those instances their advice can't be trusted.

How Stock Prices Affect Management Decisions

One of the reasons Japan Incorporated is giving American companies so much grief is because of the ninety-day glasses worn by our senior corporate officers. Three months ahead is as far as most CEOs can see. Our chief executives think in terms only of the next quarter. They want to make it better than last quarter and a whole lot better than the same quarter last year. The Japanese, who aren't subject to the same kind of shareholder pressure, can and do take a longer view. They think in terms of strategy while our managers are forced to study tactics.

There's sufficient motive for senior managers to be shortsighted because many of them have bonus programs that are tied to the performance of the company stock. If the stock goes down, no bonus; they're forced to squeak by on their seven-figure salaries. If the stock goes up they receive a big, big bonus. The few million extra means they won't face the embarrassment of applying for food stamps.

To nudge the stock in the right direction CEOs must court the investment community. Wall Street decides if a stock goes up or down. What analysts want to see is *steady improvement,* each period better than the last on to infinity. They love growth because the entire investment game is a bet on tomorrow. Investors willingly pay fifty times earnings for a company they believe is growing fast, but won't offer fifteen for a stodgy outfit, even though that company may produce steady profits.

Corporation top executives know if they can deliver improvement and growth the price of their company stock will rise and they will collect those mouth-watering bonuses.

Of course, everyone knows that performance can't be improved forever. There's a glass ceiling for everything, maybe including the universe. So the senior managers' main concern becomes whether performance will be acceptable to the Wall Street crowd during their watch. They don't care what comes after, just as long as things look good and are headed up right now. That often leads to short-term decisions by shortsighted executives. (They're wearing those infamous ninety day spectacles, remember?)

A factory may be closed rather than modernized because the tax write-off makes the next period look better. Research-and-development funds may be cut because it takes a long time for new products to make an impact on the bottom line. The company may delay buying equipment needed to stay competitive. In many cases these decisions aren't made because they're in the best interests of the company, but rather because they'll help make the next ninety days as if the company were still headed for the stratosphere.

This myopia often infects the entire organization, as relentless pressure to perform over the short term radiates from the top. Mid-level managers cut corners, take indiscreet chances, and even fudge numbers so they are able to report they are "on target." Reporting the right set of figures becomes more important than performing the job function. Once the habit is developed, each quarter's objectives become more difficult to achieve than were the last. Managers resort to desperate measures to achieve goals. The controller stops paying the company's bills on time to squeeze a few extra days' interest on its bank accounts. The purchasing agent reneges on deals with suppliers or pressures them too hard. Manufacturing lets quality control slide. The sales manager puts in telemarketing to replace the direct sales force. Obsolete inventory is carried at original value. Warranties are honored only at pistol point.

There comes a time when even the desperate measures don't work any more. Then the organization begins to implode upon itself. Managers become even more desperate. The pressure becomes more intense. People do silly things. There are layoffs. The numbers that were once fudged are now fabricated.

- ❖ That's when the surprises begin.

- ❖ That's when the chief financial officer has an emergency meeting with the company president to announce very unpleasant news.

- ❖ That's when the president suddenly becomes too busy for those friendly lunches with Wall Street analysts.

- ❖ That's when the red ink forms a raging river wider than the Mississippi.

- ❖ That's when the stock heads south.

❖ That's when the president is no longer available for press interviews.

❖ That's when many senior- and middle-management people suddenly resign or are fired.

❖ That's when suppliers won't ship anymore.

❖ That's when the sales curve becomes a straight line headed down.

❖ That's when there's talk of restructuring.

❖ That's when the company president starts complaining about trade restrictions and demands to know why we can't import rice into Japan.

❖ That's when the company tries to pile every write-off possible into one quarter (wearing their ninety-day spectacles to the last) to get all the bad news out of the way at one time.

❖ That's when the company stops paying its creditors.

❖ That's when the layoffs begin in wholesale numbers.

Why Boardroom Egos Are Destroying Jobs

The men and women who occupy boardrooms are not shrinking violets. They are successful people, they have ability, they have power, they have prestige, and they know it. However, most are not satisfied. They want more. Perhaps this desire for always wanting more is what first led to their success. We'll leave that one to the psychologists.

Typical CEOs rose from the management ranks. They were lower or middle managers who wanted to become department heads. When they became department heads they wanted to become senior vice presidents. When they became senior vice presidents they wanted to run the company. Now that they run the company, why should they be content?

The CEO and his or her cronies in the boardroom want the company to expand. A bigger company means more prestige and more power. (Lord Acton, who held a dim view of the lust for power, believed power was the ability to degrade and demoralize.) Despite the personal motives, growth is an admirable aim, and it's what Wall Street is looking for. Sometimes company growth doesn't happen fast enough to suit the ambitious, however, and sometimes it doesn't happen at all. What to do then? The power-hungry CEO's typical solution is to expand by acquiring another company. If growth can't be achieved through expanding the company's regular business, they'll buy it.

The rationale used is that the acquisition will be a good thing for one and all because the CEO and staff of the acquiring company are infinitely wiser, superior managers and all-round better fellows than the executives in the company being bought. A typical comment for the press will be that the outfit being sought has "unfulfilled potential" that will be realized by this excellent and sagacious management crew.

The publicity releases emphasize how the combined organization will be more efficient, better equipped to face the competition, more responsive to the needs of the market, leaner and meaner, better able to take advantage of economies of scale, and, heck, just a whole lot bigger. The differences in the bottom line will be dramatic. (That's a promise.)

Does the above sound like mammoth egos at work?

Egos the size of the Great Pyramid of Cheops fueled the takeovers of the Eighties. Chief executive officers with full board approval and encouraged by investment bankers in search of eight-figure fees took on enormous debt loads to buy up other companies. They used the excuse that once the dead wood in the acquired company was cleared away the new organization would be a money machine, an example to the world of a modern corporation. It would be better managed and, of course, it would make more profit. The debt service would be insignificant compared to the business Colossus being formed.

These reasons were spurious. The real quest was for power and prestige; the real need was to be bigger and more important than others. And it didn't work. The takeovers created debt loads so enormous that the slightest quivers in the economy were enough to send fine, old-line companies scurrying for the safety of Chapter Eleven.

Who picked up the tab for these miscalculations? Who paid to feed these egos?

❖ The egomaniacs didn't pay for their mistakes; they collected their seven figure salaries and, if fired, floated gently and profitably to earth on their golden parachutes.

❖ The deal makers and investment bankers didn't pay. They collected their eight-figure fees and took the 5:05 back to Scarsdale.

❖ The lawyers didn't pay. They also collected their fees and retreated to the Hamptons.

❖ The old stockholders didn't pay. They made out fine if they sold out when the takeover offer was made.

❖ The cronies in the boardroom who rubber-stamped the deals didn't pay. They risked only their honoraria to begin with.

Then who did pay?

❖ Hundreds of thousands of workers paid with their jobs and future security.

❖ Vendors and other creditors paid when the new organization couldn't meet its obligations.

❖ Junk-bond holders seduced by the high interest rates paid when the bonds lost most of their value.

❖ The American public paid because fine old companies were wrecked with little chance they could be put back together.

Why Top Management Always Opposes Takeover Bids, No Matter How Lucrative It Would Be for Stockholders

Here's a mythical story of a takeover bid:

Outmoded Incorporated's stock has fluctuated between eight and fourteen dollars a share for the past two years. Right now it's selling at ten. Along comes Intimidation Corporation, headed by a CEO who can be described as an ego dressed in an Armani suit. The ego, or rather Intimidation Corporation, offers Outmoded's shareholders twenty dollars a share in a buy-out.

Does the management team at Outmoded jump for joy at this potential bonanza for their investors? They do not. Instead, they call a war council. Everybody with a vice president's title is in the meeting. They come out grim-faced. Within a few hours they issue a statement to the effect that the offer is almost an insult. "It does not reflect the true value of the company," the CEO grumbles. He doesn't mention that Outmoded's shares have never sold for twenty dollars.

A counterattack is launched. The battles are fought in the courts, with poison pills, with delaying actions in the search for a "White Knight," and in self-serving newspaper ads (primarily in *The New York Times* and *The Wall Street Journal*) questioning the motives of the takeover company. Outmoded's management team vows never to surrender to the invaders. Death before dishonor. It promises to be a long fight.

The situation is mythical, but the hysterical reaction of management to a takeover bid is typical. Why don't they take the money and run? In most cases the management team owns stock, or at least stock options, in the company, so they would profit from the generous offer. You can bet they've strapped on their golden parachutes so they wouldn't be hurt financially if another company took over. Many members of the team would probably be retained by the acquiring company to run Outmoded.

None of those advantages compares to what they would lose by the takeover, which is power, prestige, and independence. The management team at Outmoded wouldn't be calling the shots anymore. Decisions would have to be explained to outsiders. Performance standards would be set by others. Someone else would be calling the tune while they danced. The former CEO, if he's still on board, would be president only of a subsidiary operation. Worse calamity, he might not even retain his title! There is also no doubt that the managers at Outmoded would have to adapt to the corporate culture and style of Intimidation Corporation. They'd have to learn some new tricks.

All these things are too terrible to contemplate, so Outmoded's management team will fight to the last shareholder's fiscal ruin to retain their prerogatives. They don't care if this means that the people who have their money in the company will miss out on a big windfall. Their sanctuary has been threatened, and they will resist. So they'll resist even if it ruins the company in the process. (In some instances the resistance is false, meant only to extract a better price than the original offer. NCR never hoped to really elude an AT&T determined to gobble up that computer company, but they did manage to raise the ante.)

Why the Costs for Defending a Takeover Have Almost Ruined Many Companies

Management's first reaction to a hostile takeover bid is hysteria. (For some reason offering to pay millions of dollars more than current market value for a company is called "hostile.") The complete management team is assembled to develop a defense strategy.

They aren't the only ones called for help.

High-powered public relations houses are invited to plot a campaign to smear the other company.

Self-serving, full-page ads are placed in the *Journal* and *Times*.

Investigators are hired to see what dirt they can dig up on the opposing CEO.

The lawyers march to the battlefield by battalions. Lawsuits are filed everywhere. An hour doesn't go by without a deposition being taken, nor a day without an injunction.

Consultants who specialize in advising companies fighting takeover bids pitch their tents in the boardroom. They construct elaborate, expensive defenses. "Take on a lot of debt," they whisper. This advice is often followed.

Investment bankers loan large sums for a war chest. The rates aren't all that hot, but what the heck, this is an emergency.

The management team doesn't care how much of the company's money it spends because they are protecting their territory, their jobs, their sacred rights. If this means future tough times for the company, if it brings the organization to its knees, so what?

Something else happens during a hostile takeover bid. Not much attention is given to the company's actual business. This is left in the hands of middle managers while senior management battles "the crisis." Operating budgets are cut because the top executives need every penny for defense. The business often suffers by this neglect. Some companies never recover.

The odd thing is that few critics question this behavior by those willing to bring the company to the brink of doom just to protect their jobs. The management team doesn't own the company, the shareholders do. It is the management team's recognized duty to look after the shareholders' interest, a duty that is almost always ignored during a takeover bid.

Occasionally, shareholders have sued managers who rejected attractive bids. Not nearly enough have protested. The point is, *if a power-hungry company makes a foolish offer why compound the foolishness by rejecting it?*

Why "Poison Pills" Are Against the Best Interests of Stockholders

There are species of toads whose skin secrete a poison when touched. It's a way to make themselves unappetizing to predators. That's the strategy behind the corporate "poison pill," and it's obvious that toads developed the program. With the help of consultants who specialize in antitakeover strategies many companies have gone to extraordinary measures to make themselves unappetizing to potential predators.

Sometimes the voting rules on the stock are changed if the company is acquired. Some shares would have no voting rights, others would have as many as ten votes. The result would be that the majority shareholders would not control the company. Friendly state legislatures have also assisted by outlawing certain takeovers or modifying the state tax codes to work against them.

Why are these poison pills against the best interests of the stockholders? Because they are instituted only to protect existing management. They inhibit attractive offers, and that works against the best interests of the investors. It's as if senior management has decreed that the ultimate purpose of the company is to provide them with gainful employment and to hell with those who have put up their money.

Why "Golden Parachutes" Are Unfair to Middle Managers

Another favorite tactic of senior managers is to vote themselves extremely favorable compensation terms if they are forced to leave the company. Should they be forced out because of a takeover, they will receive years of salary, lump-sum payments, often in amounts of six and seven figures. early pensions, use of company facilities and staff, consulting fees for doing nothing, and sundry other goodies. Essentially, what they've done is to bury a pot of gold that can be dug up and carried off in case of an emergency.

The company doing the acquiring doesn't mind these extraordinary payouts because they are recognized for what they are: bribes to the old crowd for getting out from underfoot.

The golden parachutes usually cover only the "key" executives. Middle managers don't get the benefit of this security. If the company is taken over they are left to fit into the new organization as best they can (while the high brass leaves the premises in a limousine laughing their heads off). Frequently, middle managers working for the acquired company discover that their job function is a "duplication" of work carried out by managers in the acquiring company. That means some of the managers will have to be terminated. Guess which ones are more likely to go?

There is just too much disparity between the rich outplacement compensation packages given to the top brass who are terminated after a takeover and the few weeks' severance pay offered to middle managers. Most middle managers realize that the people in the executive suite have written very comfortable insurance policies for themselves. They also know they aren't covered by the same policy. This knowledge has destroyed any feeling of company loyalty. Cynicism is the only reasonable attitude.

The golden parachute is just one of the many "proofs" that the modern corporation has forfeited any right to unswerving loyalty on the part of its employees. Work for a company when it suits your best interests. Leave without hesitation when it doesn't.

THE NUTS AND BOLTS STUFF EVERY MANAGER NEEDS TO KNOW

❖ 11 ❖

THE STUFF ABOUT
COMPANY OPERATIONS
EVERY MANAGER NEEDS
TO KNOW

A Brief Word On the Nuts and Bolts and All-You-Ever
Need-to-Know Sections

Each of these little "essays" on a business function or operation is less than four or five pages long. They are written to give corporate managers an insight into the typical functions that keep the company afloat. A few are perhaps a bit more than the average high school graduate can read and digest in a single minute, but not much more. Managers who haven't had the benefit of much formal business education may find these short overviews particularly helpful. (In some instances they are contrary views.)

One brief disclaimer: A few of the pages of explanation won't make the reader an expert on any of the topics tackled here. If that were possible everybody would be reading short summaries instead of spending years to master certain subjects. These essays can, however, lead to a better understanding of how business works, give an inkling of what goes on in the offices down the hall, and grant insight as to the reasons why senior management makes certain decisions. The knowledge can help the manager do a better job.

The glossary of buzz words, when mastered, can make the user *sound* like an expert on the related subject. Buzz words are captivating. They are the jargon used by insiders to demonstrate a working knowledge of a specialty. One writer called them "salvation in syllables." They are meant to separate the knowing from the ignorant, the anointed from the unwashed.

Many of the choices are acronyms because nothing defines the insider so clearly as knowing what the letters in an acronym stand for. Our selections are current, but in many industries buzz words live short, perilous lives. They change fastest in fast-changing industries. We think the ones we've selected will still be in vogue when this book is printed.

The knowledge of a few special terms doesn't define a true expert, but it will help the manager understand what the experts are talking about. This knowledge also helps the manager identify the phony, and that's important too.

What Profit Is All About

"Profit" is the most provocative word in the English language. It causes happiness for investors, or it causes agony if it's not present. In business, profit means to make a gain, and it does a lot more for a company than just keeping investors ecstatic.

In an earlier chapter of this book we said that business was a game. Profit is how the score of this game is kept. The winners show a profit. The losers do not. (If they lose often enough they get thrown off the playing field.)

There can be no profit without creating value. Value is what buyers are willing to pay for. Superior value is offering goods or services of equal quality at lower prices. Spectacular value is making sure whatever is offered satisfies the buyer. So the company that wishes to prosper will create spectacular value for its customers.

Profit is a goal, but it is also a limitation. A company's goals can't be larger than its stomach. Realistic goals must be set when targeting profit objectives.

Profit is calculated by taking total sales and deducting the cost of the goods sold. The result is *gross profit*. Unfortunately, that isn't the end of the process. Next, subtract selling and administrative expense, plus depreciation. The result is *operating profit.* There's still more subtraction. Deduct interest payments, taxes, and other expenses not related to operations. The result, sweet to behold, music to the ear, is *net profit.*

It's obvious to any manager that the three ways to increase profit are:

1. *Make more sales and thus more gross profit. However,* the effort to increase sales will result in greater sales expense.

2. *Increase the difference between the selling price and the cost of goods sold and thus make a higher gross profit. However,* selling the product for a higher price could result in lower sales because the value won't be so obvious to customers.

3. *Reduce the amounts chipped away during the journey from gross to net profit by reducing costs. However,* the effort to trim costs will impact sales, service, or quality.

It is the manager's responsibility to work out a happy balance between the suggested solutions and those nagging *doubts.* Here are the questions the manager must throw upon the scales to be weighed:

1. *What selling price will produce the best margins without eroding sales volume?*

2. *What costs should be incurred without eating away net profits?* (Costs versus benefits should always be weighed.)

Planning for profit begins by setting goals and objectives. The next step is to develop forecasts and budgets. Next, specific projects are developed in detail. Finally, because the execution of any plan always brings surprises, the results should be monitored and the plans revised. Here's a chart of the profit-planning procedure:

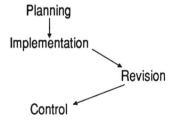

Now for a little profit-oriented philosophy: The first definition of "profit" one comes to in Webster's dictionary is, "to make progress." There are many alternate definitions listed, but we like Webster's first call because it identifies why profit is such an important concept to business. Progress keeps the engine of industry running. It is the most essential goal for any enterprise. Progress, recognized improvement, is more important than the traditional, but limited profit objective of having as much money as possible left over after all costs have been subtracted.

The company with a steady record of progress will be well regarded in its chosen industry and will be the darling of Wall Street. By definition these are the companies whose sales are growing fast, the outfits that are gobbling up market share, the organizations turning around bad situations, and the enterprises that have developed dramatic new processes. The stock for such companies will command greater premiums for their shares than the stodgy outfits who crank out better net returns or pay out higher dividends.

The real issue for any organization then becomes not just how much can be added to the bottom line for any specific period, but rather if the company is continuing to move forward. To measure forward movement requires the setting of goals beyond tomorrow's profit, another vital management task.

Thinking in terms of progress stimulates managers to look at total return on investment rather than merely near-term net when making plans and budgets. The manager who views progress as a profit goal is well on the way to personal success. Choose the course that will result in progress for your company, your operation, and yourself. That course of action will truly ensure a profit.

All You Need to Know About Finance in Fifty-nine Seconds

The invention of money rates right up there with the wheel and fire as one of the ideas responsible for modern civilization. The ancient Greeks, recognizing that money was an important business tool, stamped their metal money in the shape of tools.

Cash, profit, progress, and value are the objectives of every business operation. Finance and accounting methods reveal if these objectives are being met.

One of the first problems any business faces is where to get its hands on enough money to operate. The start-ups get it from selling shares to sucker relatives, borrowing from Grandma, tapping savings accounts, making small-business loans, maxing out credit cards, and so forth. What's amazing is not how often these methods fail, but how frequently they succeed.

New ventures scratch up capital from somewhere but they usually don't get enough. The single problem that sends most new companies into oblivion is *undercapitalization*. There's nothing in reserve to weather any storms. In fact, some new companies don't have enough in the kitty to survive light showers.

The second biggest problem for the new company is cash flow. It's the first item that an auditor will examine. Cash flow doesn't guarantee profit, but it does help ensure that the company will survive. Often, the start-up company doesn't have enough money coming in the door to pay expenses. The first question the entrepreneur should ask is, "Where will the orders come from?"

Major corporations get their money from lines of credit with major financial institutions, stock and bond issues, sale of goods, and the sale of other assets. The total amount raised from all these sources is called "net working capital."

(One major difference between American and Japanese corporations is that most American companies use equity financing, that is, selling stock, while Japanese companies tend to borrow from banks. The result is that Japanese corporations have much higher debt loads and interest payments than do American companies. This is a competitive advantage we have that isn't sufficiently explained by the American press when writing about the specter of Japan Incorporated.)

Most corporations now use debt as a way to finance new operations and capital goods purchases. Today too many corporations owe two or three times their invested capital. This is a very scary development. (We're more fiscally conservative than the Japanese, but it's still scary.)

In the next decade corporations will turn to new sources for obtaining capital. These include secondary stock offerings, borrowing overseas (Who said the suckers had to speak the same language?), and private placements.

The company's balance sheet reveals what the company actually owns and how these assets are financed. As a poetic accountant (if there is such an animal) put it, "The balance sheet is a window into the soul of the organization." Actually, it's really more like a snapshot, a still picture of the state of the company at a specific point in time.

Assets are the things the company owns that have value. For example, inventory is an asset. So is a manufacturing plant and the machines in it. A hot shot salesperson may be an asset to the company, but he or she doesn't get listed unless under contract.

Liabilities are the obligations of a company. The mortgage against the manufacturing plant is a liability. So is the long-term loan from the bank.

Liquidity is the company's ability to pay its bills. It's a very important requirement for the company that wishes to remain in business very long. Liquid assets are the things that are easy to exchange for hard cash, such as salable merchandise. Fixed assets are the things nailed to the floor, or even the floor itself.

Take everything the company owns and subtract everything it owes; the result is net worth. What's disturbing about recent trends is that so many companies have a negative worth today. (They owe more than they own.)

It's up to the corporation's chief financial officer (CFO) to provide and manage the company's capital. Their chief management tools are budgets, forecasts, reports, and the inescapable logic of numbers. Anyone who controls the purse strings is powerful, and the CFO is usually one of the top two or three executives in the company. Stay on his or her good side. Send Christmas cards.

Money is like any other commodity. The more there is available, the less it is worth. When there's plenty of money around it costs more to buy things because people would rather have the things than paper bills, which become worth less every day. (That's called inflation.) Many executives think cheap money is good for business—until it gets too cheap. Then the prices for everything increase so rapidly that planning becomes impossible.

Ten Buzz Words That Will Identify You as a Financial Genius

The world of finance, money, and accounting has a rich, specialized vocabulary that has grown over many years. It is a world that rewards conservatism, meaning that buzz words don't change as quickly here as they do in some professions. There were literally thousands of possible choices, and all would have been good selections as representative buzz words. Still, if you know the meaning of the following words, you'll be considered a member of the fraternity and entitled to wear a green eyeshade at the next office Christmas party. (We have resisted the impulse to include any economic terms. This is the devil's language.)

Risk Management. This is the practice of balancing the hazards of any business enterprise with the potential benefit. For example, extending credit to good customers is often necessary to obtain their business. However, that involves the risk that they may not pay. (Look at all the vendors left holding the bag when Macy's went belly-up.) Many companies can increase sales by lowering their credit criteria. They would also incur heavier bad-debt losses. Working out a practical compromise is what risk management is all about.

GAAP. An acronym meaning *G*enerally *A*ccepted *A*ccounting *P*rinciples. These are the accounting methods generally used and authorized by the major public accounting firms. Companies who have something to hide may not want to have an audit conducted by an accounting form who employs these principles.

CRAP. An acronym meaning *C*leverly *R*igged *A*ccounting *P*rinciples. The name tells the story. These are accounting methods meant to obscure or hide the true financial condition of a company. They are usually employed as a result of an "understanding" between the accountant and the top executives of the company in question.

The Big Eight. These are the nation's largest public accounting firms who because of their prestige and reputation for integrity are the most influential financial powers on earth. They are:

Arthur Andersen

Arthur Young

Coopers & Lybrand

Haskins & Sells

Ernst & Young

Peat, Marwick & Mitchell

Price Waterhouse

Touche Ross

When one of these outfits puts their stamp of approval on your company's financial statement, everyone usually accepts the result.

ROI. These initials mean *R*eturn *o*n *I*nvestment. It is a measurement of how much profit is made against how much was put into the pot to make it. Projecting ROI determines whether many projects get funded.

LBO. These initials stand for *L*everaged *B*uy-*O*ut. It means using debt and other people's money to take over a company. The problem with LBOs is that so much debt is assumed that if one little thing goes wrong, such as a temporary business turn down, the entire organization falls apart. Many profitable companies have been forced into bankruptcy and reorganization because they couldn't afford the debt service after raiders used LBOs to take them over.

Debenture. You've heard the word used countless times; now here is what it means: A debenture is a long term debt assumed by the corporation. It is not backed by anything the company owns, but rather is based on the credit history of the company.

Commercial Paper. These are short-term promissory notes. They are used by corporations to raise cash needed for periods of less than six months. Commercial paper doesn't bear interest. Instead, it is sold at a discount. That means the company borrows, say, nine hundred dollars. In six months it must pay back one thousand dollars.

Internal Rate of Return. A sophisticated accounting process that tries to compare the amount of cash coming in against the amount of cash that's going out. The idea is to determine just how efficiently the company is managing its resources.

Capital Budget. The capital budget is the amount of money allocated to spend on stuff that will take more than twelve months' time to realize a pay-back. When things are going badly, many companies reduce their capital budgets because it cuts immediate expenditures and doesn't hurt near-term sales or profits.

All You Need to Know About Sales and Marketing in Fifty-nine Seconds

Marketing is strategy; sales is tactics. Marketing is cerebral; sales is gut-level action.

Not quite clear on the difference between the two functions yet? Okay, here's some more. Ask a marketer what she's supposed to accomplish and she'll say "stimulate demand."

So how is demand stimulated? Marketing analyzes conditions, determines the product niche, sets the prices, selects the distribution channels, gathers intelligence, comes up with promotions, develops the image, worries about margins and market share, works on advertising campaigns, develops the sales brochures, and does all these wonderful things from a comfortable office in World Headquarters. The marketing person's burden is the dead certainty that the company's salespeople are all idiots.

Ask a salesperson what he's supposed to accomplish and he'll say, "get orders."

The sales crew, the aforementioned idiots despised by the marketers, are knee deep in the muddy trenches, face to face with customers, exchanging small-arms fire with the competition, digging up prospects, cutting deals, holding hands with big accounts, making cold calls on people who wish dearly to be left alone, worrying about deliveries, making presentations and demonstrations, smoothing over problems, and struggling with a boss who wants more action. Their curse is the damn-fool marketing staff, not one of whom has ever spent a single day in the field or ever met a quota.

Marketing does the planning. Sales is responsible for the execution. Marketing uses a variety of means to develop an interest in a product; sales actually goes out there and nails down the deal.

The functions are opposite ends of the same worm. Cut the worm in two pieces and each end might survive, but it will perform better as a whole.

A brilliantly conceived advertising campaign for a new bread combined with an attractive package design, healthy ingredients, and a terrific taste won't sell a single loaf unless the sales force is out there convincing the grocery-store chains to carry the brand. The grocery-store chains, who want as much revenue as possible from every inch of shelf space, won't be convinced until they learn about the marketing plans that will create demand for the product.

This decade's hot marketing topic is Market Share. It's important because the companies with the biggest market share are the front runners who set the pace. They determine the pricing, when new models will be announced, and how the product will be distributed. *Market leaders can afford to do more to promote the product and develop improvements because their revenue from the sales of that product are greater.* That's why companies will spend millions of dollars and experience temporary losses to establish market share. That's why there are gigantic wars between organizations over market share. (A classic example is the fight between Coke and Pepsi for dominance in the soft-drink market.)

Those companies who can't afford to fight it out in the main arena with the heavyweights will often decide to concentrate on a particular niche. This means trying to tailor a product to appeal to a certain class of customer. A good example is Volvo, whose every ad focuses on the car buyer whose first concern is safety.

The basics of selling haven't changed much over the last hundred years. Salesmanship is still making contact with a prospect, establishing interest, and asking for the order. The nature of sales organizations are changing, however, because it costs so very much today to make a direct call on a prospect or customer. Current estimates for the cost of a single direct call are close to $300, which means that the salesperson who walks through the prospect's door better have something pretty important to say. More and more companies are relying on selling by telephone (telemarketing), straight commission salespeople who are paid only on results, and third-party selling organizations. This trend will continue.

The reduction of direct field sales forces will result in a heavier emphasis on marketing to carry the load. That means a greater need for skilled marketing people, bigger budgets, more money spent on advertising, and so forth. Many companies trying to contain costs will ask their salespeople to become independent reps who won't be carried on the roster of direct employees. Others will explore different distribution channels that offer fixed costs per sale.

The demand for technically competent salespeople will remain high. They will be needed to explain the benefits of complex new products.

Ten Buzz Words That Identify You as a Sales and Marketing Expert

In most corporations everyone, including the janitor, considers him or herself to be a sales and marketing expert, so it's hard to stand out as someone with the arcane knowledge of the insider. The following list of words may help.

Positioning. This word substitutes for niche. It means selecting the portion or segment of the market you want to attack. This technique has become very fashionable as a marketing strategy because it's an alternative to spending gobs of money to gain dominant market share. That makes positioning sexy.

Demographics. The definition of this word is population studies, but in the marketing profession it really means trying to find out where the potential buyers are hiding. (Marketers will follow buyers to the ends of the earth.) For example, radio stations and magazines will try to appeal to certain age or income groups by the kind of material they present (positioning their entertainment product.) Then they sell advertising to companies interested in reaching these groups. A luxury car company might buy the use of American Express's customer list for a direct mail campaign on the assumption that the Amex card holder is affluent enough to afford the purchase.

MPIS. These initials stand for *M*arket *P*lanning and *I*nformation *S*ystem. It's a market research method that starts with deciding the purpose of the research and develops a plan all the way through implementation. It really means that the first chore in marketing research is to find out what you want to find out.

PRIZM. An acronym standing for *P*otential *R*ating *I*ndex *Z*ip *M*arkets. It's an assumption that people with similar backgrounds and tastes will want to live close to one another. (Perhaps huddling against one another for comfort and warmth.) Marketers who base campaigns on the PRIZM factor feel they can target "young" neighborhoods, "blue collar" neighborhoods, and so forth.

Model of Rationality. Marketers and salespeople are always trying to figure out why people buy things. (So they can influence them to buy something else. In marketing they're always looking for *The Answer*.) A Model of Rationality tries to explore the decision-making process that goes into a purchase. The models get pretty complicated, and the explanations as to why people buy are sometimes esoteric.

Market Driven. This phrase relates to a company philosophy of creating products and services based on the perceived needs of the marketplace. It is the complete opposite strategy of a product driven company which first develops the product, then tries to create the need for it. The market-driven person says, "Tell me what you want, and we'll build it." The product-driven person says, "We just made this wonderful doohickey and here are all the reasons you can't live without it one second longer." Market-driven companies must react to events faster, but they build sales more rapidly. Product-driven companies have more time to plan, but sometimes they get stuck with goods nobody wants.

SPINS. An acronym for a solution selling technique. It stands for *S*ituation *P*roblem *I*mplication *N*eeds Solution. In this type of selling the salesperson first learns the *situation* at the prospect company, uncovers a *problem* his company can solve, warns the prospect of the dire *implications* of that problem if it isn't resolved, translates those implications to *needs* the prospect can't live without one minute longer, and then heroically presents a *solution* that will save the prospect's bacon. Using the SPINS method takes a product out of the commodity class, which means that better profit margins can be maintained.

Win-Win Negotiating A negotiating technique that theoretically serves the best interests of both parties. In practice it means snatching the last dollar on the table, but leaving the spare change.

Consultive Selling A selling method in which the salesperson tries to rise above the level of an order taker or price quoter by serving as a consultant to the prospect. Somehow, the advice usually given is that the prospect will be far better off with the consultive salesperson's product. Often consultive salespeople use the SPIN method of finding a problem and then solving it.

Drip Marketing This means focusing all marketing activities, such as direct mail, telemarketing, and so forth, into a target market. The idea is that by concentrating all marketing efforts toward a specified group of suspects, more leads and therefore more sales will result.

All You Need to Know About Manufacturing in Fifty-nine Seconds

Manufacturing literally means manmade. It applies both to the first sharpened sticks whittled with stones more than 20,000 years ago and the latest wafer-thin computer chips. There are three basic kinds of manufacturing. They are:

1. *Unique-product manufacturing, which is what artisans and craftsmen do.* A woman hand knitting a sweater or a man turning a pot are engaged in this type of manufacture. Unique-product manufacturing began to diminish with the birth of the industrial revolution (circa 1820). Today it's enjoying a resurgence.

2. *Mass production manufacturing, which is turning out identical products from interchangeable parts, usually on some kind of line set up for the purpose.* Workers concentrate on a single task, and they, too, are almost interchangeable. (The workers soon recognized they were easily replaceable, which is one of the reasons labor unions were formed.)

   This is the form of manufacturing that America "invented." The key question today is whether it is an outmoded model. The Japanese and others have pioneered different types of work place organization that rely on skilled workers, cooperation between management and labor, and pride of craftsmanship.

3. *Process manufacturing, which is turning raw material into a finished product.* An example is an oil refinery that "cracks" crude oil into gasoline and a variety of by-products.

A manufacturing operation requires a high level of management involvement including:

1. *Strategic planning.* (Deciding what to make.)

2. *Tactical planning.* (Working out budgets and use of resources needed to start making something.)

3. *Operational control.* (Setting up the procedures for actually producing the product and supervising the execution of those procedures.)

"Job Shop" manufacturing means making a product on demand to fit a customer's specifications. A typical example of job-shop operation is a business-forms printing plant. This type of manufacturing requires set-up time for each new customer, but the output is sold in advance.

Stock items are made for inventory. The production of these items is usually more economical, but there's no guarantee they will be sold.

The goal of every manufacturer is to make it good and make it cheap. If forced to choose between the two, most companies choose cheap.

The manufacturing process of things can be divided into three stages. These are:

1. *The component stage.*

2. *The subassembly stage.*

3. *The assembly stage.*

Well-planned manufacturing starts at the bottom, with components. These should be designed to be flexible enough to be used in a variety of products. That makes the changeover into different models less expensive and time consuming.

Today, many manufacturers are farming out the component and subassembly work to other suppliers. In essence they have become assemblers. This practice can reduce costs, but it also reduces control over the finished product.

The cost for labor in this country has been used as an excuse by some manufacturers for the loss of our competitive edge. Labor cost is only one factor. In 1990 factory labor costs were $14.77 an hour here compared to $12.64 in Japan. That's not enough of a discrepancy to account for our trade imbalance. In West Germany 1990 factory labor costs were $21.53, 33 percent higher than ours. Yet, in that year Germany enjoyed a healthy trade surplus of $9 billion. The manufacturers who scream for lower wages by

American workers are looking for scapegoats to cover their own mismanagement.

The cost for making a product can be reduced by a variety of factors including capital investment (buying more modern equipment).

Product design changes can significantly reduce the cost for making that product. Changes that typically lead to lower manufacturing costs include:

1. *Reducing the number of parts in the product.*

2. *Reducing the steps to make it.*

3. *Simplifying the machinery or process for making it.*

Another important manufacturing issue of the 1990s is quality control. The Japanese have taught American customers to expect products to be well made. Other Pacific Rim countries have learned the lesson taught by the Japanese. The products now being delivered from Korea, Singapore, Taiwan, and other places in the Far East also offer excellent quality.

What American manufacturers must learn anew is the ability to produce products that offer real value.

Ten Buzzwords That Identify You as a Manufacturing Guru

Simultaneous Engineering. This is a system in which the design of a new product and the manufacturing process needed to produce it overlap. In other words, the plans to make the product and the initial manufacturing steps begin long before the design is finished. The idea is to get products to marker faster. Obviously, it requires close cooperation between the manufacturing and product-design groups within a company.

IMS. These initials stand for *I*ntelligent *M*anufacturing *S*ystem. They mean computerized manufacturing, or simply, using computers in factories to control machinery. This is a hot topic right now between American and Japanese technical committees. Both sides want a joint research project. The Japanese, however, are reluctant to share their ideas on producing products that are commercially feasible. The Americans are worried that a cooperative effort would result in our software research being pirated. In other words, each side wants to protect the advantage it started with.

Labor Productivity. This is a unit of productivity measurement that rates the dollars of output per number of hours worked. We're looking good compared to other nations. Despite all the conversation about the decline of the American worker, we still lead the world in productivity.

Cluster Groups. This is an old, outmoded idea of putting like kinds of production machinery in one location. That means lathes would all go in one corner, the punch presses in another. The arrangement made some sense in the old days when most production equipment had a lot of downtime. If the equipment were all together, expert mechanics and an inventory of spare parts could be nearby to fix it.

Now the phrase has taken on another meaning. A cluster group is also a self-contained unit given decision-making responsibility for a particular job function. More about this in the section on administrative management.

Multifactor Productivity. This is a composite measure of how an economy makes use of capital and labor. In the United States our productivity arrow is pointed down. We're still the world leader, but we're not making as efficient use of capital and labor as we once did.

Dedicated Flow Lines. This refers to a manufacturing technique in which a production line is dedicated to a single product, or a very narrow range of products. The design makes it simpler to bring components and subassemblies to that line.

Linear Processing. This term means setting up a production line so all the processing steps take place in a logical sequence. A good example of linear processing is my high-tech coffee maker. It "wakes up" in the morning at a preset time, grinds the whole coffee beans (which wakes me up), heats the water, pours the heated water over the freshly ground beans, and keeps the brewed coffee piping hot until I can get downstairs to drink that lifesaving first cup.

MITI. American senior managers utter a silent prayer, or issue a curse, whenever they hear this word. It's an acronym that stands for *M*inistry of *I*nternational *T*rade and *I*nquiry. This is the Japanese agency, infamous in some quarters, responsible for the successful strategies that led to that country's domination of many industries. It was MITI that insisted smaller Japanese firms form alliances with larger ones for greater financial clout. It was MITI that forced Japanese companies to concentrate their efforts in certain industries and product areas so as to dominate them. MITI makes long-range strategic plans for Japanese industries while our government agencies try to devise new ways to restrict ours.

CAD/CAM. These are acronyms that stand for *C*omputer *A*ided *D*esign and *C*omputer *A*ided *M*anufacture. The words themselves explain their meaning. They refer to the use of computers to assist in product design and product manufacture. CAD systems are more in use than CAM is.

Hierarchical Production Planning. This is a planning system in which decisions are made in logical sequence. It's a complicated way of saying that when planning a production operation, go from the general to the particular.

All You Need to Know About Inventory Management in Fifty-nine Seconds

Inventory and manufacturing are irrevocably tied to each other. Even the cave dwellers who sharpened sticks for another tribe couldn't get a manufacturing run started until they assembled a supply of raw materials (young branches and flint stones) to work with.

The biggest lesson to learn about inventory is that it is frozen cash and, in its current state, a drain on resources. The money frozen in this manner is called "working capital." Only when products are sold, shipped, and paid for is that cash converted into usable form. That makes inventory expensive and inventory management an important science.

A manufacturing firm will typically carry three different types of inventories:

1. *Raw materials.*

2. *Work in process.*

3. *Finished goods.*

The job of the production manager is to turn the raw materials into finished goods as quickly as and economically as possible.

The gut-level management problem facing any manufacturer is knowing just how much of a product to make. This decision determines inventory levels.

There are good arguments for turning the manufacturing spigot on full force. These are:

1. *It's usually cheaper to make something in large batches.*

2. *Raw materials and work-in-process inventories can't be converted into cash.* That can happen only when the product is finished and sold.

3. *To sell a product it must be available.* If customers can't find your company's product, they'll buy something else.

4. *There are certain fixed costs and factory overheads that keep on accumulating whether or not the production lines are open.*

A finished goods inventory gathering dust in the company warehouse, however, is a horrible misuse of company funds. Now, labor and manufacturing costs have been added to the raw-material inventory cost. As the finished-goods inventory ages, it becomes obsolete. Not only is inventory money, but obsolete inventory is money down the tubes. Making too much product that couldn't be sold has destroyed many a company.

Production demands and inventory costs are like Siamese twins, joined at the hip. The manufacturing executive juggles the needs of the marketplace on one hand and the production of the product in economical batches on the other. (That's one reason accurate sales projections are so important.) There are more formulas for calculating "ideal" inventory levels than there are for postulating infinity.

When management decides that an inventory item is obsolete, get rid of it. That item is using up valuable space, and the money it represents is still frozen.

Many managers will stubbornly hang onto obsolete merchandise, hoping some fool will come along and buy the whole shebang at full-listed value. That fool doesn't travel the circuit often enough. Despite the dust and scratches, the merchandise does not appreciate as antiques. When faced with a warehouse filled with out-of-date goods, remember that old merchandising wisdom: "The first discount is the cheapest." Cut quickly, cut deep, ship the stuff out, and spend time on those products that are still viable.

Eleven Buzzwords That Will Identify You as an Inventory Hotshot

Inventory Turns. One of the indicators that reveals how well an inventory is being managed is how many times a year the company's inventory of products is sold and replaced. Each time is considered one "turn." The more turns, the better the company's money is being managed.

Just-in-Time Inventory System. This is a system that brings raw materials, parts, and subassemblies to the production point at the exact time they are needed and not a minute before. The advantage of this approach is that less money and warehouse space is tied up in raw-goods inventory.

There's less waste. However, the system requires close cooperation and confidence between the manager and all suppliers. The Japanese love the system. (It was taught to them by an American.)

LIFO. An acronym meaning *Last In, First Out*. This is an inventory-valuation method. In this method the most recently purchased inventory is charged against sales. A LIFO accounting system measures the replacement costs of goods sold. The company using LIFO is calculating profit or loss based on the current cost of doing business.

FIFO. Another acronym and another inventory valuation method. This one means *First In, First Out*. In this method the oldest purchased inventory is charged against sales. The FIFO system works best during a period of inflation. Costs are minimized and profits are maximized.

Inventory Balancing. This is an accommodation for customers, usually resellers, when they've been sold products that just won't move. If the reseller screams loudly enough some companies will replace the dog merchandise on a dollar-per-dollar basis with stuff that is more salable. This procedure is also called "stock balancing."

ABC Inventory Classification. This is an inventory-keeping system that groups items by their annual usage, the most-used items are in group A, the next in group B, and the least-used items in group C. These records can be kept by quantity used, by the dollar those quantities cost, or both. As inventory is money, knowing exactly which items are being used is important.

Safety Stocks. If a component or subassembly is out of stock the entire production line may be shut down. The safety stock is the quantity of inventory items that should be on hand to satisfy the lead times necessary to purchase or make it.

Pipeline Stocks. These are items or materials actually being worked on, or moving between work centers, or traveling to another location or customer.

Economic Lot Size. In inventory language this is the best quantity lot to order from a supplier or the most economical lot size to manufacture.

Continuous Review. This means monitoring inventory status all the time. Each withdrawal from stock is recorded. The method requires more clerical effort, but there are no surprise shortages.

Stage Location. The actual place where the inventory is sitting on pallets. Also called an "echelon," "facility," or more simply, "storage."

All You Need to Know About Administration and Organization in Fifty-nine Seconds

Administration is the means companies use to control their business. It is the executive policy of an organization, the rules governing its operation, and the conduct of its daily business. The administrative "style" sets the tone for the organization.

All organizations have missions. That is, they are supposed to get something accomplished. The means are the ways they use to accomplish this mission. In the bureaucratic organization the mission sometimes gets obscured by the means.

Things get done by people, which means the organization must *administer* the behavior of individuals and groups. Here's a linear sketch that shows how the process works in most companies.

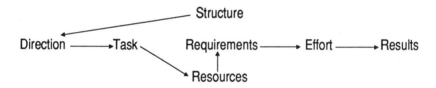

Successful administrators possess or acquire three skills. They are:

1. *Technical skill, or knowledge about a special function or specialty.*

2. *Human skills, or the ability to work within or to lead a group dedicated to a common purpose.*

3. *Conceptual skills, or the ability to see beyond a specific activity, to see the organization as a whole.*

All three are important and all are interrelated. The need for technical skills fades with each step up the executive ladder, replaced with a greater need for conceptual ability.

Administration is responsible for processing, recording, sorting, interpreting, and summarizing the company's business transactions. These functions are considered havens for middle managers, places where they can endlessly shuffle papers, enforce regulations, and generally impede progress.

Corporations today are awestruck by the size of the bureaucracies they've created. Most are dedicated to reducing the number of their middle managers. That means administration is not a safe place for a manager to be. (At IBM they call their corps of more than 25,000 middle managers "The Big Gray Cloud.")

Some companies have formed small groups of employees called "quality circles" or "clusters." This group is made responsible for an entire function from A to Z. They can cut across organizational lines to get the job done and make their own work rules, and their own decisions. What's amusing about the concept is that quality circles are nothing more than a corporation's attempt to defeat its own bureaucracy. Why not dismantle the bureaucracy instead?

The desire to hack away at corporate fat is everywhere. Big is bad today. A few years ago Peter Drucker wrote that large institutions such as DuPont and General Motors had "outlived their usefulness." Does that mean these giants are going to fold their tents and go away? Not bloody likely! What will happen is that they will restructure themselves into smaller, independent operating groups.

If corporations truly wish to reduce their bureaucracies they will have to dismantle the bulky apparatus built over decades to make sure everything was done by the numbers. More specifically the corporation of the 1990s must:

1. *Reduce the number of rules and simplify those that can't be eliminated.*

2. *Reduce the number of steps needed to get something approved.*

3. *Empower more managers to make decisions within the framework of their responsibility.*

4. *Make sure that administrators have some direct contact with customers.* Internal managers must learn how their decisions can affect business and customers' perception of the company.

5. *Tie employee rewards to customer satisfaction.*

6. *Don't expect perfection.* As Wild Bill Donovan, founder of the OSS, said, "Perfection is inefficient." He meant that the amount of effort necessary to eliminate every possible mistake is not worth the potential gain.

7. *Be willing to entertain dangerous ideas.* They may be the salvation of the company.

Ten Rules of Corporate Organizations

Working for a large corporation is easier when you recognize some basic truths about how all organizations work. Here are ten thoughts that will help you understand something about your work place and the people in it.

1. *One symptom of an organization in trouble is rampant paranoia among the work force.*

2. *Punishing failure will ensure that it doesn't get reported.*

3. *To gain respect in an organization, don't make concessions.*

4. *Directions from the top of the company tend to break down as they filter through the organization.* That means the head honcho is just as frustrated as you are.

5. *Every organization spends time and energy on company politics.* Perhaps this is true because the internal political situation is usually more interesting to talk about than the job is.

6. *Every individual in every organization spends time and energy in protecting a bit of turf, no matter how minuscule.*

7. *Bureaucracies suppress opposition.* The more bureaucratic the company you work for, the less you are "allowed" to disagree.

8. *In large companies deadlines come and go and nothing happens.* Most deadlines are artificial anyway. Why live or die by them?

9. *The more details involved with your job, the less responsibility you have.*

10. *Only about 21 percent of administrative labor costs are expended on clerical personnel.* The rest, almost 80 percent, are costs for management and professional people. This 80 percent are the "Big Gray Cloud" that is on every corporation's hit list.

All You Need to Know About Distribution in Fifty-nine Seconds

Distribution means all the channels used to get the product into the hands of the company's customers. How the product gets from the factory into the customer's eager hands will be the most critical marketing and sales issue of the next decade. Companies that make a mistake by choosing the wrong channel could find themselves out of business.

Why is this such a hot topic? Because the costs for making direct sales calls rise every day. The *Harvard Business Review* estimated the cost of a computer industry sales call at $300 per hour! Who can afford that kind of overhead just to reach a buyer whose mind is already hermetically sealed? Steve Jobs, one of the founders of Apple Computer, believes that dealers and distributors with outside salespeople can't support that kind of expense. He feels the channels of the future for the computer industry are direct mail and telemarketing.

Some of the old reliable methods for getting products to market are being challenged by new, upstart distribution vehicles that didn't exist a few years ago. For example, department stores, once considered the best way to distribute most high-ticket consumer-type products, face fierce competition from discounters, home shopping TV networks, mass merchandisers, and the like.

It's no accident that K-Mart and Wal-Mart, both of whom have surpassed Sears in sales volume, are perceived as discount operations. (Sometimes the discounts aren't all that hot, but that's another subject.) Everyone is lining up for a slice of this distribution pie. Suppliers who a few years ago wouldn't consider using a discount merchandiser because it might "cheapen the product" today fight like rabid dogs for shelf space at the Price Club.

In dealer, distributor, retail outlet, value-added reseller, and some other channels, the cost to the supplier to sell a product is fixed. A few points in margin are surrendered, but only a few direct people are needed to supervise the network.

The trade-off is that the company that chooses any indirect distribution route loses control of the sales effort. Demand for the product diminishes because the direct people aren't out in the field every day pushing it. This puts greater pressure on marketing to develop advertising campaigns and promotional gimmicks to stimulate demand.

A change in how the product reaches the market must be carefully weighed. The prime considerations when choosing a new distribution channel are:

1. *How much merchandise can this channel be expected to move?*

2. *What is the cost for getting a product into that stream?*

3. *Can this channel coexist with other channels?* (Give a product to a discounter and many department stores won't touch it because they can't compete with a discounter's price. Some suppliers deal with this problem by making products with cosmetic differences

between models. One model is offered to discounters, another to full-price department stores.)

4. *How much control can be maintained over the product pricing in this channel?*

5. *Will this distribution channel be around a few years from now?* (Some channels are drying up. Many department stores won't carry electronics and a host of other products any longer because they can't meet the competition of the discounters. The individually owned computer store and the independent office-equipment dealer are going the way of the dinosaur. Many home TV shopping clubs are not profitable and may not survive.)

When selecting distribution channels, it's important to consider the requirements for moving the company's products five years from now as well as the need to move products today.

❖ Pick channels that are vibrant.

❖ Pick channels that aren't self-destructing, with unprofitable business practices.

❖ Pick channels that show an interest in establishing and maintaining long term relationships.

All You Really Need to Know About Research and Development in Fifty-nine Seconds

The Research and Development team are those scientists and engineers occupying the laboratory they won't let you near. They're the Ivory Tower boys working on the secret stuff. The idea is to develop something that will knock the socks off the competition.

Actually the name of the department is misleading. Most company R & D operations are strictly devoted to developing new products and should be called Product Development Laboratories. Only a few, such as Bell Labs, still do basic research.

A company's dedication to the future can be determined by the amount of money it spends on product development. Sony, one of the leading disciples of Nirvana through innovation, employs more than 9,000 scientists and engineers and spends about $1.5 billion a year to support R & D. That's 5.7 percent of their total revenue. The investment pays off with *four new products introduced every business day.*

The average percentage spent on R & D for large companies is 3.9 percent of sales. Small companies with under $100 million in sales spend an average of 8.7 percent. In high technology industries the average is much higher. Last year, Xicor, a semiconductor maker, had an R & D budget equal to 25 percent of its sales volume.

The CEO anxious to make a shaky year look a bit better may cut back on development funds. This is like taking out a second mortgage on the old homestead because things are tight. It may provide temporary relief, but in the end it makes the other bills tougher to pay.

Product development teams have the same problem that a hunter has when trying to knock a duck out of the air. If he aims directly at the bird he'll miss because the duck won't be there by the time the buckshot reaches the spot. The hunter must lead the duck, that is, *anticipate* its arrival at a different point in the sky and aim accordingly.

Like the duck hunter, development teams can't aim their big guns at products currently on the market. They must anticipate what is likely to be available from the competition when the product is ready to be launched. This is a basic, almost simplistic precept, but so many companies seem to ignore it when planning development projects.

It's important to distinguish between product improvement and genuine innovation. Product improvement is almost always a good thing for the company. The wrong kind of innovation can destroy it. Completely revolutionary products can unravel structure and profitability. That's because it's difficult to predict market acceptance of a new concept, and it's hard to anticipate the impact of true innovation on the current product line. The questions that should be asked about an innovative product are:

1. *Is the marketplace ready for it?*

2. *Will the marketplace pay for it?*

3. *Does it offer real advantage to the customer over what is available now?*

4. *Are we satisfied that it really works?*

5. *Will it destroy a current product?*

6. *Will educating our customers about this innovation take up all our time and attention?*

7. *Will it mark our company as a pioneer and help distinguish us from the competition?*

8. *Will it be an easy product for our competitors to copy?*

9. *Is the competition already working on something like this?*

10. *Can it be suppressed while older, more profitable, products are maintained?* (If it offers true benefits not now available, the answer is almost always no.)

11. *What effect is it likely to have on the company's bottom line?*

Here in the United States we have relied too heavily on the research work done in the military and space applications to develop new, innovative products for industry. We won't have this crutch anymore. Industry has got to step up to the bar and start paying for what had been the free drinks at the party. If that doesn't happen we'll all be slinging hamburgers down at McDonalds.

Ten Pearls of Wisdom on Research and Development

1. *When hiring for the R & D team, stay away from too many specialists.* Their scope is too narrow to be truly innovative.

2. *Base product development on perceived need for something.*

3. *The R & D center doesn't have to be a palace.* Too many companies are building Taj Mahals badly disguised as laboratories.

4. *Be reconciled to the fact that only one out of every twenty to twenty-five ideas will ever result in a product.*

5. *Be further reconciled to the fact that fourteen out of every fifteen products will fail.*

6. *If you can afford to employ several teams working on the same project, do it.* Competition works in R & D too.

7. *At most U.S. companies senior management gives most of its time and attention to businesses and products that are already established.* Japanese managers know better. They devote most of their time to new products.

8. *Keep intelligence gathering to a reasonable limit.* Waiting until everything is known is waiting too long. Extreme caution could cost the company a jump on an important new market. Go with hunches. Treasure inspiration.

9. *Wait until the last minute before freezing specifications on a new product.* Once the specifications are set in concrete, so are the

minds working on the project. Keeping the architecture open keeps the creative juices flowing.

10. *If you recognize the NIH (not invented here) factor at work in your shop, stamp it out.* Good ideas can come from any source. A great many will come from employees who are not "designated inventors."

All You Need to Know About Credit in Fifty-nine Seconds

Credit means handing over the product to a customer without getting paid for it right now. The first person who made that kind of offer is one of the anonymous heroes of history, like the guy who ate the first oyster.

Companies extend credit for only one reason, to stimulate sales. Cash on the barrelhead is a much more prudent policy. Why don't companies insist on cash with order? Because business would dry up as the customers defected to other suppliers.

That makes the extension of credit a function of sales and marketing. Credit is a marketing tool. So why doesn't it fall under marketing? Because the marketing and sales managers can't be trusted. They would grant credit to everyone. Anything to get the order out the door.

To keep from shipping stuff to companies who can't pay and to keep from perhaps going broke with bad debt losses, the company puts in a watchdog.

That's the credit manager. This is someone hired to evaluate the risks involved in granting credit terms. To make sure there's no pressure by the sales department to okay questionable deals, the credit operation is usually controlled by the financial officer.

The tough question that credit managers face is, just how much credit is prudent? To get the answers, they rely on credit reports, past payment histories, customer balance sheets, financial statements, bank and trade references.

They tend to be cautious because they get no praise by giving a customer a large credit line, but they can expect a tongue-lashing from the CFO if bad-debt losses exceed certain limits. Guess whose head is on the chopping block if a major customer with a large outstanding balance declares Chapter Eleven?

To limit risk, credit managers will establish a maximum amount a customer is permitted to buy before paying part of the balance. In theory this means no one customer can wound the company too deeply. In practice, much of the credit risk of most companies is represented by the outstanding balances of a few large customers. That's because the credit limits are elastic for good customers. They get "stretched" near the end of the month when the sales department needs a few more shipments to look good.

Many companies will offer discounts if the invoice is paid within a certain number of days. Typical terms on an invoice are "3/10, net thirty." That means a 3 percent discount if paid within ten days, with the net amount expected in thirty days.

If the balance is not paid within thirty days it is said to be "aged." Credit managers tend to worry once an account is more than sixty days overdue, and they worry a lot if no payment has been received in ninety days. Every day the account ages lessens the chance it will ever be paid.

Credit managers use refusal to ship as a weapon to get payment on invoices that are long past due. Sometimes this works, especially if the customer needs spare parts, and sometimes it sends the customer into the waiting arms of the competition. Of course, if the customer hasn't paid his or her bill with your company, he or she won't pay the competition either.

If refusal to ship doesn't work, the credit department begins sending strident letters, each more threatening than the last. The collection process used to be a lot nastier than it is now, and companies are limited as to what they can do or say to obtain payment. They do have recourse to legal action if the bill is large enough to warrant it, or they can turn the account over to a collection agency if the amount is small. The losses due to bad debts that are never collected are considered part of the cost of doing business. They are charged to sales.

When times are bad and orders tough to come by, marketing will appeal to finance to turn on the credit spigot full force. Easier credit means more sales. (There's no shortage of outfits out there happy to operate on your company's money.) Some companies think this is a good idea. They adopt very liberal credit terms on the theory that they're better off if the product is sitting in the customer's warehouse rather than in their own. Once the product has been shipped, at least it shows up on the books as a sale and a receivable.

Other companies will reluctantly offer General Motors a $5,000 credit line—after they've seen a recent balance sheet and trade references. The pressure from sales to grant credit more liberally conflicts with the pressure from finance to be more fiscally conservative. What happens in most companies is a compromise that satisfies neither faction. That's why nobody is, or ever will be, satisfied with the performance of the credit manager.

THE MANAGER'S GUIDE TO UNDERSTANDING TECHNOLOGY

Reviewing the Last Decade and Predicting the Next

The last decade has seen a relentless advance of technology, spurred in large part by a small, wafer-thin square of silicon called a computer chip. This seminal product is causing revolutionary change in the world of commerce. Once lucrative businesses confront new challenges. Entire industries face upheaval and confrontation from unlikely sources.

If there's one sure prediction for the next decade it is that digital technology will rewrite the rules for competition. No one is exempted. Companies that thought they owned the "franchise" for a particular market may find themselves bushwacked by newly formed gangs of marauding banditos. Gone forever will be those sweet, exclusive pockets of profit that made some organizations so fat and comfortable over the years.

One of the byproducts of this revolution is an overlapping of capabilities. If a company uses digital technology to design a computer, they can certainly adapt it to design a communication network. Industries that once existed completely separately now find they have become unlikely adversaries, fighting for a share of the same market.

This competition has already happened in four giant industries most affected by the computer chip: computers, communications, entertainment, and electronics. Senior management of the major companies in these industries are busy drawing attack plans and lining up allies. That behemoth communication company, AT&T, not only designs computer hardware as well as communication gear, but it paid billions to acquire NCR so it could reach new markets. Sony, the consumer electronics colossus, overpaid for Columbia Pictures to gain entry into the entertainment field.

Electronics isn't the only area undergoing profound technical change. The biosciences are probing at the secrets of illness, aging, and life itself. The search for inexpensive and renewable energy sources appears close to finding realistic answers. At least part of the reason for these advances coming upon one another so quickly is that sophisticated computing power is available at every scientist's fingertips.

Executives who don't keep abreast of these technological advances may find themselves on the business slag heap. For the young manager, this knowledge is a mandatory requirement for advancement. For the middle-aged manager, the lack of it is almost a guarantee of outplacement.

In this chapter we've tried to explain, in nontechnical terms, a bit about the technology at the root of the revolution. The reader will definitely not be qualified as an electronics engineer upon completion of this material. He or she may, however, have a better understanding of the forces fueling these extraordinary changes.

The Short-Short Course in Computers: What They Do, How They Work, What Their Limitations Are, and Why You Shouldn't Be Intimidated by Them

The most important thing to remember about computers is that they are incredibly stupid. Contrary to popular myth, they neither "think" nor do they understand. Their so-called "brains" are off-on pulses, something like a light switch, which are used to create and transmit a binary code. If they can be said to *know* anything, it's a simple yes or no.

A newborn baby comes into this world with the capacity to wiggle its fingers, move its arms and legs, open or shut its mouth and eyes, feel hunger or pain, eat, digest its food, cry, sleep, and relieve itself. These are instinctual abilities shared by most mammals; the baby knows nothing. Its mind is a blank slate, ready to receive the world's images. Now imagine this same baby without the basic instincts of all humans, its mind also a blank; but this infant has the ability to calculate at incredible speeds and remember whatever it has been told, and it is able not only to recite everything, but to feed it back in a variety of ways. That unique newborn is a computer, and it's one baby that you definitely don't want to throw out with the bath water.

How Computers Work

Computers are nothing more than a series of electronic circuits. They are born (come out of the box) with no knowledge, so they must be told how to do absolutely everything in a logical, step-by-step process. This telling is accomplished by a set of instructions called *programs* or *software*. The instructions must be quite literal, and they must be absolutely complete. (When teaching a six-year-old child how to tie shoelaces, you might begin by telling the child how to hold the laces. That instruction would come in somewhere down the line when programming a computer for the shoe-tying task. First, you'd have to tell the computer to bend over.)

The programs are fed into the computer (the *hardware*) via *floppy disks*. These are flexible magnetic disks that look like phonograph records. There are floppy disks which hold up to 1.4 million *bytes* of memory, but the demand is for even more memory so larger capacity disks are on the way. *Hard disks* can hold more than 100 million characters and *optical disks* much more than that.

The programs are stored in *internal memory*, which also holds the data that the computer manipulates. There are two kinds of memory, *read-only-memory (ROM)*, which contains permanent instructions, and *random-access-memory (RAM)*, which is temporary storage inside the machine for the program currently being used. The programs control the brain of the computer, its *central processing unit,* or *CPU*. In the case of a microcomputer, this chip is called a *microprocessor*. This chip contains thousands of electronic components compressed into a very thin silicon wafer. The way a computer handles the instructions it has been fed is called its *operating system*.

Information is entered into the computer via various *input devices*, such as keyboards and scanners. Then the computer goes to work with this information, "massaging" it in some way.

What's wonderful about a computer is just how quickly and accurately it can move things around. For example, on the word-processing program being used to create this manuscript, if several sentences or paragraphs are added in the middle of the text, everything else that comes after the additions is automatically shifted down to make room. That makes changes much easier than in the old typewriter days when everything that came after an addition would have to be retyped. The reason this capability is so valuable is because as Michael Korda points out in his book, *Power*, "Information is never in the form in which it is needed." The computer allows the user to put information in any form desired.

The work a computer produces is often printed on an *output* device, such as a dot matrix or laser printer. The operator views the work in progress via a *cathode ray tube (CRT)*. This device looks just like a television screen, which it is. Computers can send information to one another via dedicated or ordinary telephone lines. Tying a group of computers together is called *networking*.

Machines, computers included, should never be used as a substitute for decision making. They can assist in the decision making process by providing information to the decision maker in a variety of forms, but they can't make judgments, except on predetermined parameters; they can't consider personalities; they can't discount data from a questionable source, unless they've been specifically told to disregard it; and they can't play hunches. They are limited, both to the data that's been fed them and to the programs they use.

Summary on Computers

In summary, a computer is a very dumb machine that consists of *input, memory, central processor, operating system,* and *output.* (See page 216.)

Computers are very good for number crunching and for manipulating data. There's nothing better for repetitive clerical tasks. They are no substitute for creativity or judgment. They offer no insights, take no risks, and contribute no dreams.

Hint for the computer user: When relying on computer data to make decisions, always remember the programmer's axiom: garbage in, garbage out.

What's Just Over the Horizon for Computers

There's a race going on more important than any Olympic contest. It is the mad dash to be the first to produce a computer with "teraflops" speed. For those of you with a vague hunch that teraflops might somehow be related

INTERRELATIONSHIP OF COMPUTER COMPONENTS

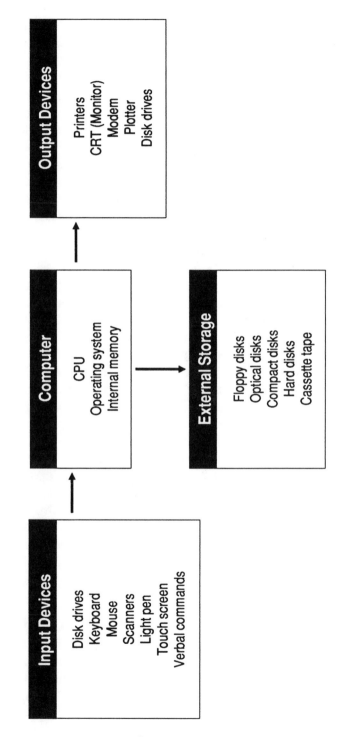

Input Devices

Disk drives
Keyboard
Mouse
Scanners
Light pen
Touch screen
Verbal commands

Computer

CPU
Operating system
Internal memory

External Storage

Floppy disks
Optical disks
Compact disks
Hard disks
Cassette tape

Output Devices

Printers
CRT (Monitor)
Modem
Plotter
Disk drives

to belly flops, the word means one *trillion* floating point calculations per second. The contestants to be the first to create this wonderment are, of course, the United States and Japan. Both governments are providing assistance to companies working on the project. At this point the contest is too close to call.

Besides the obvious use for calculating the U.S. national debt, who needs all that speed? Scientists do who study meteorology, molecular structure, and subatomic physics. In turn, these disciplines lead to a better understanding of climate, diseases and their cure, manmade materials, such as metal alloys, plastics, new kinds of ceramics, and much more. NASA could use a teraflops unit and so could the Department of Defense.

A teraflops computer would allow complex calculations that might require years on one of today's slowpoke supercomputers. (Fastest processing speed yet achieved is 13.9 billion floating-point operations per second at Caltech on a specially designed system called Delta.) This kind of computer would allow more detailed studies in product design, in climate control, in semiconductors (allowing even faster computers to be designed), in brain-cell activity, and so forth. All these studies, and a thousand others, could be conducted in countless variations. The sheer power of these computers would unlock many mysteries.

The key to attaining teraflops speed is through "parallel processing," that is, linking an endless number of ordinary computers together in a kind of assembly line and giving each one a portion of a task to perform simultaneously. The Delta unit at Caltech used parallel processing to achieve its record-breaking run.

The problem facing the developers is the expense. One machine would cost well over $100 million. Today's market doesn't seem to be able to support that price. When the Univac was first developed, however, the potential total world market was forecast at ten to twelve machines. So the race is on to be first with the teraflops. Its arrival will unlock a new era of science. The benefits will filter down to the computer hacker because the knowledge gained to build computers with teraflops speed will be used to design PCs equal to today's mainframes.

Fourteen Buzzwords That Will Make You Sound Like a Computer Expert

The computer industry is a buzzword-rich environment. We couldn't narrow the selection to a mere ten words. Thousands of examples could have been selected, many a good deal more exotic than the few we've chosen.

However, these are a representative sample. If you know what these words mean, most computer people will grant that you have at least a nodding acquaintance with the subject.

Flash Memories. A new kind of memory chip based on "flash" technology. They can erase and store information much faster than current methods of long-term information storage. By the year 2000, the market for flash memories is expected to exceed $10 billion annually.

Semiconductor. The core technology behind the computer revolution. This is a silicon chip etched with electronic circuits. A typical 6-inch wafer yields about 5 million transistors. By the year 2000, industry experts are predicting chips with a potential capacity of 3.5 billion transistors.

RISC. An acronym that stands for *Reduced Instruction Set Comput-*ing. This is a process for simplifying the basic commands built into microprocessors. The simpler the command structure, the faster the computer can run. The battle is on among powerful competitors to build the fastest and simplest-to-use RISC chip.

Fuzzy Logic. This is an attempt to make computers reason more as humans do. Computers are precise, but if they don't have all the data, they're lost. People are prepared to make decisions even when they don't have all the information because they make judgments based on approximations. Fuzzy logic is the attempt to program computers to approximate.

LAN. This is an acronym that stands for *Local Area Network.* A local area network is a communication system that ties a group of computers together so they can share information and data.

DOS. This is an acronym that stands for *Disk Operating System.* Remember that all computers must have an operating system that feeds the instructions to the various components? DOS is the system used by IBM computers and all IBM clones. The advantage of standard operating systems is that software can be written and used by a whole class of computers.

Megabyte. "Mega" always stands for one million of something. In the case of megabyte, it means one million bytes of information. That seems like a lot, but as computer users become more sophisticated their appetites for faster speeds and larger memories are like a woman's appetite for closet space: No amount is ever enough. A megabyte doesn't excite anyone any more. A *gigabyte,* which is one thousand megabytes, now that's another story.

Desktop Publishing. This refers to a computer's ability to combine text and graphics on a single page. It was made possible by the introduction of laser printers and is very practical for applications such as newsletters. Desktop publishing cuts down, and sometimes even eliminates, costs associated with typesetting.

Laser Printer. A laser printer operates something like a photo copier in that it transfers images from a drum to paper. It is faster and more versatile than daisy-wheel or dot matrix printers. The image quality is excellent. Laser printers are the popular choice for desktop publishing and graphics applications. *Postscript* laser printers allow the user to select a variety of font styles and can almost be considered limited printing presses.

Mouse. A mouse is an on-screen pointer that makes it easier to give commands to a computer. Instead of typing in a command via a keyboard, the computer user moves the pointer to a picture (icon) representing that command.

Hard Drive. A hard drive is an external memory attached to a computer that has more capacity than the memories available from floppy disks. Hard drives for PCs come with capacities exceeding 120 megabytes.

Nanosecond. No, it's not baby talk; the word means one billionth of a second. As processing times become faster and faster, they are often quoted in nanoseconds.

Worm. This stands for *Write Once Read Many*, and the acronym refers to a special kind of external memory. These are extra-large-capacity memories that can hold much data but are difficult to change. Vast amounts of static information, such as an entire set of encyclopedia, can be contained on WORM memories and retrieved by the computer user whenever needed.

Megahertz. We remember that "mega" stands for one million, right? So megahertz must mean one million hertz. Still not enlightened? Hertz, when it isn't a car rental company, is an international unit of frequency, equal to one cycle per second. A megahertz is one million cycles. The word is used when defining the operating speed of computers. Right now, anything above 25 megahertz is considered moderately fast for a personal computer.

How Facsimile Machines Have Destroyed the Concept of a Paperless Society

Remember the self-proclaimed "futurists" of the early Eighties who talked about the "paperless society"? In this Utopia, which was supposed to be just over the horizon, hard copies of any kind of communication were going to become quaint antiques. Woe to the filing-cabinet manufacturers, because all information would be stored electronically. Not another tree would be cut down in this future because there would be no need for any written form of anything: *The computers would do all the work and keep all the records.*

A funny thing happened on the way to that future. Along came these devices called facsimile machines. Unlike computers, any idiot can operate one. What they do is to send a representation of a document (a facsimile) over ordinary phone lines. Bring one into the office, plug it into the phone, feed in that important memo, dial a number, press a button, and a few seconds later, presto, the home-office facsimile machine halfway across the country has received your thoughts, in writing, about that important contract amendment. The process is fast, easy, and painless.

Businesses developed an appetite for fax machines in the mid-1980s, when the price on the product dropped enough to make them economical for just about any office. In 1990 about one million fax machines were sold. By mid-decade, the populations of fax machines is expected to be about ten million. They're used in offices and homes everywhere. They've created a blizzard of paper just at the time when the experts said paper would disappear.

What made people fall in love with fax machines? *They satisfy the need to know right now.* Want the data? Here comes a fax! (A sociologist might observe that they pander to this generation's desire for instant gratification.) The futurists who predicted the paperless society ignored the human preference for hard evidence of what has transpired. Instead of peering at images on computer screens, people prefer holding actual copies of important documents in their hot little hands. They feel more comfortable putting these copies in filing cabinets for safe keeping, rather than relying on the fidelity of an electronic charge deposited on what looks suspiciously like a phonograph record.

When a document is placed into a facsimile machine a scanner "looks" at the page for degrees of darkness. The scanner is minutely examining each square inch of the page recording black or white or shades of gray. The scanner now has stored an electronic representation of that page.

Next, that electronic page representation is "packed" tightly so it won't take too long to send over a telephone line.

The electronic packed page is in digital form, but telephone equipment sends analog signals. (Analog signals can be pictured as sent from point to point in a string or rope.) The electronic digital page must be converted to analog form so it can be sent over the phone line. That conversion is handled by a box inside the fax machine called a *modem.*

Next, the telephone number for the receiving fax machine is dialed. The two fax machines "shake hands." If one machine recognizes the other's handshake, the electronic page is then sent.

On the receiving end the reverse of the transmission process happens. First, the signal is reconverted from analog to digital form. The electronic page that was sent is then "unpacked," and a representation of it is printed in its original form.

HOW FAX WORKS

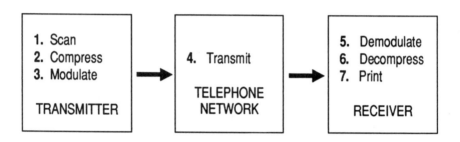

Facsimile transmission isn't a new concept. The technology has been a worm in the tequila bottle for about one hundred and fifty years. The old wire photos used by newspapers and police departments were a kind of facsimile transmission. The first photograph was transmitted via fax more than eighty-five years ago.

The equipment is becoming more sophisticated. Plain paper fax, machines that don't require special thermal paper to print images, have become much less expensive. One machine at a central location can send messages to other fax units all over the world.

The use of these machines will continue to grow because they save time and money. There's no doubt that their proliferation will impact the overnight mail-delivery industry. (Remember what we said earlier about established industries facing challenges from completely new directions?)

Transmit These Eleven Buzzwords to Sound Like a Fax Expert

Broadcasting This is the ability to send fax transmissions to multiple locations. It's very handy if the home office wishes to communicate the same message to various branch locations.

Gray Scale. The higher the gray-scale level (shades of gray), the more detailed the photograph will be. Sixteen-level gray scale is good, thirty-two is better, sixty-four is overkill. (64 shades of gray are more than the human eye can discern.)

TAD Interface. Allows connection of a telephone answering machine to a facsimile unit, meaning the phone line can be shared. Very handy in a home office.

Baud Rate. Refers to the number of bits passed along the transmission network per second. The faster the baud rate (9,600 bits per second is the most common) the faster your message gets sent and the less phone costs will be incurred. (Providing the fax machine at the other end can "catch" the incoming message at the same speed at which it is sent.) Transmission speeds are increasing with each new model introduced.

Polling. The ability for a remote fax to request transmission from another unit. Very handy when the home office wishes to get reports from the branches. They can be sent in off-hours when phone costs are less.

Modem. This handy product, also used by computers when they communicate with one another over long distances, converts digital signals into analog signals so they can be transmitted over a phone line. At the other end another modem reconverts them.

CCITT. This is a United Nations group, the *C*onsultive *C*ommittee on *I*nternational *T*elephone and *T*elephone, that works on international standards for fax machines. It would be impossible to communicate with fax machines in other countries without these international standards.

Password Check. A security code that prevents the reception of unwanted documents. Very important today because "junk fax" has become very popular. (Most junk fax is advertising sent directly into the heart of offices via facsimile transmission. It's an alternate to direct mail and a challenge to that industry from a new direction.)

Pixel. The "picture element," or degree of blackness on a page. If the picture element is only black or white it is called a *pel*. On a standard $8\frac{1}{2} \times 11$ sheet of paper a fax machine will scan 3.7 million pels.

Confidential Mailbox. Allows the user to receive confidential fax messages directly into memory. The recipient gets a hard copy by using a code number. Very important if you don't want everyone in the office reading a classified document.

Error Correction Mode. An internal mechanism that monitors the reception of fax messages for errors. If there is one, that portion of the message is transmitted again.

How Personal Computers and Communication Devices Are Changing the Concept of a Centralized Work Force

The factory, a popular idea since the nineteenth century, is a place where people come to make something. It is a central location where equipment, power, raw materials, and labor can be brought together under the watchful eye of management.

The "paperwork factories" of most companies, that is, the company departments that perform administrative tasks, are also centralized for many of the same reasons. The office equipment can be placed in one location to be shared by all, workers can be closely supervised, and communication can be personal.

Personal computers, facsimile machines, and most of all, improved communications, are causing some companies to rethink the idea that all office workers had to be brought together just because that's the way things had always been done.

The office staff doesn't work on a production line as do factory workers. They don't really need to be standing in a certain place to receive work, make a contribution, and pass it along to the next point. Many companies have discovered that office tasks can be done anywhere and the results communicated to a central point. Many companies have discovered that office tasks can be done anywhere and the results communicated to a central point. What workers did in cubbyhole offices separated by movable partitions, they can do out of a spare bedroom. So why not try to save valuable office space? The answer to that question led to the birth of telecommuting. It is an idea whose time has come.

"In and out" boxes are being replaced by electronic messages that can be sent to a PC sitting on a desk at the worker's home just as easily as it can be sent to that same PC sitting on a desk in the office. The at-home worker with a computer and a fax machine, and perhaps a personal copier, doesn't need the availability of other office equipment. (Want to tap a growing market? More than $29 billion worth of office equipment was purchased for home-office use last year.) The telecommuter can be in constant communication with management and peers. Working at home saves commuting time. Have you noticed that rush-hour traffic on the highway is slightly lighter these days? Desk space is saved at the central facility. There's also an implied freedom in working at home because supervision isn't sitting on the employee's shoulder.

All these reasons, and others, are why there's such rapid growth of workers using their homes with the blessings of management. There are now more than 5.5 million corporate employees working out of their homes. In some cases the "home" is hundreds of miles from the central office.

The disadvantage, of course, is that the home worker has less supervision. The traditional management suspicion is that the absence of the cat encourages the mice to frolic. Who is to know if the worker decides to turn on the TV and watch the ball game or a soap opera in mid-afternoon? That's why the "dispensation" to work at home has largely been granted only to planners, designers, certain specialists, and engineers, trusted individuals whose work ethic is unquestioned, and to sales people who aren't supposed to be in the office anyway.

There are other negatives. For those who enjoy the social contact in an office, telecommuting doesn't work. Camaraderie and office romance are definite casualties. If people don't get together, they don't develop a team spirit. If men and women don't get together, they don't get together.

However, the trend toward corporations allowing employees to work out of their homes is growing. The number of home-based corporate employees is expected to double by 1995. It will continue to increase as company management becomes satisfied that work output and quality don't suffer.

It is unlikely that the corporation of the year 2000 will contain the stadium-sized offices, washed in the glare of fluorescent light, with row upon row of steel desks lined up like so many tanks on a battle line, with a worker hunched behind every desk. That vision of plunking hundreds of office workers down in one place and sticking glue to their seats has rightly been dumped in the dustbin. (One by-product of the development of the at-home corporate worker is that it will be a long, long time before the current glut of office space disappears. Commercial real estate will not recover anytime soon. The space just won't be needed. Another result it that the prediction of glutted freeways around every major metropolitan area may not come to pass. These are still additional reinforcements of the lesson of the Nineties: All industries face challenges they didn't realize existed.)

Interactive Television: The Couch Potato Strikes Back

Ever want to swear at your television set? Within the next year or so the opportunity will present itself. A company called TV Answer is using advanced cellular radio technology and satellite communications to develop an interactive television network. The system will allow viewers to "talk back" to their television sets. They will use a special device connected to their sets to shop, bank, order merchandise or food, respond to surveys, participate in educational courses, and take advantage of a host of other services.

A special computer, built by Hewlett Packard, will be hooked to subscribers' TV sets. The unit will be about the size of a video recorder. The television set will ask a series of questions or give the viewer a number of choices. The viewer will punch in a response in the same manner as another program is now selected. This response will be recorded in a central location.

American business is excited about the concept of interactive television because it gives them a crack at people inside their own homes. Companies that conduct surveys see a time when they can obtain instant answers on *burning* issues. Ten seconds after consumers registered a preference for product A over product B, the unfortunate loser could be headed for the products' graveyard. (Not unlike the elephants' graveyard in that no one knows exactly where it is.)

Marketers could use the system to determine if special promotions were working. Political pollsters could survey the attitude of the great unwashed on a particular issue or candidate. In fact, there's no reason why actual voting for political elections couldn't be done via interactive television. Of course, there's a danger of government policy conducted on the basis of popular opinion. (Press A if in favor of going to war in the Middle East, B if in favor of air strikes only, C if in favor of sanctions, and D if in favor of continuing negotiations.)

The initial services are intended for mass markets only. Local franchises, authorized by TV Answer, will operate in specific geographic areas. They will relay the signals from the "black boxes" connected to TV sets to a national data center that will be connected to the broadcasting TV programs. The appeal is immediacy, know what's hot and what's not.

However, there's no reason why this system couldn't be refined to provide real one-on-one interaction via a television screen. That means a student could interact with a teacher, a doctor with a patient, a salesperson with a prospect. The campus for the college of the year 2000, or the doctor's examination room, may just be an overstuffed sofa.

Why Every Large American Corporation Will Find Itself in the Education Business

High school dropout rates in our major cities now average 25 percent. No more than 5 percent of our high school seniors can do college-level work. Between 20 to 30 percent of all U.S. workers lack the skills required to handle their *current* jobs. A goodly portion of the work force doesn't have the reading skills necessary to decipher an average instruction manual. In tests conducted in the mid-1980s among thirteen nations, U.S. high school seniors finished at or near the bottom in subjects such as biology, chemistry, and physics.

One of the advantages American corporations enjoyed over much of the rest of the world for most of this current century was the availability of a skilled work force. Our educational system at the high school level provided a steady stream of entry-level workers who could follow verbal and written instructions, do basic arithmetic, and operate simple equipment. They were moldable as their employers chose to mold them. Those students coming out of college had some exposure to logic and language and independent work. Those coming out of technical schools had a fair knowledge of a technical discipline. The brightest were quickly snatched up by business for executive-training programs. (They still are, when bright ones can be found.)

Today, at a time of high unemployment, the single biggest problem facing business is finding qualified workers. There are plenty of available bodies, but they are bodies unqualified for much of anything. Our educational system has failed American youth, and one of the big losers, aside from the kids themselves, is American business. The educational system must take the rap because the kids today are just as teachable as those of thirty or forty years ago.

The decline in American educational standards is coming at a time when the rest of the world is upgrading theirs. By the year 2000, worldwide high school enrollment will approach 450 million students. Another 115 million will be in college. The graduates from these programs may actually know something, such as being able to read and cipher, compared with the average U.S. high school senior whose diploma merely testifies to four years of reasonable attendance.

American industry is faced with the job of doing what the educational system failed to do. The alternative, importing talent in a time of high national unemployment, has been happening for some time in the technical disciplines. Importing talent cannot be expanded on a large scale to other corporate levels without weakening our already threatened middle class.

American companies now spend between $30 and $44 billion a year on training. About two thirds of this goes to professional-management training. Executive development alone accounts for 12 billion, with slightly more than 3 billion going for MBA development. It's clear from these figures that businesses are investing their "human resources" training dollars at the top end of the corporate ladder. (One of the oddities about this emphasis on training at the top rung is that professionals, more than any other class, avoid learning. The "expert" is resistant to change, particularly change that may result in less control.)

When training is provided for the "lower ranks" it is usually job specific, that is tied to a particular task or to the introduction of a new piece of equipment.

This strategy of training the people at the top worked fine as long as there was an adequate supply of workers who could handle the tasks that needed to be done at the bottom to keep the company humming.

The sad truth is that most U.S. companies just don't have their educational priorities straight. What is needed by industry is a better prepared entry level work force. It's obvious that the educational system in this country isn't filling that need. Radical change in the system is not likely because public education policy is the food and drink of demagogues.

Companies today spend only about $1 billion yearly on remedial education. (That means the basics of readin', writin' and 'rithmetic.) Twenty times that amount is needed *as a start* if we plan to be competitive with the rest of the world in the next century.

Fusion, Superconductivity, and Optical Fiber Super Highways: Are These Controversial Topics for Real? What It Means for American Business If They Are

Nuclear Fusion. What are we going to do when we run out of oil, coal, and natural gas? Go back to wood-burning ovens and stoves? Our energy will have to come from somewhere, but where? Nuclear fission, touted as the answer twenty years ago, creates radioactive waste that won't go away for hundreds of years. We simply don't know what to do with aging nuclear plants as they are decommissioned. They're too big and much too hot to put into plastic baggies and leave at the curb for garbage pickup.

For those who believe solar energy is the wave of the future, photovoltaics, the direct conversion of sunlight into energy, has a long way to go. The idea that solar energy could be "farmed" in millions of family plots, like so many vegetable gardens, is simplistic. Meanwhile, the past few centuries have seen us gobble up most of the solar energy patiently stored on this planet over the last fifty billion years in the form of fossil fuels.

Nuclear fusion appears to represent the best bet as the energy source of the future. For those who slept through high school physics, fission, the method nuclear plants use now, creates energy through the splitting of atoms. Fusion creates energy through the merging of atoms.

Fusion is the reaction that takes place on the sun hundreds of times a second. It's what makes our sun this planetary system's fireplace. It's fair to say that fusion is the energy process responsible for life on earth.

What makes fusion an attractive energy source is that this process promises an endless supply of energy, but it is also safe. There is no possibility of a meltdown because the process shuts down if something goes wrong. There is also much less radioactivity and that of a much shorter duration. It will not create global warming, so fusion appears to be an environmentalist's dream.

So how far away are we from this dream? Experimental reactors have created small bursts of energy through fusion, but more energy is consumed in the process than energy is released.

A few years ago there was a great deal of excitement when scientists in Utah claimed "cold fusion" through chemical reaction. Scientists who have repeated the experiments feel something is happening that is difficult to explain, but they're not sure it's fusion.

Fusion as a practical method for creating energy will come during the next century, but not near the turn of the century. That means industry must struggle along with fossil fuels and conservation measures for a long time.

Superconductivity. The more technology is introduced into a complex world, the more important it becomes to deliver energy to the four corners of the earth. As fossil fuels are depleted and man-made methods, such as nuclear fission and fusion, are used to generate energy, an efficient delivery system becomes vital.

Energy, in the form of electricity, can be moved from point to point over lines containing conductors, which are metals such as copper. Some of the energy never makes it from point A to point B because, even in the best of conductors, the material "resists" its passage.

Scientists have know for some time that cooling the conductive material dramatically to minus 452 degrees Fahrenheit makes the resistance disappear. That's because in ordinary electrical current electrons flow one by one. At very frigid temperatures electrons travel in pairs. They bowl the opposition right over. The problem with applying this knowledge is that maintaining such freezing temperatures uses as much energy as is saved by eliminating resistance.

In the past few years scientists have discovered certain ceramic materials that permit superconductivity at much higher temperatures. There's been success at minus 54 degrees, which by superconductivity standards, is almost Palm Springs weather. The cryogenic systems needed to sustain these temperatures is less rigid, which makes superconductivity more practical.

What superconductivity will mean to the business world is:

1. *Cheaper power plants.* It won't cost so much to build them any more.

2. *The ability to deliver power to remote locations without losing any in transition.*

3. *Cheaper power.* There will no longer be a delivery charge in the form of energy lost during transit.

4. *More powerful computers.* Electronic circuits can perform without the hindrance of resistance.

5. *Development of other technologies, such as magnetics.*

6. *Faster communications in the form of optical fiber-optics.*

Optical Fiber-Optic Communication. Dig under any city's streets and you'll find telephone cables thick as Arnold Schwarzenegger's thighs. Slice through one of these cables and you'll discover hundreds of individual shielded copper wires, each capable of carrying electronic pulses. The wires are put together in a bundle called a coaxial cable. The signals these lines carry need amplification every few miles to compensate for losses through resistance.

Coaxial cable is the roadway used by the communication systems of today. It is a slow two-lane highway marred by potholes and detours and speed traps at a time when our information-based society needs a super-highway.

The concrete for that superhighway is being poured. A new communication network based on lasers and carried by hair-thin glass fibers is in the works.

What lasers can do is to send a beam of light without distortion. What optical fibers can do is to carry enormous amounts of data over long distances. Each thin glass fiber in a fiber-optics network can carry thousands of signals at different wavelengths. These glass fibers have a much higher payload than does the copper filaments used today, and they operate at close to the speed of light. They also offer other advantages, such as being free of interference and static.

Scientists are using these recent developments to create an information freight/express train. The train is a freight because of the amount of information it can carry. It's an express because of the speed at which the information can be delivered.

The result will be an information infrastructure that will make all kinds of data available to every home and office in the country. There's an old adage to the effect that "knowledge is power." By the year 2000, knowledge will be available to almost everyone who wants data and is willing to pay for them.

Why Biotechnology Is No Cure for What Ails You

One of the great moments in motion-picture history is when Doctor Frankenstein shouts, "It's alive!" as his monster stirs for the first time. Later, when the angry peasants discover the monster lacks the social graces they burn down the good doctor's castle. That's the way many investors feel who have been stung by putting money into biotech. They view it as a monster with a voracious appetite for more and more capital.

Biotech permits the transfer of genes, those factors that control the synthesis of all protein, from one living organism to another. A popular name for the process is "gene slicing." The early biotech companies of the mid-Eighties promised much, raised tremendous amounts of capital, and went broke faster than bacteria multiplying on a laboratory culture.

Despite the early inability to make profits, biotech companies are still a magnet for money. Today, about half of all U.S. drug companies' research funds go into biotech projects.

Biotech promises to create wonderful new drugs that can cure anything from acne to AIDS. They are the medicine men of the twentieth century hawking the elixir of life in a throwaway bottle. Even a new super aspirin that prevents blood clots is under development. There have been a number of successes. Drugs developed through biotechnology are already being used to treat cancer, anemia, heart disease, and many other ailments.

Biotech scientists can change the structure of plants and animals to produce vegetables with longer shelf lives, fruits that are sweeter, pigs with less fat. (I'm waiting for genetically created spareribs with a tangy barbecue sauce.)

The problem has not been in new discoveries—there have been many—but in actually bringing products to market. There are problems with the U.S. Department of Agriculture and the Environmental Protection Agency. Both government agencies insist on rigid testing before allowing a product into the market. The customer for these brand new drugs, the health-care industry, isn't all that enthusiastic about the costs. The result is that biotech companies just don't produce enough revenue to support their research. That's why they look for new sources of capital as eagerly as they seek scientific discoveries.

The reason more funds keep pouring into biotech companies is because they seem on the threshold of incredible advances. Who wouldn't want to fund a company that promised a cure for cystic fibrosis or Alzheimer's disease?

The promise of biotech is a world without disease, a world that extends the lifespan, a world of plenty because of "engineered" plants and animals to feed us. The reality is an industry that keeps demanding more money to fund development and doesn't deliver any profits. The companies have developed no method for splicing away the torrents of red ink.

Still, it's much too early to count out this industry. It offers a glimpse of sky so blue, so dazzling, the critical eye is absolutely blinded.

❖ 13 ❖

MISCELLANEOUS KNOWLEDGE MANAGERS MUST HAVE AT THEIR FINGERTIPS

This chapter is a hodgepodge of information and facts that will help the beginning or mid-level manager carry on an intelligent business conversation in the corporate cafeteria, in the elevator on the way up to the office, or even in the executive dining room.

Knowing this stuff will not startle your peers or managers with your perspicacity, but it may help persuade them that you understand how business works. That is the first step toward gaining their respect. The chapter may also help compensate for any gaps in your business education.

Why Many Companies Incorporate in Delaware

Almost half of the *Fortune* 1000 companies are incorporated in Delaware. They didn't choose to register in the Diamond State because of the balmy climate (which it doesn't have) or the seafood at the shore. So what is the reason? People and companies tend to go to places where they feel welcome and wanted. Delaware is a very friendly place to be if you happen to be a corporation.

Let's begin with an explanation of incorporation. A corporation is an entity, an artificial creation that exists independently of its individual owners (the stockholders). It's a handy invention in several ways. First, though a corporation is obviously a group of individuals, it can conduct business as an entity. That means it can make and sell products, own property, enter into contracts, and so forth.

The owners' liability is limited only to the amount of money they have invested. Limited liability is another all-time great idea. It means an investor's risk is absolutely limited to the amount he or she has chosen.

Unlike a partnership, the corporation survives if one of the shareholders pulls out, sells his or her shares, or even dies. In a way, that makes it perpetual. (A corporation can apply for a charter limited to a certain time frame, but few do.) The corporation can continue to function just as long as it meets the needs of its stockholders and customers.

Registering a corporation in a state is fairly easy. All that is necessary is to present the articles of incorporation to the Secretary of State or the Department of Corporations and pay the relevant fees. The articles need not give away much information. All that's required is the following:

1. *The name of the company.*

2. *The kind of enterprise planned.*

3. *The number of shares.*

4. *The voting rights of shareholders.*

5. *The amount of money in the kitty at the start.*

6. *The identity of the registering agent.*

7. *The names of the first board of directors.*

(The CIA could function with that amount of limited disclosure.)

Registering in a state has nothing to do with geographic desirability. Just because a corporation is registered in a state doesn't mean its corporate headquarters must be located there. That means companies tend to choose states that offer them the best deal. Most corporations registered in Delaware have their headquarters somewhere else.

States are eager to have corporations register within their borders because they are a source of revenue. New corporations pay organizational fees to the state where they register. Existing corporations pay an annual franchise fee based on the worth of their capital stock. For Delaware, these revenues are substantial. Other states eye them with envy, but many politicians are reluctant to be so friendly to big business.

The reason corporations prefer to register in Delaware is because the state imposes fewer restrictions on company operations than do many others. Delaware permits incorporation for almost any legitimate business purpose. Companies can conduct their business in any way they choose just as long as they behave in an ethical manner.

Low taxes are another big reason why corporations prefer Delaware. The annual franchise fees don't approach the amounts other states charge. In effect, Delaware is being very competitive in the registration business by offering corporations a low tax structure and few interfering regulations.

Still another reason companies like Delaware are the clearly defined corporate statutes that provide guidelines as to what the state considers permissible. These statutes tell the companies up front what behavior they can get away with and what action will result in a slap on the wrist. The statutes make it easy to predict the outcome of litigation, and litigation is a major expense for corporations these days.

In summary, Delaware offers cut-rate prices and a hands-off attitude to corporations. Their laws take some of the uncertainty out of doing business. In these uncertain times that's reason enough.

What a Leveraged Buy-Out Is

A leveraged buy-out is a triumph of ego over gray matter. It is a crazy skin game, and many suckers have been fleeced by it.

In a leveraged buy-out the buyer pledges the seller's assets as collateral for the loan needed to make the purchase. Essentially, that's what happens when an individual buys a house. Most of the money to pay off the seller comes from a financial institution, which takes actual title to the property and issues a mortgage that the buyer must pay off.

The loan value of corporate assets, however, are often inflated when predators are after a business kill. That means the predators often don't have to put up much of their own cash. The leveraged buy-out artist ropes in the suckers by promising to pay more for a company than others think it's worth. They're using the target company's exaggerated value to acquire the company, hoping their target can generate enough cash flow to pay off the debt service. The recent string of corporate bankruptcies has, in part, been created by leveraged buy-out deals that went sour.

Why would any company agree to sell under those conditions? In many cases the management of these companies had no choice. Their stockholders demanded that the deal be consummated. Management's responsibility then becomes to play hard to get until an even better deal is struck. That means a more onerous debt service that becomes impossible to meet.

Using the home analogy again, let's say an individual had a home valued at $100,000. The person had no intention of selling, but someone came along and offered her $200,000. She might start packing her bags and counting the money. Later, she learns that the buyer can't pay off the bigger mortgage, but so what? She has her money.

The seller in a leveraged buy-out gets paid, usually at an inflated rate, and walks away laughing. The sleazy investment houses who put the deal together pocket their millions and cast their greedy eyes on other opportunities.

The buyer, who has just acquired a company for very little risk, begins selling off pieces of the new acquisition to pay the debt service or begins making "improvements" by trimming costs. Out the window go all those projects with long lead times. Out the door go the executives and middle managers who contributed to making the company an attractive takeover target in the first place. The improvements are intended to make the bottom line look better so the stock will inch up enough to justify the acquisition.

It seems as if both buyer and seller are satisfied with the deal, so who loses? There's a long list of losers.

The lenders who put up the capital to finance the buy-out were the losers because they lent more than was prudent. They got stuck with junk bonds that lost much of their face value.

Employees of well-run companies were the losers because new management often resorted to desperate measures to meet their debt service. Many of the companies didn't survive.

The public were the losers because many of their favorite institutions were destroyed.

Our national economy was the loser when one by one the slick leverage artists began to default on the oversized loans taking the lending institutions with them, sliding into a sinkhole that collapsed everything around it. It's unfair to say that leveraged buy-outs are alone responsible for the S & L mess, but they certainly contributed.

Lenders with hundreds of millions in capital to invest aren't stupid, so what made them give away their funds to these ill-starred ventures? Greed mostly. The interest rates offered for these loans were much higher than those that could be obtained in legitimate deals. The bottom lines for these lending institutions looked absolutely sensational—for a time.

Now, some of the heads of prominent lending institutions find themselves explaining their actions to congressional committees. Others have exchanged their pinstripes for prison stripes. Their disgrace is a lesson the financial community will remember for a long time—at least until the next boom, the next financial scheme that is too good to be true.

The Difference Between Markup and Margin and How to Calculate Each

It's surprising just how many competent business people don't understand the difference between margin and markup. This is a dangerous ignorance because the distinction is vital to anyone who is concerned about bottomline profit.

Margin is the *difference* between the cost and the selling price of the merchandise.

Markup is the amount *added* to the cost to arrive at the selling price.

Do these explanations appear as if exactly the same thing is being stated in two different ways? Perhaps a better way to explain the distinction between the two is to offer an example of how each is calculated.

Markup is calculated by multiplying the percentage of profit desired by the cost of the item. Here's an easy example based on a product that cost $200 and a desired profit of 20 percent. (Don't worry, the math won't be rigorous, and we won't complicate it by adding in various costs of doing business.)

Cost of product	$200.00
Plus markup of 20%	40.00
Price of product to customer	$240.00

Simple, neat, and easy! So why isn't markup a good enough system for all resale situations? The seller who wishes more profit need only factor in a higher markup percentage.

What if the product is not moving, however, and the seller wishes to close it out? She's willing to break even just to remove that dog from inventory. Does she mark it down 20 percent as the walkaway price? Here's what happens when she tries that approach.

Sale of product	$240.00
Less markdown of 20%	48.00
Discounted price	$192.00

The seller now actually loses money! (Because she's also marking down the profit margin built into the selling price.)

Markup becomes cumbersome and misleading when trying to calculate discounts for sales promotions and distress sales. That's why many businesses, particularly retail, prefer to work on margins.

Lets' repeat the first example using margin instead of mark-up. (The math is still painless.) Margin is calculated in a two-step process. First, subtract margin desired (20 percent) from one hundred—100 percent minus 20 percent equals 80 percent. Next divide the cost of the product by 80 percent.

$$.80 \overline{\smash{\big)}\ \begin{array}{c} \$250.00 \\ \$200.00 \end{array}}$$

A $250 selling price reflects a *margin* of 20 percent on a product cost of $200.

Assume the same disaster; the product is a dog that must be marked down by 20 percent for quick sale.

Sale price of product	$250.00
Less markdown of 20%	50.00
Discounted price	$200.00

The seller breaks even. Using margin to calculate profit and markdown to determine discounts makes it easier for sellers to know how deeply they can cut prices for a sales event or to get rid of a product that isn't performing.

What Price-Earning Ratio Means

The price-earnings ratio is the market price of a stock related to its net earnings after taxes. A company that earns $1 a share and is selling for $1 would have a 1 to 1 PE ratio. If a company with that kind of PE multiple were listed on a major exchange, you'd think it would be a good idea to mortgage the kids and buy all the shares you could get your hands on. There would, however, have to be something drastically wrong with a company selling for so low a multiple. The stock market is like anything else. If something appears to be too good to be true, it is.

One of the big puzzlements for beginning investors is why one company's stock will sell for ten times earnings while another, perhaps in the same industry, will command thirty times earnings. The important thing to remember is that PE ratios for publicly owned companies are not indicators of how well they are currently performing, but rather reflect Wall Street's opinion as to their future potential.

Companies with very high PE ratios of 40 to 1 and more are "high flyers," those that hold much promise because of technological developments or an attractive merchandising scheme or a perceived market edge. The key is *anticipated growth.* Wall Street is an eager purchaser of tomorrow. When trying to convince a customer to buy a stock, many brokers will offer predictions on the PE ratio *next year* based on anticipated earnings.

The problem with predicting growth is that the predictions don't always come true. The high flyers crash and burn when the anticipated results don't happen. A low PE multiple means The Street discounts that company's ability to grow. It doesn't mean that the company isn't well run or profitable. For example, utilities traditionally sell for low PE multiples. Yet, most are profitable, most have locked-in customers who can't go elsewhere for that particular service, and most pay their investors excellent dividends. The reason they're not valued higher is because they're subject to regulatory control and have limited opportunity for expansion.

PE ratios are important factors in buy-out situations. How much a company earns determines how long it will take the buyers to recoup their investment, which in turn helps determine the selling price.

During times of relative prosperity PE ratios tend to be higher than during times of recessions. During this recession, however, we're seeing the exception that proves the rule. The market and PE multiples have never been higher than right now. The reason is the lowering on interest rates made stocks more attractive, and there's a lot of money out there looking for a home.

One popular personal investment strategy is to invest for growth when young and invest for income when close to retirement. That's not a bad plan for anyone.

What Makes a "Hot" Stock Hot

Students of the stock market like to refer to a classic situation, a market in tulip bulbs in eighteenth-century Holland. Tulip bulbs became a medium of exchange, a commodity like wheat or corn or gold. The trading became frenzied. Brokers bid up some individual bulbs to what would be the equivalent of thousands of dollars today. Each day the bulbs would increase in value by up to 100 percent.

What prompted the traders to pay thousands of dollars for a single tulip bulb was not the perceived value of the flower the bulb would produce, but rather the belief that they could hold it for a few days, then sell it for even more to someone else. It's what Wall Street calls the "greater fool theory." When a stock is hot, no matter the price, there's always a greater fool out there willing to pay more.

The market for tulip bulbs eventually burst, and those brokers left with inventories were ruined. There weren't many tall buildings in eighteenth-century Holland, so I assume the bankrupt traders jumped into the canals. This leads to a basic investing precept: *Every market runs out of fools eventually,* so don't be the last fool in line.

The herd mentality, buying something because everyone else is buying it, is one of the biggest factors in a market for a hot stock. Most hot stocks, however, need additional fuel to sustain their heat. This fuel is "inside" information, often in the form of:

1. *Whispers of an important product development.*

2. *Rumors of a buy-out or takeover.*

3. *Hints about a possible stock split.*

4. *Noises that management may increase the dividend.*

5. *Indications that an important investor or group is about to take a big position in that stock.*

6. *Suspicion that the company is about to land an important order.*

Note that all of the above rumors were *indications* that something important was about to happen, not the actual event. While the whispers whirl through the corridors of Wall Street the stock will continue to rise. Once the announcement is made confirming the rumor, the stock will probably go down. That's because many traders rely on the old axiom, "Buy on the rumor, sell on the news." Remember always that traders on Wall Street buy tomorrow. Once today is here, they sell.

The one factor that can keep a stock hot for a protracted period of time is sustained growth. Any company that can maintain profitable growth will enjoy a steady increase in the price of its shares. If the growth is geometric it need not even be profitable.

Why You Should Buy Stock in Every Company You Work for, Even If It's Only a Single Share

The first thing to do after landing a job with a publicly traded company is to call a stockbroker and buy stock in the corporation. Buy a hundred shares if you can afford it—the broker's percentage of commission will be smaller—but buy at least one share.

There are several reasons why owning a small piece of the place where you work makes sense. The first is that it gives you a different perspective from the average employee. You are one of the investors, and your attitude will be slightly different, more proprietary, even though you may not realize that you are behaving differently.

The second reason is because shareholders automatically receive copies of the annual report, and perhaps quarterly earnings statements as well. These reports may break out sales and earnings by division, information that is often not available to employees at middle management levels and below. You'll receive notice of intended elections to the board of directors. If the company is in the midst of a major acquisition, or is engaged in significant litigation, the annual report will contain the details. A large write-down may be explained.

The report will also probably contain a brief address by the chief executive officer charting the company's direction for the next fiscal year. Surely all this information about your company is worth the cost of a single share of stock.

As a stockholder you are also entitled to attend the annual meeting. The refreshments are usually lousy, but if there is major opposition to the way the company is being run, you're likely to hear about it at the stockholders' meeting. Some of them get very lively. It's also a chance to observe the CEO in action, as most will act as company spokesperson during the stockholders' meeting.

Owning stock in the company just makes you better informed about things going on in the organization that may be far above your management level. Besides, it's a heck of an investment because now that you're on board, the value of those shares is bound to increase.

Why the Japanese Reputation for Long-Range Planning Is Overblown

Japanese senior managers enjoy the reputation for being better long-range planners than their American counterparts. That's just another stereotype that mars the chances for the two nations' business communities to ever fully understand one another. Japanese managers don't have crystal balls with fewer defects. They don't see farther into the future than anyone else. Their advantage lies elsewhere, in the methods the Japanese and Americans use to finance business.

American corporations are financed primarily by their investors who buy stock, while Japanese companies are financed largely through bank borrowing. The reason the difference is significant is because stockholders want the value of their shares to rise in the near term, while the bankers want the loans to be repaid and to establish customers who will grow larger and need to borrow more. That means the CEOs of Japanese and American companies face two very different constituents and different kinds of pressure.

Product market share and long-term growth are right at the top of the Japanese manager's agenda. Near-term performance and increasing the price of the stock at the next tick preoccupies the American senior manager.

If there's any doubt on where the U.S. investment community wants the emphasis, the compensation plans for American senior managers are often based on a bonus scheme tied to share value.

If you're a CEO for an American corporation with the potential for a seven-figure annual bonus by inching the stock up a few points, what is your focus likely to be? That's an easy question for most CEOs to answer. They worry about the bottom line for the next quarter and about making this fiscal period look a bit better than the last.

One way the Japanese drive competitors to their knees is through the relentless introduction of new products and models. While American and European manufacturers try to squeeze a certain lifespan out of a product to pay for its development cost, the Japanese amortize the development costs over much shorter periods. The result is they spit out new products at a dizzying pace, each new model a bit sexier than its predecessor. The competitor who sets his sights on a particular Japanese product is always aiming at a moving target.

The American manager knows all about market share and the profits that can be made once the competition has cried "Uncle!" The problem is the American manager doesn't have the luxury of waiting several years to reap the benefits of a long range plan.

It would seem from the preceding remarks that the Japanese corporate model is much better than the American. It does have advantages under certain conditions. These are:

1. *The home market is closed (it is) so that brand-new products can be nurtured in a noncompetitive environment.*

2. *The export markets are open (they are) so that product development and tooling costs can, in effect, be sent offshore.*

3. *The world economy is expanding (this is in doubt right now) so that corporate growth can be sustained.*

4. *Access to cheap money is maintained.* For a long time the cost of funds were much lower in Japan. Nevertheless, most Japanese companies are highly leveraged and must continue to grow to survive.

When these conditions no longer exist Japanese managers won't perform any better than their American counterparts do.

The Government Agencies That Directly Affect the Way Your Company Does Business

Before the West was tamed armed men on horseback enforced frontier justice at the point of a gun or the end of a rope. They called themselves "regulators" and acted as accuser, judge, jury, and executioner. The odd thing is their ilk are still riding the range. These days the gangs hole up in Washington, DC, identified with strange code letters such as the EEOC or OSHA. Like all vigilantes they sometimes hang the innocent along with the guilty, and like all vigilantes they really don't care. A hanging gets the point across marvelously.

No company can afford to ignore the role federal government regulatory agencies play in business today. They're behind each corporation's shoulder, examining and passing judgment on every business activity, from making the product to decisions on who can be hired and fired.

The following list includes nine of the most powerful federal agencies who regulate business. They are among the thousands swimming in the alphabet soup of agencies in the nation's capitol. Knowing who they are, where they're located, what their charter is supposed to be, and name of the person in charge is a small start in learning how to deal with them. Good luck. You'll need it.

Occupational Safety and Health Administration (OSHA)

200 Constitution Avenue   Gerard Scannell
Washington, DC 20210   (202) 523-9329

During the Spanish Inquisition no one accused of heresy was ever declared innocent. Even those who got off lightly were required to confess their guilt, do penance, and pay huge fines. OSHA, which enforces and sets policy for occupational safety and health standards, operates with much the same philosophy as did the Spanish monks. No company that voluntarily agrees to a safety inspection by OSHA officers ever escapes with a clean bill. There are *always* charges. The Senate is now considering new safety laws that, among other things, would give workers the right to protest any fines assessed by OSHA that the workers felt were too lenient. A safe work place is a vital concern to everyone, but the mood of Congress continues to be antibusiness. Legislation that gives OSHA more power, and business more paperwork, will see more jobs flee our shores.

Equal Employment Opportunity Commission (EEOC)

1801 L Street N.W.
Washington, DC 20507

Evan J. Kemp
(202) 663-4110

Find the problem with asking this question of a prospective employee: "Do you have any friends or relatives now working for the company?" The EEOC, which has the charter to end discrimination in the workplace, might find the interviewer's question inappropriate and perhaps discriminatory. The "wickedness" of the query lies in the fact that most companies now employ a preponderance of white, middle-class males. Asking the job candidate if he of she knows anyone now on the payroll suggests a bias toward the group that Washington appears so determined to stamp out. (The only hope for white, middle-class males is to be declared an endangered species.) Hiring practices, dismissal procedures, an equitable work environment, affirmative action by the federal government, these are all grist for the EEOC mill. It grinds exceedingly fine.

Securities and Exchange Commission (SEC)

450 5th St. N.W.
Washington, DC 20549

Richard Breeden
(202) 272-2650

Perhaps it's no accident that the former head of enforcement for the SEC was a wife beater who seemed to be a heck of a swell guy to co-workers. This agency seems to operate on an axis that is part suave charm, part brutish force. The SEC supervises public disclosure of financial information about companies whose securities are offered for sale. It enforces regulations to prevent fraud in securities markets, supervises the operation of the stock exchanges, regulates the activities of security dealers, participates in bankruptcy proceedings, investigates inside trading, and so forth. All these things are necessary to keep the market clean. Unfortunately, the big trading swindles seem to happen under its nose.

Consumer Product Safety Commission

5401 Westbard Avenue
Bethesda, MD 20816

Jacqueline Jones-Smith
(301) 504-0100

This agency establishes and enforces product safety standards. It recalls hazardous products. Sometimes it is overly zealous, but it serves as a needed watchdog.

Environmental Protection Agency (EPA)

401 M St. S.W.
Washington, DC 20460

William K. Reilly
(202) 382-4700

Will my wife's hairspray destroy the ozone layer and give everyone skin cancer? Will Minneapolis have a subtropical climate in a few years? These are minor questions compared to the big riddle: Is the EPA controlled by hysterics? The EPA administers federal environmental policy. It enforces standards for air, water, toxic substances, pesticides, hazardous solid waste, radiation, and so forth. It investigates violations and has the power to impose fines. It's unfair to say that the EPA is the captive of such outfits as the Sierra Club and Greenpeace, but it isn't all that unfair.

Interstate Commerce Commission (ICC)

12th St. & Constitution Ave.
Washington, DC 20423

Edward J. Philbin
(202) 275-7582

If your product is shipped from state to state via surface transportation or inland waterways, the ICC is involved in your business. It regulates carrier licensing, rates, service standards, and the like. It's supposed to handle complaints but, as anyone who's had a problem with a long-distance moving company and tried to get some action from the ICC knows, that's a joke.

National Labor Relations Board (NLRB)

1717 Pennsylvania Ave. N.W.
Washington, DC 20570

John Trusdale
(202) 254-9056

This agency's influence has waned along with the clout that labor unions once had in our nation's capital. The NLRB prevents and remedies unfair labor practices. It supervises union elections and right-to-work laws.

Federal Trade Commission (FTC)

6th Street & Pennsylvania Ave. N.W.   Janet D. Steiger
Washington, DC 20580   (202) 326-2100

The FTC appears to be dedicated to ensuring that U.S. corporations don't achieve the size and financial muscle necessary to compete in world markets against the giant Japanese trading companies. It loves its work. Its formal charter is to promote policies designed to maintain competition, break up monopolies, and police unfair restraint of trade and deceptive practices. The FTC also enforces the Truth in Lending and the Fair Credit Reporting acts.

Internal Revenue Service (IRS)

1111 Constitution Avenue N.W.   Fred Goldberg
Washington, DC 20204   (202) 566-4115

The only thing that separates IRS agents from collectors for juice racketeers is that the IRS agents don't carry baseball bats in the trunks of their cars. Your kneecaps may survive an encounter with an IRS agent, but not much else will. The IRS administers and *enforces* internal revenue laws. It enforces them in a cavalier fashion that borders on the illegal and sometimes ignores due process. The agency has a vested interest in making the tax laws as complicated as possible. That in turn fuels another industry, tax lawyers and accountants, who couldn't otherwise find useful work. To strike terror into the hearts of these bureaucrats whisper the dreaded phrase, *"Flat tax!"*

Good Guy Agencies

So we won't be accused of antigovernment bias, here's a listing of just a few of the many government agencies that perform valuable services for the business community.

General Services Administration (GSA)

18th & F Streets N.W.   Richard Austin
Washington, DC 20549   (202) 708-5082

This is the agency where the goodies come from. The GSA develops and implements federal government acquisition procedures. It reviews contracts and sets procurement policy. In other words, it buys stuff. The U.S.

government is the biggest customer for goods and services in the world, and the GSA is the gateway into that market.

Small Business Administration

409 3rd St. S.W.   Patricia Saik
Washington, DC 20416   (202) 205-6605

This agency offers invaluable services to the small business. It sometimes serves as loan guarantor for companies that couldn't otherwise obtain financing. The SBA also offers a host of advice and counseling and management assistance services. One of its other activities is to supply loans to flood, and other catastrophe, victims.

Economic Development Agency (EDA)

Main Commerce Building Joyce Hampers
Washington, DC 20230   202-482-2000

The EDA administers assistance programs and technical aid to distressed areas. It awards public works, grants to public institutions, and assists local and state governments with economic-adjustment programs. What it tries to do is stimulate the economy of poorer sections of the country by pumping in federal funds for various public projects.

All the agencies on the list suffer from the same flaw: the bureaucratic mentality. That makes them difficult to deal with for anyone who hopes in vain for straightforward answers to direct questions. That doesn't mean they can't be valuable if you can develop the patience to deal with them.

Ten Resources to Get Any Information You Wish

Someone once said, "The real benefit of a college education is that it teaches you where to go to get the information you need." The following reference books will cut down the search time for most business projects.

Standard & Poor's Register of Corporations, Directors and Executives

If you're looking for the name of a corporation, where it is headquartered, and the identity of the honchos who run it, this reference work will give you the information quickly. The *S & P Register* is almost a business bible.

The Congressional Quarterly

This reference work put out every day lists all government agencies, their locations, phone numbers, and who runs them. Most of these agencies put out reams of material available to responsible parties, so the *Congressional Quarterly* is a tap into an information cornucopia.

Moody's Handbook of Common Stocks

This work gives the background, statistics, dividend yield, recent developments, and prospects for companies listed on major stock exchanges. Reading *Moody's Handbook* is a good way to get a thumbnail sketch of any company that strikes your fancy.

Thomas Register Lists

Want to know who makes sprockets? The *Thomas Register* will contain page after page of sprocket manufacturers. They list the manufacturers of just about everything. There's a good deal of advertising in the *Thomas Register* so reading it can be annoying.

Corporate Affiliations

Interested in finding out if an apparently small company is controlled by a conglomerate? Does your competitor have a big brother waiting in the wings waiting to take you on? *Corporate Affiliations* lists the subsidiaries of corporations. They tell the reader who actually owns and runs subsidiaries.

Brands and Their Companies

This reference work put out by Stetler is a list of brand names and the names of the companies who own the copyrights. This list is handy if there's a brand name not currently in use that you'd like to revive.

Exporters Encyclopedia

If you're planning on marketing overseas this reference work put out by Duns Marketing contains a goldmine of information relative to shipments for foreign markets. Don't leave port without it.

Who Owns Whom

I like this reference work by Dun & Bradstreet because of the cute name. The book offers details on foreign ownership of companies, including their subsidiaries. It's handy if your company is looking for foreign partners.

Rand McNally Banker's Directory

You can't borrow money if you don't know where the banks are. This book tells you, by region. It won't let you know if you're likely to get a loan.

Moody's Lists, Municipal & Government Manual

This book lists state, county, and local government agencies. If you are selling to the federal government, you can sell to local agencies as well.

Where can these reference works be found? A good library will have most of them. Incidentally, most libraries won't lend out reference material. You'll have to use the book right there in the library. If one is particularly useful, buy it.

If these books don't contain what you're looking for, ask the librarian. There's no better resource than a helpful librarian.

❖ 14 ❖

PREDICTING
THE FUTURE

Edmund Burke, an eighteenth-century British statesman, said, "You can't plan the future by the events of the past." Yet, that's exactly what all so-called futurists try to do. They forecast tomorrow based on an interpretation of yesterday. The problem with that convention is that it inevitably misses the sharp turns of history. Human society steams in a direction, gathering inertial speed until what lies ahead seems bound to be a repetition of the past with a few refinements. Then a bump in the road sends us caroming off on a new course. No one predicted the rapid breakup of the Soviet empire. No one is likely to predict the next sharp turn, when it will come, or where it will take us. With that caveat of fallibility, here are a few predictions for the next decade.

What the Aging of America Will Mean to Business in the Next Decade

A hundred years ago the average American died before age fifty. Today, the average life expectancy is approaching seventy-five years. New medical techniques, more exercise, better diets, and an increased awareness in healthy lifestyles keeps expanding our lifespan. Children born today should live into their eighties.

Despite a recent baby boom, American women are beginning their child bearing later in life, and they are having fewer children. The result is a gradual "middle-aged bulge" of our population. The attendance keeps creeping up at senior centers while declining at youth camps. Age spots are replacing beauty marks. We are a young country now only in our ideas.

A mature population strains the nation's social services. Medicare, Medicaid, and social security payments now eat up a full third of the federal budget. Within a few years these services will account for half of federal expenditures. Who will pay these costs? The young, of course, but there will be fewer of them. That means a bigger tax burden for those remaining in the work force, including a bigger burden on business.

A corollary development is that people are retiring earlier. They're cashing in their 401K plans and their IRAs. Calling it a career at age fifty-five and even earlier, they're accepting the severance packages offered by large corporations anxious to downsize. (It's after age forty the realization hits home that there's "only so much time left.") We're faced with a nation of retirees, puttering around golf courses in plaid trousers, putting in flower beds, gassing up the old RV, and driving halfway across the country to attend the big antique show.

Many retirees embrace second careers, doing the things they enjoy, which is what they should have done the first time around. The result is a flurry of home-based businesses, true cottage industries involved in everything under the sun.

What's it all mean for business? One thing that it means is that, despite the trend toward early retirement, the work force will be getting older. Mandatory retirement age is now seventy, meaning people can stay on longer if they choose. Antidiscrimination laws make it difficult to get rid of employees who are a bit long in the tooth. They'll be needed anyway, as fewer young entry-level people are available. The opportunities for advancement won't be there, however, because in the smaller-sized corporation that is today's model the demand for professionals weakens. That means job stagnation resulting in a vaguely dissatisfied, somewhat cynical work force putting in the hours for a paycheck. Senior management faces a real challenge in how to motivate this kind of work force.

Senior citizens are already a potent political force, and their "clout" will increase with their numbers. Look for the so-called peace dividend to be siphoned off into additional services for the elderly. The age of eligibility for maximum social security benefits is already slated to rise to sixty-seven in the next century, but payments into the fund to match the payouts mean high taxes are here to stay, regardless of any political promises to the contrary.

Inexpensive housing and low living costs become priorities for the early retirees. There is already a migration back to small towns and mid-sized cities, particularly in the mid-South, by this population segment. Communities who learn how to appeal to the retired will prosper. The planned "old folks" developments won't fare quite as well, however, unless their housing costs are rock bottom. The retired will be cautious in their expenditures. The aging of America also means increased need for health-care facilities.

The home-based businesses of retirees are markets for compact versions of traditional and new kinds of office machines. The discounters of this kind of merchandise, such as Office Club and Staples, will prosper.

The early retired also represent a source for contract labor. When companies downsize they frequently find that they have cut too deeply and must go outside the organization to get certain tasks done. Look for a proliferation of business cards with the word "consultant" printed on them. More retirees will be recruited to work part time at the entry-level tasks once assigned to very young employees.

This last is not pleasant to predict. Expect a growing resentment among the young for the elderly who are more numerous, who chew up the tax dollars, who set the political agenda, who may be absorbed by the past, who appear to have more leisure time, and who compete for a dwindling number of corporate positions. Jokes about the elderly will replace those about lawyers and Poles.

The Coming Comeuppance of Japan

The *shinkansen* is the Japanese bullet train that races across the countryside at speeds of more than 100 miles an hour. The Japanese economy has been a *shinkansen*, a bullet train without a braking system, rushing across the world, devouring markets as an energy source for even greater speed, reaching financial destinations in record time. It's been a wonderful, non-stop ride, but any train without brakes is headed for derailment.

Suggesting the demise of the Japanese economy at a time when it seems unstoppable requires an explanation. To understand why they will fail, it is necessary to know why they succeeded. Here are the ingredients that went into the Japanese success formula. (Stir well before using.)

1. *They purchased other nations' raw materials in exchange for Japanese finished products.*

2. *They provided government subsidies and protection for emerging industries.* In many cases their definition for an "emerging" industry was one that didn't dominate the world market.

3. *They constructed layer upon layer of import barriers to stifle outside competition.*

4. *Their banks kept the cost of corporate borrowing very low.* A high rate of savings among Japanese citizens kept the money supply ample and cheap.

5. *They kept their currency undervalued, reducing the cost of their export goods.*

6. *They indoctrinated a zealous work force into sacrificing their every waking hour for the good of the organization.*

7. *They were blessed with a xenophobic local customer base unwilling to buy anything foreign.*

8. *They maintained a centralized planning committee (MITI) that guides and coordinates industrial development.*

9. *They established an "old boy" distribution network that discriminated against outsiders.*

10. *They perfected an overall business philosophy that takes the longer view.*

11. *They conditioned the population to endure a low living standard while corporations thrived.*

12. *They spent very little for national defense, giving the government more money to pour into the private sector.*

13. *Their stock market made spectacular gains year after year.* Stocks with inflated values could be used by corporations for loan collateral.

The formula has been a world beater for years. The recession affects Japanese companies as it does everyone, but the formula continues to work. Recently, however, it has been contaminated by new ingredients that alter the mixture. These ingredients are:

1. *By the end of this year "EC 92," Western Europe's twelve-nation community, will have integrated most of its markets and econo-*

mies. There will be less room for Japanese products, which are already restricted in many European market segments. For example, their market share for automobiles is restricted to 11 percent of the total market.

The Europeans are now engaged in writing product and testing standards for just about everything. You can bet the farm that new European standards won't favor Japanese products. American products face a similar challenge. As the world's number-one super power, however, we have a bit more muscle to force concessions. Japanese imports to the twelve-nation EC will decline.

2. *Japan, Inc. will discover another customer, one anxious to buy anything that comes off a production line and holds together for more than an hour.* That eager customer is Eastern Europe. The problem will be getting paid by nations who are virtually bankrupt. Never willing to pass up an order, the Japanese banks, in concert with the government, will establish liberal credit policies for former Eastern Bloc nations. Their companies will continue to move product and hope for the best. This will be a mistake. Eastern Europe has disintegrated into a goulash of autonomous states, none of them with the ability to repay international loans. There will be extensions and concessions, but the loans will begin to default in the mid-Nineties.

3. *The Japanese attempt to grab a larger share of the American market to compensate for losses in Europe will be frustrated by a growing protectionism and a rising resentment of things Japanese by the American consumer.* Our trade negotiators will finally begin to get tough. By mid-decade Japan will be forced to really and truly open its markets to American and European products. This will further erode its competitive advantage.

4. *One of the things the Japanese learned with utter chagrin during the Gulf War was that they were totally reliant on American military might for free access to vital raw materials such as oil.* Expect them to finally acquiesce to American demands that they conduct their own defense.

When they arm, they're going to want to do it in a hurry. The Japanese expanded military budget will take up a larger portion of the GNP, leaving less for reinvestment. The cost of commercial financing will rise.

5. *Most Japanese trading companies are so highly leveraged they must continue to expand to survive.* The shrinking markets for products and the rising cost of financing will create a few bankruptcies and many mergers. As smaller companies are folded into larger ones, the "more efficient" organizations will require smaller work forces. Unemployment will become a factor in the Japanese economy.

6. *Japanese banks are overextended because of real-estate loans on property that has decreased in value.* (Sounds a lot like the S & L mess, doesn't it?) Their capital is heavily concentrated in corporate stocks. As stock prices drop, so does bank capital. That will limit their ability to make new loans. As this book is being written, Japanese banks have virtually stopped making loans to the United States through the purchase of government debt obligations.

7. *Every few weeks American newspapers and magazines carry stories about job-related stress in Japan.* Surely, with twelve- to fourteen-hour workdays their employees have been dropping at their posts for years. Why the publicity now? Could it be because the workers are finally beginning to resent the relentless pressure put upon them by their employers? The younger generation now coming into the work force just won't be willing to make the same sacrifices for the corporation. Productivity will be affected. (Despite the negative publicity, the American worker has always been more productive than his Japanese counterpart.)

8. *The Japanese have been coming to the United States in ever greater numbers as tourists and resident workers.* They've seen our superior standard of living first hand and carried the tale back home. The Japanese government and major corporations won't much longer be able to swindle the workers into working harder but receiving less. There is already a demand for improved living standards. That means less work, more leisure time, and lower prices on consumer goods, and that means inflationary pressure.

9. *The Japanese are reputed to be good managers, but they've never been forced to handle labor-force reductions.* After forty years of expansion they may have a difficult time learning how. The massive cutback of employees will destroy forever the idealized notion of the corporation as a surrogate parent.

10. *A few years ago there was a small panic when the Japanese began buying American real estate.* Now it seems that they were taken to the cleaners, overpaying on some properties by hundreds of millions of dollars. There will be defaults on the loans that financed these purchases.

All these factors, and others, suggest that the Japanese days as a supereconomic powerhouse are coming to an end. Don't worry about them; we won't be diverting CARE packages from Nigeria to Nagoya. Japan will continue to be a significant economic factor, particularly in the Far East. However, America will revitalize many of the industries given up for dead.

The Challenge Posed by the New European Community as Both Potential Customer and Competitor

Europe is heading toward a confederation of 12 Western European countries with one market, one currency, one set of standards governing products, one set of rules regarding social and environmental issues. Many of the national borders between these countries, as they relate to commerce, were scheduled to be torn down. It may be a more significant removal of barriers than the razing of the Iron Curtain because it will create a single market of more than 340 million consumers. The economic output for the 12 charter members of the EC exceeded $6 trillion in 1990. (The economic output of the United States was just over 5.3 trillion.) It is a marketplace we cannot ignore.

The plan is to create a sort of United States of Europe bound together in a loose federation. It is vaguely similar to the original concept the founding fathers had for this country of strong, independent states. Each European "state" will retain the rights of sovereignty. They'll still fly their own flags, sing their old anthems, speak their own languages, maintain their own armies, administer their own laws, and control immigration. (Products will move freely across borders; people will not.) What these countries will share are one another's markets and integrated economies. Gone will be tariffs and duties and custom inspections and regulations that prohibited the flow of goods from one country to another. A common currency is scheduled to be in place just before the turn of the century. That, of course, requires a common bank.

The jury is still out on whether so many diverse nations can achieve unity of purpose. It's hard to imagine the French cooperating, unless they call the tune. Germany, as the most powerful economy in Europe, has all the financial muscle and it won't give it up easily. There's bound to be a squabble as to where the international bank is headquartered because that nation will become the financial center of the federation. The wage discrepancies between the richest and poorest nations in the federation will give the poorer nations an advantage in a free-trade situation. That means there must be some kind of wage stabilization. The question of not permitting membership to Eastern European nations is still not resolved.

These questions, and others, make it almost a certainty that the end-of-1992 deadline for unification will not have been reached. That doesn't mean it isn't coming eventually.

If the idea works, a powerful new economic entity will have been created. It will become an economic competitor to the United States at the time we have our hands full with Japan and the other Pacific Rim countries.

Most Europeans feel they don't need the United States as a watchdog anymore. They chortle at the idea of Americans with their noses pressed against the glass, begging to get in someplace where they're not wanted.

Jacques Delors, president of the EC Executive Commission, states, with some relish, that "Americans will have much difficulty with Europe if unity succeeds." Another of his remarks is "Europe will be open, but it will not be given away." These statements and others by officials of the EC suggest hard trade negotiations are ahead.

Protectionism may come in the form of product standards, testing, and safety codes that favor European products at the expense of "outsiders." These standards, through the requirement for elaborate certification, may become effective trade barriers. There may be the requirement for local content, which essentially rules out foreign manufacturers.

We can also expect a political movement that transcends national borders to boot the United States off the continent. If there's anything the European community will agree on it is that they'd like to see less of competitive U.S. companies that are currently taking away market share.

If the Europeans want a decreased U.S. presence we should oblige them, at least to the extent of decreasing our European bases and troops. With the troops gone, a source of irritation will be gone. Closing the bases, however, will be monumentally expensive because the involved countries have demanded that we "clean up" the sites. The estimated costs are so high even the Pentagon is staggered.

Right now we enjoy a trade surplus with Europe. A united Europe won't be any better at manufacturing computers and construction equipment, developing new drugs, designing software, digging coal, growing grain, raising chickens, making movies, turning out hit records, and so forth, than were the individual nations. We'll do all right competitively with these kinds of products and others as long as we have free access to the market. The key to obtaining a square deal is through negotiating access to our own rich markets.

A unilateral free-trade agreement, such as our current arrangement with Japan, is a compact between a swindler and a sucker. We can't afford to let diplomats trade away access to our markets for some dimly perceived geopolitical advantage and nothing more. We must have equitable access in return. That means removing negotiations on these matters from the diplomats and giving them to hard-nosed business executives.

American companies now exporting to Europe must realize that they won't be able to business at the same old stand much longer. They must develop new strategies, new partnerships with European countries, new presences in European communities if they wish to maintain their export business. At the same time American companies must recognize that new, powerful competitors will be formed. These competitors will be nurtured and protected in much the same way the Japanese government nurtures emerging companies. They'll grow quickly because the market they serve will no longer be fragmented.

The bottom line is we won't be able to export our costs much longer, only our values.

EC Members

Germany	Portugal
France	Belgium
United Kingdom	Greece
Italy	Ireland
Netherlands	Denmark
Spain	Luxemborg

Careers to Avoid in the Nineties

The theme of this book is that middle managers are in grave jeopardy. The corporate pressure to reduce personnel, to "rightsize," will continue to the end of the decade. The planners, the number crunchers, the liaison people, the market analysts, the coordinators, the interfacers, all those who can't describe their job function in one simple sentence are in particular trouble. They're on their way out, and they won't make a comeback.

Many professionals also face rough sledding. A full army division could be formed from the number of out-of-work bankers. We're graduating far too may lawyers at a time when many of the nation's largest law firms are cutting back on personnel. (Unfortunately, lawyers' "make work" projects are those inane legal actions that clog the court system.)

The technical disciplines, always considered recession-proof, will be severely affected by the cutbacks in the defense industry. Engineers will no longer be able to waltz away from a contractor who lost a big government deal to join the outfit that won it.

The jobs that can be replaced by machines should be avoided. These included bookkeepers, telephone switchboard operators, date input clerks, meter readers, bank tellers, typists, and the like.

The careers that should absolutely be avoided are those that don't bring the worker any personal satisfaction. If you hate the job, don't do it.

The "Hot" Careers of the Next Decade

Over the past twenty years the best job in the country was to be a member of Congress. The prestige and perks were great, the power almost unlimited, the accountability nonexistent, the pressure to perform slight, and, once in office, incumbents were almost always reelected. However, with the Supreme Court upholding term limits, with the cost of a campaign now well over seven figures, and with the general loathing and contempt voters seem to now feel for elected officials, a career in politics may not be the job of the Nineties.

For those interested in income, short hours, adulation, and a job in the fresh air, being a baseball player is the job of the moment. Those making a paltry $3 or $4 million a year are sulking as being underpaid and unappreciated. Baseball players make those big salaries, however, because there are a limited number of people who can hit a small round object traveling at 95 miles an hour. (Which proves that labor is like any other commodity: Price is related to demand and scarcity.)

Daydreams aside, what are the safe jobs of the nineties? If the operative word is "safe," *there are none.* The lifetime career in management with a single company is becoming an oddity. There are, however, many specialties in demand right now. Among them are:

Computer Programmers and Systems Analysts

As computers proliferate so do the need for people who can write specialized programs. As companies modernize and simplify their systems, they'll need analysts to show them the way. One danger: Computers are becoming easier to program. The profession could be in danger from do-it-yourselfers.

Private-Sector Educators and Trainers

Public schools face budgetary problems and cutbacks that are likely to impact the quality of education. Many dissatisfied parents will be sending their children to private schools, or for remedial training. A voucher system that would allow parents to have a greater voice in where their children were educated would also increase the demand for private-school education. Companies that once maintained large internal training programs will be meeting their needs through training contractors. All these factors will result in a greater need for trainers and private-school educators.

Human Resources Management

Fortunes really improved for former personnel managers once the title on the office door was changed to "Director of Human Resources." With equal opportunity laws, affirmative action, possible discrimination suits, and the walking-on-eggs care required when making personnel cutbacks, the human resources manager has become an important member of the management team. As a job has become almost a property right, the human resource managers make their way through minefields of federal and state laws. For a major company, the position is close to requiring a law degree.

Paramedics and Nurses

The problem isn't so much a lack of trained medical personnel, but rather where they are located. The available jobs are in the inner city and small towns, but the trained people prefer the suburbs of major metropolitan areas where they can treat rich folks. Many small towns are so desperate for trained health care professionals they'll settle for someone who doesn't have a full medical degree.

Environmental Advisor

Advising companies on hazardous waste, clean-up, air-quality requirements, landfill, recycling, water treatment, chemical risks, and environmental standards should be a growth industry for the remainder of the decade and beyond. Aside from doing what is socially acceptable, complying with environmental regulations is necessary for any company that doesn't wish to be in jeopardy of huge fines.

Independent Sales Rep

As companies trim back their direct selling costs, many will turn to independent reps. This has already happened in midsize and smaller cities as companies choose to concentrate their sales forces in major metropolitan areas. The reps are usually paid on straight commission, so the company pays only for results. The commission rate is higher than for those who are also compensated with a base salary. The rep who is professional and performs will be able to pick up lucrative lines unavailable only a few years ago. The key to success in repping is to be very selective about the lines chosen and keeping the operation local.

Tax Accountant

Want a guaranteed career plan with a six-figure income? Get a law degree, attend school a few more years for your C.P.A., hire on with the Internal Revenue Service for three or four years to learn the ropes, and then hang out a shingle as a tax lawyer/consultant. It will take a bit of time, but the money will roll in.

Tax specialists will be in demand because every "simplification" of the tax code has made it more complicated to file a return. It is in the interest of the I.R.S., and a host of specialists, to keep out tax regulations difficult to understand. They don't want the general public initiated into the mysteries. There's no more chance of a flat tax rate than there is of a flat earth.

Line Management

One of the keys to survival in the next decade is to be doing a job where performance can easily be measured. The line manager, responsible for a team producing so much per month in the form of sales, profits, widgets, or whatever will remain a key employee even if the number of team members are reduced. The qualifier, of course, is that the manager must perform well.

Technical Support

On-site product service is becoming one of those quaint old customs, like bobbing for apples at Halloween. It's just too expensive these days to send a warm body to a customer's office to find the cause of a problem or offer instruction in a product's use. As an alternative, many companies are using 800 numbers the customers can call. At the other end are technical-support personnel who handle the phones. The use of these kind of services will expand and so will the requirement for knowledgeable people who can diagnose a problem over the phone and talk a customer through a solution.

Telemarketers

Swampland isn't the only thing being sold over the telephone today. As companies trim back direct sales forces to reduce sales costs, they're being replaced by people who contact the customers by phone. Today, this kind of selling has become as respectable as going to church on Sunday. The telephone marketer can offer the monthly specials, keep a running record of the customer's buying habits, try to establish a rapport, and even open new accounts. There will also be continued opportunities for telephone sales-department managers and sales pitch scriptwriters.

Truck Drivers

Want to wave bye-bye to corporate life, settle back in the cab of a big Kenworth, plug in the old C.B. and take off down a six-lane superhighway to some romantic spot halfway across the country? Trucking is still the transportation medium of choice for moving goods from one point to another. There will always be a need for an operator who can back a semi-trailer into an alley with only six-inch clearance on either side. If you think it's a life without pressure, however, think again. Many interstate operators own their rigs, which means there's pressure to keep up the payments. So wolf down those biscuits and gravy, tip the dyed-blonde waitress, and get back on the road.

The Hot Cities of the Next Decade

The early Spanish explorers of America heard tales from the Indians of the "Seven Cities of Gold." They spent years trying to find them, but the golden cities were always just over the next horizon. These seven golden cities of the next decade can be easily found on most any map.

San Antonio, Texas

This isn't a climate report, though San Antonio is one of the warmest places in the United States. What makes San Antonio hot is its position about 100 miles from the Mexican border, 100 miles from Dallas, and not much further to the high-tech center of Austin, Texas. About $28 billion in annual trade now moves north and south of the Rio Grande. About half the trade flows through San Antonio. The coming Free Trade agreement between the United States, Mexico, and Canada should increase that number dramatically.

What Mexico wants most from the United States are high-tech products and a technology transfer to stimulate their own high-tech industry centered in Guadalajara. San Antonio is in an excellent geographic position to broker both products and technology.

Trade moves in both directions. The *maquiladoras*, assembly plants set up in duty-free zones in and near Matamoros, Mexico, ship their finished goods into the United States through the ports of Brownsville and San Antonio. All of this means San Antonio will bustle.

Housing is cheap, the Riverwalk is charming, and the Alamo inspires. Bring your short-sleeved shirts and cotton suits.

Austin, Texas

It's hard to pick up a California business journal today without reading a story about the demise of Silicon Valley. The high-tech firms that just a few years ago created a completely new industry are disenchanted with high taxes, a cost of living in the stratosphere, and a state government determined to be environmentally correct. There's an exodus going on worthy of the Old Testament as companies scatter out of Cupertino and San Jose and Scotts Valley to towns in Nevada, New Mexico, Arizona, and elsewhere.

The place hoping to replace the Valley as the capital of high-tech is Austin, one of the fastest-growing towns in Texas. The city is a state capital; the University of Texas is there; two research outfits, Sematch and Microcomputer Corporation, have located there; two of the fastest-growing PC suppliers, Dell and Compaq, are there; the Apple Computer customer-support center is there; it's located near the metropolitan markets of Dallas and Houston and close to the Central and South American export markets via San Antonio. It's a great place to be an electronic engineer.

In summer you don't need a car because the humidity makes it possible to swim down the street. However, the real estate market is still affordable and the Oklahoma-Texas football game is enough excitement for everyone.

Portland, Oregon

When Californians run away from home one of the places they run to is Portland, Oregon. This rapidly growing city appears almost recession proof. Unemployment is a few points under the national average. It has become an outpost for Pacific Rim countries, serving as a port for the shipment of agricultural products overseas. Japanese firms such as Fujitsu, Matsushita, and NEC have set up assembly plants in the area. A local high-tech area flourishes. Portland will keep on growing, which means the job opportunities will be above the national average.

The ocean is about an hour's drive away. Two rivers, the mighty Columbia and the Willamette, grace the city. There's been a real estate boom in recent years, but homes are still low priced by West Coast standards. The climate is mild, but in the wintertime it does mist and drizzle and dribble.

A tip for anyone considering the Portland area is to investigate the town just across the Columbia River, Vancouver, Washington, the tax escapee's paradise. Vancouver enjoys the lower property taxes of Washington and much lower energy rates. Washington has no state income tax and, best of all, residents of Vancouver can do their shopping across the river in Portland, Oregon, which has no sales tax.

Memphis, Tennessee

Why do the Japanese seem to locate all their assembly plants in the mid-South? They do it because cities such as Memphis are centrally positioned and make ideal distribution centers. There is a good supply of nonunionized labor. These are also the reasons why Federal Express chose Memphis as a headquarters.

The combination of strategic location and an eager labor force will keep Memphis jumping. Both the city of Memphis and the state of Tennessee bust their butts to bring in new companies. The mid-South is likely to replace the Midwest, now known as the "rust belt," as the major manufacturing area of the United States. An influx of retirees will also bring in dollars. Small companies offering products and services of use to major manufacturers will do well here.

Memphis, like many metropolitan areas, is two different cities. The inner city is blighted and dying while the suburbs bustle. The tax rate is relatively low and housing costs are moderate. Taxes and housing are even lower in Northern Mississippi, just a fifteen-minute drive from Memphis.

The Mississippi washes the city's feet. It's hard to look at this wonderful river and not dream about floating on a raft all the way to New Orleans.

Orlando, Florida

For those troubled by insomnia, Orlando offers more than 70,000 bedrooms. They serve the millions of tourists who come to visit Walt Disney World and other attractions. Entertainment has supplanted raising citrus and catering to retirees as the area's principal enterprise. Movie studios, such as Universal, have moved in and so have people. Orlando is one of the fastest growing cities in the United States. What keeps them coming is a warm climate, a reasonable number of jobs, and a feeling that the best is still ahead.

It's true that most of the available jobs are in the low-paying service industry, prices for homes have increased dramatically, and residents complain that the city can't keep absorbing the flux of newcomers. But Orlando will continue to be a magnet that draws people from the Northeast corridor.

San Diego, California/Tijuana, Mexico

San Diego has a picture-postcard harbor filled with gunboats and so many retirees, the mortuary business is the hottest game in town. Tijuana is the place to go to buy a social disease or get drunk cheap. Those are the stereotypes of these two border cities. When the Navy dominated San Diego and Tijuana pandered for American tourist dollars the stereotypes contained much truth.

All that has changed. If taken as a single city San Diego/Tijuana is one of the most important commercial centers of the world. Together they have a population of more than three million people. The area has become the import/export center for the state of California (the world's sixth largest economy). It serves not only Mexico, but much of Central and South America as well.

Once dependent on the U.S. Navy, San Diego bustles with a myriad industries. There are high-tech companies and tourist attractions and financial-services firms and defense contractors and fruit growers and service companies and a dozen others. It is also a haven for swindlers and fast-buck artists, but that is another story.

Just a trolley ride away from downtown San Diego is Tijuana, Mexico, a city teeming with two million souls. Tijuana has cleaned up its image, though it is still possible to indulge the flesh if one wishes. To the casual visitor, Tijuana offers poorly made, low-priced trinkets, inexpensive restaurants with Montezuma's revenge featured on the menu, cheap liquor, and sports-betting parlors illegal in California. To the business person, Tijuana offers *maquiladora* assembly plants, experienced importers, hand crafts, a marketplace for American goods, and a gateway to the interior of Mexico.

The two cities have a love-hate relationship. By night, Mexican *campesinos* swarm across the border in numbers so large the Border Patrol can only wave at them in desperation. Once here the illegals pick our fruits and vegetables, work in our sweatshops, clean our houses, watch our kids, and do all the other grunt work that Americans of today won't touch. Their low-cost labor keeps down the cost of many things, particularly agricultural products.

On the weekends Americans return the favor, swarming south to take advantage of the exchange rate for an inexpensive holiday. For a few dollars they get drunk in the cantinas, eat Pacific lobster in the restaurants, buy hand-crafted goods in posh shops, or plain junk from peddlers in the street, fill up their gas tanks with cheap Mexican petrol, and head back across the border with one heck of a hangover.

As the U.S.–Canada–Mexico free-trade agreement takes shape, the two cities become even more vital to the economy of the entire West. The partnership will increase the local demand for U.S.-made products and services. One estimate projects that the free trade agreement will create 130,000 new jobs. Most of them will be located right here, on either side of the border. There may be more opportunities for entrepreneurs in this locale than anywhere else in the United States.

Large corporations, including many Japanese firms, are exploiting the cheap labor available in the duty-free *maquiladora* plants. For example, Ford Motors has its top-of-the-line Crown Victoria assembled in Mexico. (One of the reasons, aside from low labor costs, is that it helps Ford beat EPA standards for gas mileage because technically the car isn't manufactured in the United States.)

Housing costs are positively painful in San Diego. It's still a bit of a hick town, with a remnant to the old link with the Navy to be found in the occasional downtown tattoo parlor. The state legislature never saw a tax it didn't adore. However, the weather is the best there is anywhere. *Anywhere*!

Melting Down the Iron Curtain and Selling It for Scrap

When Russian cosmonaut Sergei I. Krikalev rocketed into space in May 1991 he was launched from the Soviet Union. When he returned in March of 1992, after ten months in the Mir space station, Krikalev landed on foreign soil in Kazakhstan, one of fifteen republics in a Commonwealth of independent states that once made up the USSR.

The time warp at work was the disintegration of the Soviet empire and the collapse of communism in less than a single year. Gone are the satellite states of Eastern Europe that provided a buffer for the Soviet Union in the event of war. Gone is central planning and the bureaucracy that stifled individual initiative. Gone are the state-run enterprises that produced shoddy goods. Gone are the military adventures. Gone is the evangelism that tried to indoctrinate the entire world to the joys of socialism.

In their place are a confused people with an uncertain future who mistrust their leaders. Their goals are ill-defined, their economy has disappeared, the safety net provided by the old Communist state is shredded, and the ruble is worth little more than the paper it is printed on.

The Russian people are looking to the West for near-term relief in the form of food credits and direct loans and for long-term assistance in the form of investment and advice in how to convert to a free-market economy.

Advice is one thing—we've always been very free with that—loans and investments are another. There's no doubting that this is a marketplace with a hunger for Western goods; the question is, how will Russia and the rest of Eastern Europe pay for these goods? Every state-run enterprise will be for sale to the highest bidder, but they don't have much that we want. Their factories were not forced to be competitive and so turned out poor-quality products. Their agriculture was so inefficient it never could feed their own people. (On a recent tour of a Soviet cooperative farm Illinois farmers found more than 1,000 people working acreage that would be handled by no more than 5 people in the United States.)

The political situation is likely to be unstable for some time. The military is disgruntled by an 85 percent cut in arms purchases. There will almost certainly be conflict between military leaders and civilian authorities. The old party *apparatchiks* hope to make a comeback. Ethnic differences have flared. The richer republics, such as the Ukraine, are likely to try to distance themselves from other members of the Commonwealth. The large Moslem population in Azerbaijan and Kazakhstan feel they have more in common with Islamic nations than they do with the other independent republics. The situation is so fragmented, no one can forecast what will happen. An investment in Russia right now is an investment in chaos.

What they can offer, however, is the kind of technical ability that was able to keep a man in space for more than ten months. Their science and engineering was able to keep pace militarily with the United States throughout the Cold War. What we must do is find a way to redirect the efforts of these engineers and scientists. That's the key to the future for Mother Russia.

Members of the old Warsaw Pact nations are in just as big a pickle because they no longer enjoy the subsidies formerly provided by the Soviet Union. Yugoslavia has self-destructed through ethnic strife. Poland and Czechoslovakia are trying to distance themselves from the others.

Romania, Bulgaria, and Albania, dominated by petty dictators, were never really brought into the postwar era. They have the longest way to go.

Despite their problems, because the former Soviet satellites are smaller entities and culturally closer to Western Europe their economies will recover faster. Czechoslovakia, with its manufacturing base, and Poland, with its ties to the United States, will be the first to recover. They'll show the way for their eastern neighbors.

What former Warsaw Pact nations have to offer right now are a well-educated work force and an eagerness to embrace capitalism. That work force can supply cheap contract labor to the Western EC community. They'd serve the same purpose that the Pacific Rim countries of Korea and Taiwan and Singapore served to Japan. All these countries first built products for large Japanese corporations, learned the ropes, accumulated capital, and gradually developed their own export networks. That same system could work for Eastern Europe.

The United States is the winner against the "Communist evil empire" in that we are the only combatant still left standing. The danger is now an inclination to support liberal regimes behind the torn-down curtain lest they regress to communism. It will be throwing money down a rat hole because there will be little chance of getting that money back.

Life in These United States at the Turn of the Century

Large corporations will begin to rebuild their work forces, rightsizing won't last forever, and the need to create bureaucracies is an instinctual obsession right up there with making babies. The entrepreneurial urge will remain strong, but capital will be even more difficult to raise. The events of the past several years have led to an aversion of risk by financial institutions that won't pass quickly. The Japanese are already pulling their money out of the country, and they figure to be the only exporter of capitol in the mid-Nineties.

Young companies and emerging industries will be responsible for much of our economic vigor. The idea of the corporate entrepreneurial executive will be considered silly, a passing fad inconsistent with corporate unity. Corporations will assume many of the responsibilities for basic education that have been abrogated by our educational system.

There will be a backlash against technology. We won't become Luddites, but there will be a pronounced nostalgia for old things. (Save anything mechanical.) Big government will still plague us, and we'll still be voting for those who promise to get it off our backs. Children of the new baby boom will be entering junior high. The environmental movement will lose some of its stridency. Women will take to corporate politics like ducks to water. It will still be possible to make a million writing a good book or a software program. A thousand and one local factions will be critical of life in these United States, but this will still be the place where everyone wants to come.

These will be good times.

2001, Approaching the Next Millennium

Nature abhors a vacuum, and geopolitics abhors a world with a single superpower in it. Rushing to fill the void will be a United Germany. During the first half of the Nineties the Germans will concentrate on resolving the problems of unification. They'll be among the first to take advantage of the cheap labor forces available in Eastern Europe because Germany now has the highest labor costs in the world. Access to an inexpensive labor force, quality engineering, precision manufacturing, plus their protected position in the EC will make the Germans the next bad guys to dominate entire market segments.

The German military buildup will begin in the late Nineties because they can afford it, because it keeps the factories humming, and because the Germans are never willing to rely on reason alone to resolve differences. Austria and Czechoslovakia will come under German influence. The rest of Europe won't like the developments, and the EC confederation will come under political pressure. The French will threaten to pull out.

Japan will stagger a bit when trading partner after trading partner proves to be an unreliable creditor. (First Eastern Europe, then China.) They'll still be powerful enough to be the most prominent Pacific Rim economic force, but they'll face strong competition from Korea if the Koreans can resolve their reunification issues. Taiwan and China will reunite. The Chinese will screw up Hong Kong. China, as Churchill said, is still a "riddle wrapped in an enigma," but it is likely they will remain communist.

Iran will become the most influential country in the Middle East, but it will be because of its size, military strength, and religious leadership rather than because of economic domination. The quarrels that have been going on for the past century will not be resolved in the next ten years. Egypt will abandon any pretense of an agreement with Israel.

In this hemisphere, the North American free-trade agreement between the United States, Mexico, and Canada will invigorate the economies of all three countries. The pact will be expanded to include all South American nations.

The result will be three economic superpowers and one theocracy with spheres of influence, markets based on proximity, and reliance on natural trading partners. Of course there will be poaching and forays into one another's markets. It will work for a while as long as the world is relatively prosperous. Then comes the next bump in the road and sharp turn of history taking us off to . . .

INDEX

C

HD
38.2
.U6
G-37
1993